Every Mother Is a Daughter

EVERY

The neverending quest

MOTHER

for success, inner peace,

IS A

and a really clean kitchen

DAUGHTER

(recipes and knitting patterns included)

PERRI KLASS

and

SHEILA SOLOMON KLASS

BALLANTINE BOOKS NEW YORK

Published in the United States by Ballantine Books, an
imprint of The Random House Publishing Group, a division
of Random House, Inc., New York.

BALLANTINE and colophon are registered trademarks of
Random House, Inc.

Library of Congress Cataloging-in-Publication Data
Klass, Perri.
Every mother is a daughter : the neverending quest
for success, inner peace, and a really clean kitchen (recipes
and knitting patterns included) / Perri Klass and Sheila
Solomon Klass.
p.   cm.
ISBN 0-345-47718-9—ISBN 0-345-47719-7 (pbk.)
1. Mothers and daughters.   2. Women—Psychology.
I. Klass, Sheila Solomon.   II. Title.

HQ755.85.K565 2006
306.874'3—dc22   2005048189

Printed in the United States of America

www.ballantinebooks.com

9   8   7   6   5   4   3

Text design by Laurie Jewell

Acknowledgments

Perri and Sheila: We would both like to thank the people who helped us imagine and carry through this project, especially our enthusiastic literary agent, Elaine Markson, and our wonderful editor, Nancy Miller. It can't always be easy to handle a mother–daughter act, with all the interesting overtones, but we got only support and encouragement. We are very grateful to the Ucross Foundation for giving us a time and place to write and think together.

Sheila: I am indebted to my late husband, Morton Klass, first for marrying me long after my parents had given up hope, and then for leading me to Trinidad and India to share the joys of the anthropological life. I owe thanks to my daughter Judy Klass and my son, David Klass, whose long-term memories were invaluable, and to them and to Giselle Benatar, my daughter-in-law, goes my gratitude for their support, willingness to listen, and unfailingly creative suggestions. To Perri, daughter, traveling companion, and coauthor, I am most grateful for her guiding hand on darkened paths and for her imperfect but durable patience. When it comes to adventure, foreign, gastronomical, or other, and to unmitigated fun, this child is very much her father's daughter.

Perri: I would like to thank Larry Wolff and our children, Orlando, Josephine, and Anatol, for cheerfully sending me off on various jaunts with my mother—to India, to Trinidad, to Wyoming, to Atlantic City—and for cheering the two of us on as we worked on this book. And when it comes to acknowledging my coauthor, well, what can I say? How do you thank your mother? In addition to expressing my gratitude for her company—and her example—on journeys of all possible types, I would like to thank her for bringing me up to understand the powerful joys of writing and authorship.

Contents

Introduction

Perri: I fantasize sometimes about making my mother enjoy things. Perhaps *making* is the wrong word. I long to introduce my mother to some of the small special pleasures and indulgences of life. I imagine opening up her life in lovely little ways and encouraging her to accept certain pleasures. It's probably slightly patronizing on my part, but sometimes I fantasize about her face lighting up in surprised delight: *How good this tastes, how soft this feels!* It's not that my mother doesn't have her pleasures, reliable and reliably enjoyed, but they don't tend to be built in any way around self-indulgence or, God forbid, luxury. So yes, I know I can take her to sit in cheap seats and watch a good play or give her a paperback copy of an interesting novel she hasn't heard about or treat her to one of the fabulous $2 grilled meat sandwiches at the Vietnamese *banh mi* shop near where I work, and I know she'll respond with delight and satisfaction: what a wonderful production, what a good book, what a great $2 lunch!

I fantasize, though, about getting her to loosen up and enjoy a little frivolous luxury. I don't live a life full of truffles, champagne, and limos myself, but I'm not above enjoying something because it's luxe—especially when someone else is paying.

I was traveling on business once, and someone was putting me up at a fancy Manhattan hotel. I arranged for a room with two beds and invited my mother to come spend the night. *We'll order from room service*, I thought. *We'll raid the minibar! I'll tell her it's all covered, even if it isn't. Let her taste the slightly illicit joys of expense-account travel.* In any event, we ate a huge dinner in a restaurant, with plenty of wine, and got back to the room in no need of room service dessert or minibar miniatures. But we spent a comfortable night on spiffy sheets that neither of us would have to wash, and I planned to overwhelm her with a luxury breakfast. In the morning, as we were getting up, I noticed that hanging on the bathroom door were two matching white terry-cloth hotel bathrobes, plush and soft and carefully labeled with the little tickets that say, *This robe is here for your comfort during your stay. If you would like to purchase a robe, $100 will be added to your bill.* "Hey, Mom," I said, as she went into the bathroom to take a shower, "put on a bathrobe, and let's lounge around. These bathrobes cost a hundred bucks a pop—let's live it up." She looked dubiously at the bathrobe, and at the tag, as if this whole idea of putting robes in people's hotel rooms was rather frivolous and ill-advised and probably a silly experiment that would never be repeated. However, she took her shower, actually put on the plush robe, then she sat down in one of the hotel chairs—but only for a moment. I went into the bathroom to take my own shower, planning to come out in the matching robe. By the time I did, she was fully dressed for the day, including her shoes.

Later that day, I teased her about the bathrobe—it was too expensive, she couldn't wear it, did she know some people routinely spent much more than a hundred dollars on a bathrobe? She shook her head; it wasn't that. "I've never done that in my whole life," she said, "put on a bathrobe and lounge around. When I get up, I have to get dressed—I think it comes from my own mother, this feeling that once you were awake, you shouldn't waste time, you should immediately get to all the chores you hate most. My mother had all kinds of disparaging terms for women who wore slippers—I grew up thinking that when you get up the first thing you do is wash and brush your teeth and then you get dressed."

I treasure my mother for all the things she most enjoys—all of which, I think, have been reliably passed on to me. We agree, I think, on the important small pleasures: I would rather discover a wonderful new novelist than just about anything, I revel in the joys of cheap ethnic lunches, and of course I love bargains, from clothing bought on sale to used and remaindered books. We even agree on the important big pleasures around which life should be based: children, family, work, writing, food, travel, and books. But I am also a creature of my times (a rich yuppie, my mother would tell you; her slang tends to be a little out of date, but the mild contempt would come across). I am fully capable of enjoying high-end travel, expensive restaurants, premium cocktails, and wine that tastes better because you know how much it cost. (Though the truth is, of course, that I have never grown up enough to take any of this for granted. Real grown-ups accustomed to the everyday luxury of expense-account travel probably don't fantasize about room service and the minibar. They're too busy doing business with the in-room fax and high-speed Internet access or keeping up with their workouts in the fitness center.) The small rewards, I think, of working hard and doing your job well, are the occasional treats you give yourself—or the occasional extravagances that life throws your way, and that you let yourself enjoy.

My mother, Sheila Solomon Klass, is seventy-seven years old. Since my father died, she has lived alone in Manhattan. Technically, she is retired from her job as an English professor at Manhattan Community College, but she still teaches a writing course every semester, carrying her briefcase full of papers home on the A train after every class and spending hours marking them in red pen.

My mother grew up in Brooklyn and never learned to drive. She is a fierce fan of the New York City subways. Many people consider the New York subway system frightening—too loud, too dirty, and very dangerous. To my mother, it is home turf, comforting and safe and infinitely navigable. She has no sense of direction anywhere else on Earth, but put her in some subway station and her brain transforms into a global positioning system—"We can take the IRT two stops down and then change to the crosstown and get the R or the N," she'll tell you, with confidence, and with accuracy—and then if there's any doubt, she'll fish an up-to-date subway map out of her handbag. My mother complains that her eyes are getting worse and worse. She has always insisted she can't read road maps or help with navigation, yet she has no trouble at all with the multicolor spiderweb of the world's most complex subway system.

For my mother, the subway has come to represent an absolute matter of principle: It represents her deeply cherished independence, as well as her desire to abjure personal luxury and avoid spending money on herself. Even late at night, when almost anyone who had a choice might decide that the subway actually *was* a little dangerous, my mother proudly rides alone. Even in terrible weather, she refuses to take the easy way out by spending the extra few dollars on a taxi. Of course, I think my mother should take the occasional taxi. I feel that at seventy-seven, a retired professor is entitled to take a cab home after midnight from Midtown (a fifteen-minute ride) instead of the A train (a forty-five-minute process involving a change of trains because the express doesn't run late at night, and of course then there's a dark walk on each end). Or she could call a car service instead of setting out, in the snow and ice, on yet another of her complex, multitrain journeys.

My mother considers me a total wimp. And anyway, she will tell you, she hates taxis, hates the uncertainty of giving directions to the driver or straining to see what is showing on the meter or calculating the tip. When it comes to taxis, my mother and I are locked into one of those endless-loop conversations, with me uselessly saying that if she can't see the numbers on the meter, she could just ask the driver. I also often wonder aloud that if her eyes are too bad to take a taxi, how can she see well enough to maneuver in the subway? My mother counters that my problem is that I'm afraid of the city.

It's not exactly that my mother is cheap. Well, actually, in certain ways, she's unbelievably cheap. Although she is profoundly generous with her children and her grandchildren, she absolutely does not spend money on herself. My mother allows herself no indulgences and, as far as I can see, no sensual pleasures. If I lived alone, I tell her, I would treat myself to fancy little gourmet items to eat, the kind of takeout luxury goods that keep New York City rich and fat. "But I *like* Campbell's tomato soup," my mother will say, stocking up. She claims she no longer eats it right out of the can (saves washing a bowl), but I'm not so sure. My secret live-alone indulgences would probably involve whole triple cream cheeses consumed in one sitting; my mother secretly eats the tomato soup out of the can.

Sometimes I think that even though my mother is a writer, she regards writing about herself and her feelings as just one more soft self-indulgence to avoid. She writes *fiction*—sometimes set in faraway places, or long-ago times. She'll throw herself into researching the American Revolution as the background for a historical adventure or reading up on the life of Louisa May Alcott for a novel about her childhood. But she does not write out the cries of her inner soul—or if she does, she doesn't show them to anyone. Needless to say, she would never go into analysis or counseling or join anything that smelled like a support group. She lived in the suburbs through the 1970s when everyone else's mother was in therapy or taking Valium or getting Rolfed or studying est or some other kind of self-actualization. My mother lived through it all without ever understanding what the fuss was about. After my father died, someone suggested a grief group, or a widows' group, and my mother reacted with fine disdain. Why would she need to talk about her private business with a bunch of strangers? It was her business to grieve—grieve she would and grieve she did—but why would she need a *group*? As her daughter, I fully understand these reactions. I am not much for group process myself, and I have a bad tendency, which I probably got from her, to regard talking about oneself as self-indulgence.

Even so, Mama, here we go. You are probably the person I understand best on this Earth, in some mysterious mother–daughter way; you are the person I come from—literally, the person I came out of, forty-seven years ago, your first child, your first daughter. I changed your life; I made you into a mother. You were standing at my side when my own first child was born and I became a mother myself. In fact, my life has recapitulated yours in many ways—here I am, midlife, mother of three, settled down in a couple with a bearded academic guy, busy with a full-time job I care about, trying to write as much as possible around the edges. Every single piece of that job description was also true for you—and yet from moment to moment and from day to day, my life is completely different from yours. Still, you drafted this road map—or subway map, if you prefer—and there are moments when I feel I am only following it. So let me push you now, a little, into the self-indulgent joys of self-reflection. Who knows, we may yet spend a week at a luxury resort somewhere, raiding the minibar and wearing the bathrobes and getting to know our inner sybarites. In the meantime, let's try to unknot a few of those endless argumentative loops and try to understand how we have shaped each other and have reacted to each other—and reacted *against* each other as well.

Sheila: Every time my daughter Perri comes to town, it's a treat. She lives five hours away, as the bus creeps, in Cambridge, Massachusetts, and she's a mother and a doctor and she heads a literacy foundation, so she's busy. *Hoo-hah,* as we said at Brooklyn College in the 1940s whenever we were in danger of being impressed. When I phone her, all too often I have to talk to a machine even though I am her venerable old mother. I hate machines, for they have no respect for hearing difficulties.

So if it looks as if Perri will be in New York or nearby, we try to connect. If she's staying over, I put her up in my unfashionable but comfortable apartment in Washington Heights, where the mirrors and the brass are not polished, nor is anything else, and the beds are made so loosely your feet slip right in between the sheets without breaking your toes.

This visit was notable because she was on a business trip, which included a paid-for hotel room on Central Park South. If you didn't grow up in the Brooklyn slums, those words *Central Park South* probably won't mean as much to you. But I first started dreaming about Manhattan when I was twelve and went over the Williamsburg Bridge on a class trip to the Central Park Zoo, where two orangutans made love and our old teacher, Miss Young, who'd never heard of sex, nearly died of embarrassment. "Look away, girls. Look away, look away," she urged. It sounded like she was singing the chorus of "Dixie." I knew this island was where I wanted to live.

At twenty-five, I finally managed to move across the East River, and I remain dazzled by the city. Central Park South bounds the bottom of the great park and is usually lined with horse-drawn hansom cabs, which lend a certain elegance but give off a fulsome odor. A half dozen splendid hotels grace the street, their doormen veritable major generals in their military dress and stance. They summon cabs with peremptory whistles that once started revolutions in Moscow. Of all the noble buildings, the Plaza, on the Fifth Avenue corner that is the eastern boundary of this elegant thoroughfare, has always been the grande dame. I had used the ladies' room there hundreds of times, and I can attest to its pleasant and luxurious ambiance. My visits to the Plaza ladies' room were always leisurely excursions, for I could never just run in and out. Not when Roxanne Jewelers offered rare and costly baubles nearby, and Neuchâtal chocolates summoned and seduced with their scent. It's true, as Perri would point out, that I never bought anything at any of these places—you can imagine the prices! For me, it was a wonderful, exotic museum. I loved to study the Palm Court's eclectic menus. Most recently the word *gratinated* caught my eye. As in *gratinated cannelloni*? I am eager to use the word myself, though I have not yet had the occasion.

Thus, when Perri called and said she had this two-bed luxury room booked in a classy Central Park South hotel and wouldn't I come and join her, I thought, *Oh, my God! The Plaza! I couldn't. After all these years of using their ladies' room. It's too much.* I was really overwhelmed, so it was fortunate that Perri's hotel turned out not to be the Plaza but a slightly less glitzy palace down the street. *Of course I'll come. I'd love to.*

We meet for dinner at the Szechuan Palace on Ninth Avenue and eat too much. There is no music in the restaurant, so we can do what we do best: We talk. Perri Elizabeth Toolsi Devi Klass is my oldest child, forty-seven years old. *Toolsi Devi* is her Hindi name, assigned to her by the Hindu priest in the Trinidadian village where she was born—it's a sacred plant. Perri shares with me a love of books and writing, and a singular purposefulness and obstinacy, which guides each of our lives. My late husband, Mort, Perri's father, taught her to read very early, and she has just never stopped. She read her way through boring classes and through all the planned activities in various summer day camps. Whenever we arrived at camp to pick her up during the water sports period, there she'd be sitting in a boat, reading her book. She wouldn't weave potholders or glue jewel boxes out of Popsicle sticks either. Other kids might do other things, but Perri read. She nearly drove several camp directors crazy. I don't know anyone who's read as much, though her three children, given time, may beat her record.

But this is not a paean to Perri. She has instructed me to complain about her not to sing her praises. Okay: She was a miserably rebellious adolescent,who not only closed her bedroom door to keep us out (me, mostly—in those years, she preferred her father) but also erected a huge Chinese screen inside. She needn't have bothered. I couldn't make it over the wreckage on her floor anyway. She has thick, luxuriant, curly brown hair, and she chose to wear it long, tease it, and conceal her face under it for about five years once she hit puberty. She also decided to completely reject the boring conventional local high school, to which she would not go. She took another route, an ad hoc alternative school taught by frantic parents (including her own), which landed her at Harvard at sixteen. In some ways, she never wholly came back home after that.

Fiction, both the reading and the writing of it, has been her passion, as it has been mine, but I'm a slouch compared to her. She combined it with a love of science, which led her to medical school, and a love of children, which led her to pediatrics.

So here she is, smart, tough, sensitive, and a great joy, for it seems to me she has made her own boundaries and not accepted conventional ones. Not even the sensible ones I subtly continue to suggest, such as limiting projects to what is humanly possible. She is doing what she wants to do: doctoring, mothering, running a literacy organization, and writing. Is she perfect? Ha! Nowhere near. She's often tired and therefore grumpy. Her sleep pattern does not exist. I never know when she'll drop off. Or awaken suddenly and get up to work. I am talking about the middle of the night during the workweek. Her refrigerator is a wilderness. She lets her kids forage for their own breakfasts, and she herself has given up breakfast entirely.

Her tastes are eccentric. She loves Broadway musicals and old movies, but it's hard to get her to any movie made in the last half century. Try to discuss politics with her? After a very few minutes, she loses patience. Her favorite put-down is, "Oh well, everyone needs a hobby." She does not suffer fools gladly—particularly foolish mothers. I've learned just how to handle her: I don't listen.

But mostly, if she'll let me say so, she's funny and kind and not at all self-deluded. She always finds time to read a manuscript and provide an honest reaction. She's full of original, offbeat ideas for traveling, for dining, for gift buying. And best of all, she always knows of wonderful new short stories and novels to read.

So here at dinner in New York, we've eaten our fill and discussed my grandchildren and her siblings and books and plays and a multitude of minutiae. She moves the conversation on to the possibility of this book we might write together. We've already successfully partnered for several magazine articles and enjoyed ourselves immensely. Once we even collaborated with Perri's daughter, Josephine.

"I think a book would be fun to do together, Mama," she says. "I think we can write an interesting and honest book."

"But, Perr—the only time I ever tried to collaborate on a book with anyone was a disaster. You remember, Papa and I tried to write a novel? I felt it was mostly me typing while he dictated, and I got angrier and angrier till I wouldn't continue. It nearly caused a divorce."

"You can't divorce me. Come on, Mama. Would you like to try? Are you up to it? I want us to try and write about mothers and daughters."

"Up to it?" I'm so enchanted at the prospect, I can't think straight. "Was Jane Austen up to writing *Pride and Prejudice*? Was Charlotte Brontë up to writing *Jane Eyre*? Was Louisa May Alcott—?"

"Calm down, Mama. They wrote novels. Fiction."

"So what?" I offer a stinging, alcoholic rebuke. "You think my life was real?" This oblique answer ends the discussion.

"Mama, I'd better get you to the hotel while you can walk."

A canard. I could have tangoed all the way across town.

We headed for Central Park South. (In this book, whenever I am traveling with my children it is by taxi. On my own, I use public transportation.) Our room was a choice one, way above tree level where we could admire the park. I never look out of hotel windows, but I knew Perri was eager for me to enjoy this luxury, so I tried. I opened the heavy drapes, but I couldn't see anything.

"It's gloriously dark," I said, trying to sound awed. It was the best I could do. We talked as we washed and we brushed our teeth, and then we talked some more, which was the fun of it. Finally we went to sleep in the hotel's comfortable beds after we'd pried loose the linen.

Came morning, I rose at six-thirty, my usual time, and leaving Perri asleep, I went to have my shower. This took a very long time because the bathroom plumbing fixtures were unfamiliar, and though there was plenty of hot water, I could not figure out how to get it up into the shower. I am not one for cold showers. The pull of gravity seemed to be forcing all the hot water down through the bath faucet into the tub. After a while, I abandoned the complex instrument panel on the shower and settled for a bath. All right. It wasn't their fault I'm a dolt with faucets.

I saw the white bathrobes hanging on the door, and I was entertained by the message that I could wear one now and, if I liked it, I could have it to take home for $100. Ha! When would I wear it at home? And why? I dress immediately on rising. Anyway, who needs a *white* robe? It's impractical. I'd have to be laundering it constantly. White is the worst possible color for a robe. Scarlet or black or deep purple with designs are so much better. Oscar de la Hoya, the Olympian prizefighter, and I share the same taste in glorious bathrobes. Except I know where to get them marked way down.

Well, Perri was awake by the time I emerged from the bathroom (in my underclothes) and she came up with this idea that I should lounge around in a robe till she finished her shower, and then we might have a room-service breakfast. Into the bathroom she went, and I sat there considering it. If I put on the robe and I spilled coffee on it or somehow damaged it, I'd be embarrassed . . . I'd feel I'd have to buy it . . . I didn't want it . . . The hundred-dollar price was exorbitant . . . I was indignant at the whole set-up . . . Why does everything in America have to be about shopping? . . . I hate shopping. . . .

I can't help the way I think. I'm always convinced that all commercial establishments like hotels are out to get me. They're just waiting for me. Offer me a deal, and my personal alarm system goes off. It is very hard to do business with me.

I reluctantly got dressed. I was sorry, because I knew that Perri would be disappointed. I couldn't help it.

How can I explain it? You see, Perr, you have to understand . . . At my back, I always hear . . . to abuse a line from Andrew Marvell . . . what I always hear is: *It's a trap for people like you, Sheila. They saw you coming. They think you're a sucker. How much is it? Too much. Who needs it? It's an utter waste. Don't get talked into it.* . . .

I'm me, Perr, and the me I am was fundamentally shaped by the Depression years and all the shalt-nots of an Orthodox Jewish home. I'm a relic. Anyone would have thought that by now, after such a full and lucky life, I'd be rid of old ghosts and idiotic habits. I'd be safely anchored in the American middle class. I'd be a shopper. But that's not what happened.

You and your brother and sister embody Papa's and my dreams. You are middle-class kids, and I am amazed at how profoundly different you are from us, while still so much the same in so many important ways. Papa was closer to you in that than I. He was smarter at eluding old binds.

The tired old waiter in Hemingway's great story "A Clean, Well-Lighted Place" tells the young impatient waiter, "You have youth, confidence and a job. You have everything." Everything. Yes. That's what we wanted for our children, for all of you. . . .

When Perri came out of the bathroom, we settled down to study the breakfast menu, me fully dressed and she in that overpriced white bouffant terrycloth bathrobe. I hoped she was sitting delicately and carefully. Eight dollars for a glass of freshly squeezed orange juice! The prices really were not to be believed. Even though we weren't paying, I couldn't—I just couldn't—swallow an eight-dollar glass of orange juice. I am the granddaughter of a woman who, if she dropped a slice of bread or any edible morsel on the floor, she picked it up and kissed it before throwing it away—her apology to God for the sin of wasting good food.

Perr, you were really a good sport. When I didn't want room service, you didn't seem surprised. You put on your street clothes without protest. Meanwhile, I hung up that albatross of a bathrobe, faultlessly. I was relieved to have it back on its hanger, back on the bathroom door.

Sure, I'd love to write the book with you. That is, I'd love to try to write it. That *try* is a mixture of old Depression uncertainty and the fact that the honest self-reflection required is a virtue I've only lately come upon. Women my age were just too busy to think when they were young. Whole decades passed, it seems to me, without my noticing. Sound strange? Nonetheless, it's true. Only now do I have time to really think.

Looking at you and your brother and sister, and all of our grandchildren—the fruit of our Tree of Life—I sense the grandeur and the mystery that is family, and I'm eager to explore it and understand it better. I'm fascinated by the possibilities of autobiography. For a working title, would you consider Papa's favorite, *The Klass Struggle*? I know a million good, cheap New York places, easily accessible by subway, where we can meet and comfortably sit and talk while we're writing our book, wearing our street clothes, wearing our shoes, properly dressed for a good day's work.

PART ONE

*Every Mother Is
a Daughter*

CHAPTER ONE

Past, Present, Future

Perri: This book is about mothers, but I would like to begin with my father. Since his death, sudden and unexpected, in 2001, I have been carrying on a variety of conversations with him. Some of these take place in my car when I am driving. Ever since his death, I have found myself talking to him, often out loud, while I drive, sometimes filling him in on how my life is going or chewing over a dilemma or updating him on the world. For the first year after he died, those conversations—well, I suppose you might call them monologues, but I find it more comfortable and comforting to think of them as conversations, to imagine him there, in some sense, listening in—usually ended with me in tears in my car, trying to drive carefully, facing yet once again the hard, cold fact that I would never again hear my father's voice.

But not all conversations—or even all monologues—take place in the spoken voice. I am a writer, and writing is what I do with my emotions, my stories, my insights, such as they are. I started writing essays about my father—an essay for a knitting magazine about knitting sweaters for my father, an essay for a newspaper travel section about travel memories of my father. I found I had many such essays in me— I still have notes for a piece about my father and food, for example, and another about my father and P. G. Wodehouse. And I think of the process of writing these various essays and articles as somewhere between tribute and conversation; the person I am really telling these stories to, I think, is the person who isn't here to read them. By writing about him, I know, I am trying to conjure him and keep him with me.

Losing a parent is a life lesson you can't learn from anyone else's experience, or even from the collective human experience of all the millions of human beings who have lost their parents before you. That my father should be gone—so suddenly, when no one was in any way ready—that his voice with all its stories and opinions should be still. That I should go on now to live my life as a fatherless daughter. And in my bleakest moments, I had to acknowledge and accept that someday I would be not only fatherless but also motherless; the lesson I had learned was that parents die and leave you. Remember that comforting false assurance we all offer our children when they're young and they first find out about death—*Don't worry, darling; I won't die for a long, long time, not till you're all grown up?* Well, the part we don't tell them is that no matter how many decades you've accumulated when the time comes, you don't necessarily feel all grown up, or even moderately ready to carry on alone.

What I am trying to say, and I feel some trepidation in saying it, as if it might bring bad luck, was that for the first time, I began to have flashes of life without my mother as well as my father. I began to imagine myself writing similar essays about my mother—I could easily imagine the topics. My mother and writing, my mother and food, my mother and her iconic ethnic jokes. And I found myself rebelling against the whole idea of writing about my mother. My mother is a writer, and she is still very much alive and writing. What I wanted was not a collection, someday, of articles in my own signature voice celebrating her, eulogizing her, trying my best to capture her essence—what I wanted was the real thing. My father was gone, but my mother was available, and it was suddenly clear to me that I should take full advantage of that availability, that we should try together to come at the various interesting mother–daughter life issues, in our two different and distinct voices.

In some ways, we spend our lives telling stories about our mothers, making up handy cartoon moms. In high school it's often the whine—*Oh my God, my mother! The things she says, the things she wants, the way she acts!* Later on, maybe you make up the story of the mother who is never satisfied, who wants you to be something you never will become, or else the mother who thinks you're perfect, the mother who blames you for ruining her perfect grandchildren, or the mother who thinks that you and they can do no wrong. There is the aging eccentric mother (or sometimes the relatively young eccentric mother), the heroic matriarch, the disappointed lonely old lady. But all of these—true or exaggerated or downright false—are stories told in a daughter's voice.

I don't want to speak for my mother; I want her to speak for herself. I want to figure out together some of the overlaps in our lives, the ways in which we echo and resemble one another, and also the ways in which we seem to come from different species. I want to know how I look to her, and rather than telling the world someday how she looked to me, I want to tell it to her and see how she reacts. I want her to let me know when I am fudging it—or bullshitting—or confabulating and creating a false mother, a cartoon mother, a Hollywood mother. And after all, though many mothers and daughters struggle with these issues and these overlaps, here we are, my mother and I, both of us writers, both of us stubborn, both of us set in our ways. We live relatively close to one another, we talk on the phone almost every day—why shouldn't we try writing it all down?

So, Mama, are you ready? I have been looking into my soul, and I have come up with some questions, which I know already that we will probably not answer—that probably no one will ever answer once and for all. But I am interested in circling round these together, worrying at them, trying to bite off pieces. And I invite you to offer up your own list for our mutual consideration:

First is a question about the past: Mama, you invented yourself. You came from a family where no one went to college, where girls were not supposed to be educated, a poor and extremely orthodox family, and you made yourself up: a college student, a young woman who lived alone in Greenwich Village, a writer, a teacher, half of a working two-professor couple. You know, travel, literature, art, culture—the whole deal. I live a life in many ways similar to yours, but I had nothing to invent; all I had to do was jump through all the hoops that were being held out to me, as I was cheered on and patted and encouraged by everyone in the world. Get good grades, go to a good college, go to medical school, have the kids, buy the house, see the world, develop a taste for fancy food. How do I understand the strength and the vision that it took for you to imagine a life that no one you knew had lived, and then bring that life to pass? Mama, I think you may be what we call in pediatrics and child psychiatry one of the supersurvivors, the one child who comes out of the devastated (and devastating) home and family and somehow not only survives but thrives. And I think that whatever I am, I am first and foremost a good girl, doing what was expected of me, doing what would bring me parental approval. What kind of life might you have lived if your parents had cheered you on and smoothed your path? Would you somehow have gone even farther, or was it the struggle and the originality that made you what you are? And if I had grown up in the family in which you grew up, would I have had what it took to change the life plan? Or would I just have been the good girl, playing by those rules?

Sheila: You give me too much credit, Perr. I didn't invent myself. I stumbled upon myself. Desperation and fear started me as a child thinking that I had to escape my surroundings and drove me out of my parents' house and into my life.

I began to realize when I was very young that I would not survive in the bitter conflict that was my parents' marriage. Imagine a home where the adults never say a kind word to each other. D. H. Lawrence has a wonderful story in which the walls continually whisper, "There must be more money!" Our walls shouted it. Imagine a New York slum flat with no heat of any sort in winter and no ice to keep food from spoiling in summer, an unhappy overworked mother who (forgive me for this harshness, but that was how I thought of it) never shut up about how badly she had married and how her three children added to her misery by being noisy, dirty, careless—by being children. A scraped shoe, a torn dress, an injury in some game brought forth wrath and punishment. She hit me till I hit her back, and then she stopped.

I was basically by temperament a happy kid, I think, but my childhood seemed designed to make me feel unworthy of anything.

To be fair to my mother, she worked endlessly to keep us fed and clothed and healthy and Jewish and, hardest of all, to make us seem respectable. It was this last heroically impossible effort that was most destructive. Everyone knew we were poor, and she minded terribly.

I looked around me at the adults in my life and noted that most of them were unhappy. I read a lot and loved fiction and drama and poetry. I saw a few movies. I began to dream of other people's kind of lives. My aunt Amy was my most successful relative; she was a public school gym teacher, having put herself through training school. Her job held even through the Depression, when my father—and everyone else—was out of work. I didn't admire or even like her, but I've wondered if she was the model who led me to teaching or at least to the vision of a secure civil service job as the ultimate paradise.

As soon as I could, I got out. I ran away once, when I was a high school junior, then I left permanently when I was a college freshman. I never lived at home again. I had two siblings, both unhappy as well. My sister quit high school to work in a factory, then married a neighborhood boy to get out of that house. And my brother ran away at sixteen, enlisted in the army, and was killed in the Korean War. Our living conditions were unlivable.

I found my way because I was desperate and because I was lucky. I came upon sympathetic people and unearthed oddball jobs. I took the entrance exam and qualified for Brooklyn College—an absolutely free public college. I started college, I moved out of my parents' house— and I loved every minute of this new life. The first taste of it was enough to nourish the dream through all the hard work and waiting. Happiness and beauty beckoned.

And Perri, just as you give me too much credit, you give yourself too little. Sure, you grew up in a middle-class suburb, in an academic home of modest income, but you made good choices. And what makes you think you were such a good girl? You were not an easy teenager. You wanted independence and privacy and freedom. It was hard for us, and it was not an easy time for any parents, I don't think. All around us, your contemporaries in that same middle-class suburb were getting stoned on drugs. Don't you remember that a couple of nice good kids you knew and liked in your high school actually died? And then there were the kids who grew into chronic shoppers fascinated by the New Jersey malls or turned into mindless jocks. We were afraid for you.

The seventies were a restless, frightening time, yet you kept your head. You chose books, you chose medicine, you chose writing. Suddenly you wanted to go into New York on your own. Not to buy drugs or hang out in Times Square, but to study Arabic and Hebrew. It meant letting you go by yourself into the city on the bus several times a week for classes, which was worrisome, but we let you, and you did it. Suddenly you wanted to volunteer to work with recovering addicts. You came home from those meetings stinking of cigarette smoke because the addicts smoked compulsively; you've always detested that smell. Suddenly you wanted to spend a whole adolescent summer volunteering on the hospital ship that gave slum kids free physicals. Superb choices.

You wore incredible clothing—the same torn jeans and T-shirts for years, it seemed to me, and you made your hair as wild as you could. It was a kind of uniform for you and your friends. You hated your high school and balked at going. As in my own life, luck intervened; our town, Leonia, started an alternative high school. You breezed through it in three years and were off to college at sixteen. You finished high school and went off to college and almost immediately met Larry, and the two of you began to work out your own destinies independent of the Jersey suburbs from whence you came.

I'm not clever enough to figure out what we each could have been in other lives. You were smart and strong, and I think you would have made your way, but it would probably have been a very different way.

Me? Who knows? I might have been Leo Tolstoy, after all. But I might have been an inveterate mall shopper. Both possibilities entertain me.

I do believe that a combination of factors determine our destinies. I ran away from home into a babysitting job with kind people who fostered my dreams of college and becoming a writer. My kid brother ran away and joined the army, where he managed to finish high school, and was making himself a good life when the Korean War broke out. He died at seventeen during the second week of the war.

I have always been a worrier, apprehensive and afraid of what might happen in any new situation. Papa, on the other hand, equally concerned and capable of more terrible mental scenarios than I, somehow managed to muster the strength to keep us all going. He had utter confidence in your good sense and judgment, and he reassured and encouraged me.

If I ever did any brave thing, I did not do it bravely, but desperately.

How and why we are who and what we are is a great mystery. It is perhaps what makes writing fiction so fascinating because an author is constantly seekng reasons for the way her characters behave and coherent explanations for what finally happens to them. In real life, of course, there may not be reasons we can see, or coherent explanations—and when we look back and try to construct them, we are partly explaining what happened and partly making up stories.

Petti: It's hard for me to read my mother's answer without wanting to correct it, or annotate it, or even interject my own wise-ass responses (*Well, if that's what you thought of the New Jersey suburbs, drugs and mall rats and mindless jocks, why the hell did we have to live there, huh?*), but I'm trying to restrain myself. How I remember my adolescence (crabby, sullen, dressed like any other vaguely countercultural middle-class child of the era, accumulating virtuous extracurricular activities for my college applications) may not match how she remembers it—but she is entitled to her memories—and to the memories of her fears. I have adolescent children myself these days, and even though it seems to me that these are somewhat easier and gentler times, I have certainly become acquainted with a whole new range of middle-of-the-night anxieties.

But as I read my mother's account of her childhood, I am again struck by that same sense of wonder—how easy I had it, how I spent my teenage years fighting mock and meaningless battles, in comparison to someone who was actually, in a certain sense, fighting for her life. My struggle was to get out of the comfortable New Jersey suburbs—or, in a more real sense, to grow up and learn to like myself and stop being so damn sullen, and to choose the life that appealed to me from a broad buffet of offerings. My mother chooses to consider me improbably heroic for having managed to do so—but then, my mother is also the only person in the world who considers me a computer whiz (because I can use Google, send e-mail, and sometimes even send attachments), so I wouldn't accept her opinion as in any way objective, if you know what I mean.

On the other hand, I'm struck by certain similarities. I also went away to college freshman year and never really lived at home again—I was only sixteen, but I was driven toward some longing for autonomy. My mother thinks she never lived at home again because home was unlivable, but it's possible that there was something positive pulling her, as well as something negative pushing from behind. A need for independence and a desire to make your own way—and make your own world—can push you along even if home is not so bad. She thinks I invented myself, and I think I did what I was supposed to do—but certainly I wanted to be out there in the world, and certainly I wanted to be, like my mother, a person who makes up stories.

Okay, so much for the past. Next, of course, is a question about the present: Mama, you are in the second half of your seventies, and I feel that you are stronger than I am, tougher, more determined, more frugal at every turn. I never worried, growing up, that you would one day break down on us. *I* could break down—I feel that someday I could just say, "Hey, I can't do this"—and my children would be unsurprised. "Oh, Mom's giving up," they would say—it would go perfectly well with the mother they know who sometimes just collapses on the couch and falls fast asleep and therefore isn't available for good-nights. I don't think that my children regard me as a force of nature, as my brother and sister and I regarded you—and as I still regard you. What drives you so that you never let down your guard—or your standards? I mean silly little things—like never leaving dishes in the sink or garbage in the garbage pail overnight—but I also mean the promptness with which you pay bills, answer letters, respond to assignments. I go into any new job a little worried about whether I will get it done and get it done on time, but you, I suspect, have never been a day late in your life with turning in the grades for your courses, submitting a writing assignment, or responding to an invitation. What internal drive is missing in me?

Sheila: Ah, Perri, you idealize your mother. What I see as the flaws of a compulsive coward you see as virtues. I pay bills and R.S.V.P. well before the deadline; I am shamefully early at social events; I do my grade sheets days before they're due, and, in general, I behave with robotic obedience to the orders of society because I fear the consequences.

I know what drives me; it's the conviction that somehow I'll mess up and be destroyed, that the city marshals will throw all our furniture out on the street again because of nonpayment of rent the way they did in 1933. The only one I ever knew who worried more than I in these situations was your father, who, as you well knew, was so anxious he often ended up on flights earlier than the ones he'd booked because he was at the airport so many hours in advance. It takes rigorous discipline to keep such paranoia under control; he was better at it than I am.

I am not strong. Fear of failing and letting people down is what drives me. Since Papa died, I have wondered often about the purpose of my life. Yes, I have incredible, loving children and beautiful grandchildren who are a great pleasure. But the eye doctor tells me I am legally blind and indeed, the world is a much darker place for me, and each day starts with a collection of pills and a blood-pressure machine and ends similarly—except that in the evening, I have to remember to put in my eyedrops. The future is literally and figuratively dim. And lonely, because children and grandchildren must have their own busy lives. Alas, I hate TV, the solace of so many of my cohort, and reading becomes more difficult, though with my special lamp and my special magnifying glass, reading still keeps me great company.

We must make our own terms with life; I feel life has been generous to me. So while a nearly blind, seventy-seven-year-old woman cheerfully negotiating the streets and subways of New York City may be a curious sight, my great joy is that I am still independent, and that I continue to teach fiction writing at my college and to share my pleasure in the craft with students who are wildly unpredictable, and often talented and funny, and sometimes troubled. I enjoy helping them learn how to use words. Last semester one of them ended her course evaluation sheet with the enthusiastic coda "Professor Klass: Your Creative Writing Workshop was the ultimate orgasm!"

Such an evaluation is reason enough to laugh and to keep going. I suggested to the chairman of the English Department that we advertise my course that way next semester; the registration will be overwhelming.

So there's next semester to look forward to. I will get my grade sheets in early, and the future, somehow, will manage itself.

Perri: Oh, Mama, I wish I could make your eyes work better. I understand how ironic and how unfair it is that someone whose great pleasures are reading and grading papers should struggle in a gradually dimming world. *All she wants,* I want to argue before some cosmic arbiter, *is to read normal-sized print in a good light and to mark her students' papers. Is that really so much to ask?* I read what you wrote, and I feel a sense of daughterly outrage, and also a certain sense of medical helplessness and apology—there *ought* to be a way to fix your eyes. But I don't think you give yourself credit for the will that drives you—that continues to drive you.

But of course we are none of us, in the end, irresistible forces of nature. And that brings me to my last question, the one about the future: Mama, what does it mean that I cannot face, cannot contemplate, the idea of life without you? Do you know that I think that in some ways, I am still spending my life trying to make you proud? Well, to make you and Papa proud, but now Papa is gone. When something good happens to me, I want to let you know, whether it's a prize or a publication, whether it's one of the children doing well on a test or in a Little League game. I know you'll be honestly pleased and proud (even if it's something as alien to your sensibilities as the Little League game), that you're cheering us all on and rejoicing in our triumphs. And sometimes I just cannot imagine what the point of life would be without that. And I guess I want to ask how that looks to you—both about what drove you if you didn't feel that way about your own mother, and about how you feel now, in your seventies, about what lies ahead.

Sheila: Don't worry, Perri. After I'm gone, I'll still be around. My mother and father and my brother have lived in my mind vibrantly all these years. My parents' eccentric thinking, their Yiddish expressions, their superstitions and tastes are vivid. My brother's sweet innocence is alive in my memory. He is forever sixteen. I've thought about my parents and our bitterness and have come to a better appraisal of them over the years. Their lives were hard; they probably did the best they could.

I wish, just as your father did—and he was the anthropologist, who specialized in religion, after all—that I believed in an afterlife and had a strong religious faith, but I don't. He used to say, wistfully, that he was tone deaf about religion, and I know exactly what he meant. What a glorious comfort it would be to believe!

You and your brother and your sister added so much joy and wonder to our lives. A large measure of our pleasure, I suspect, was our recognition in you of the values and skills we esteemed. In so many ways you are your individual selves, yet you are us. To have three children who write beautifully, write with pleasure and wit and intelligence, is an unbelievable legacy. You are right that your accomplishments and your children's give me inordinate pleasure. It's only fairly recently that I've begun to recognize how proud I am and how wonderful such vicarious success can be. I've developed the conviction that my children's and grandchildren's achievements are more thrilling than my own. I'm not sure about that, but I believe it's so. Perhaps it's because of the wonder of it; I mean, after all, when I first knew any one of you, you were absolutely helpless. And look at you now.

I think you will always know, when you've done something grand and good, how much joy it would have afforded me even if I'm not around. You know me well enough to be able to measure an accomplishment and say to youself, *Mama would be so proud!* And I would.

When I think about death, I certainly don't like the thought, but somehow I'm not afraid. It seems like the natural order of things. I watch my body changing; it's served me well, but it's old and getting tired. I get angry with it when it fails me, but seventy-seven years is a long time. My father, battling emphysema in his last illness, told me he was tired and ready to rest. I didn't understand then, but I'm beginning to now.

I'm enormously grateful for my good life, for my wonderful husband and my children and grandchildren. I have loved teaching, and I've found the City University of New York—where I got my own free college education and with it my entrée into the world of books—the perfect venue for my own professional life.

I had hoped to be a great novelist—to be Leo Tolstoy—but it didn't happen. But I have published seventeen books, and I am proud of them. And I recently finished a new novel, and who knows? It might be the big one—Leo Tolstoy, watch out!

Since this is not fiction, it can't have a standard happily ever after ending. In fact, it can't have any ending yet. As the Sondheim song says, I'm still here.

CHAPTER TWO

Whistler's Mother and Mine

🌿

Sheila: In May 1939, in the seventh grade at P.S. 16 in Williamsburg, Brooklyn, we wrote "My Mother" compositions for Mother's Day. A copy of "Whistler's Mother" tacked up in the classroom made me feel this was a lovely holiday but somehow not Jewish. Whistler's mother sat resting. She looked kind of old and wore a funny lace doily on her head. His mother looked as if she never yelled. My mother yelled all the time. She never sat. I quickly figured out the saintly portrayal the teacher required for an A and wrote it. On the Friday before Mother's Day, I crumpled up the fiction and threw it away after school, not daring to bring it home.

My older sister, my kid brother, and I (with help from an aunt) raised the small sum necessary to buy a geranium plant as Mama's reward for being our mother, knowing she would be secretly pleased but would scold us for wasting the money. That was the bittersweet way she received all offerings.

Mama never complimented us, nor did she enjoy us. She was afraid of putting a *kineahora* on a child; if she admitted to some beauty or rare quality or success, she would challenge Fate and summon the Evil Eye.

I spent my childhood wishing I had a nicer mother.

I never wanted to grow up to be like her. Even as a kid, I knew this was disloyal and unnatural, but I couldn't help it. My mother was miserable, and I wanted to be happy. Physically, as a child, I was sort of an amalgam, a dark-haired daughter of brunette parents without singular features. I didn't resemble either parent particularly. As I moved into middle age and my hair quickly turned white, I began to look more and more like my mother, and this troubled me because I remembered her always looking so unhappy. Glimpses in the mirror would repeatedly send me to my husband, Mort, to ask, "Don't I look just like my mother?"

"Not when you're happy," he always responded loyally. "When you frown, yes. But you don't look anything like her when you smile."

How would I know how she looked when she smiled?

I consciously try not to frown. I enjoy jokes and I make jokes. I love puns—the worse the pun, the better. I am very loud and quite eccentric and determined not to spend my life in lamentation.

When we kids forgot ourselves in some game or enjoyment and laughed raucously, in would rush our mother to quiet us, always with the same reproof: "Quiet down! What's wrong with you? You think life is for pleasure?"

A rousing "Yes!" should have been the answer—after all, we were children—but of course, no one dared to think it, much less say it. My mother was the mistress of rhetorical guilt.

I am not my mother. And yet . . .

Besides dealing with the mirror, I've had to filter out the echoes. Over the years, I have recognized her voice emerging from my throat, mostly when I was angry—and I have been appalled. It was the unreasonable voice of someone who did not listen; it went on endlessly listing old crimes. It meted out large dollops of guilt for small accidents, for insignificant errors like an overdue library book (two cents a day), for tardiness, for forgotten tasks, that were magnified by constant repetition. It was not so much what she said that drove me crazy as her tone: a wronged, good person being abused. That I carried this voice in my head and that petty situations evoked it from me as if I were a ventriloquist's dummy disturbed me enormously. Again, I was determined not to sound like my mother, who used her voice as her single weapon in her unending outraged combat against the poverty that was her life. She literally never stopped talking.

Except when she and my father had trouble. Then she wouldn't say a word to him, and the sudden, heavy silence in the house, the absence of her constant voice, was frightening. Silence moved in as a threatening presence and hovered for a long time, during which we children were used as instruments by the two combatants, usually within earshot of one another. Gruff commands: "Tell your mother!" "Tell your father!" directed us to repeat words already heard. A few times, I tried to say "But he hears you" or "But she hears you." My reasoning was met with angry glares by both parties, so I learned to comply. It was madness, but it was the pattern I learned, and I detested it.

However, I grew up knowing no other way. So when I met my husband-to-be, if we had differences, I retreated into unreasonable balky silence. He, however, hated stupidity—he had been raised in a similarly warring household where silent grudges were held for years—so he would insist that no matter how angry or uncomfortable we were, we had to talk. I didn't know how to do that. I had to learn, and it was not easy but I couldn't maintain aggressive silence against someone who loved me and was clever and funny and charming, and who kept talking. He made me laugh, and we talked.

The epithets my mother reserved for those who wronged her, in both Yiddish and English, these insults that I heard more than a half century ago, are currently long-playing selections on the soundtrack of my mind. The top ten are *nudnik* (bore), *schnorrer* (beggar), *schnook* (dope), *apikoiris* (heretic), *chochem* (wise guy), *pascudniak* (lousy person), *goniff* (thief), *schlemiel* (luckless fellow), *meshuggenah* (crazy man), and *Moishe Poopik* (Mr. Nobody).

In my mind, today, as I think about my mother, these angry epithets alternate with the endless everyday commandments:

Thou shalt not wear out clothing, particularly shoes.

Thou shalt not slam the door.

Thou shalt not turn on the lights before it's pitch dark.

Thou shalt not leave any food on the plate because the children in Europe are starving. Corollary: All kosher food is edible and delicious no matter how it looks or tastes, so finish it.

Thou shalt not trust anyone who is not in the family.

Thou shalt not talk to neighbors, who are all enemies out to get us.

Thou shalt not use so much hot water, soap, toothpaste, writing paper, ink, shoe polish, toilet paper—in fact, anything that costs money.

Thou shalt not speak above a whisper.

Thou shalt not tread heavily on floors or stairs. Walk on tiptoe.

Thou shalt not get nits.

Thou shalt not play the radio so loud it can be heard.

My mother had a pathological hatred of noise. It was fundamental to her pardon-me-for-living mentality. If we didn't make noise maybe *they* wouldn't notice us. *They* would think we were educated. *They* wouldn't find us intrusive. *They* might even consider us *refined*. Each slam of a door evoked a harangue—and we all slammed doors. The one childhood resolution that I have managed to keep absolutely is this: I swore to myself that I would never scold or punish anyone for closing a door. And I still shut doors forcefully myself. I'm still a slammer.

I have come to understand that much of the madness that reigned in my mother's house was self-designed. For example: She did all the laundry for us, a family of five, by hand, yet insisted on using tablecloths for all meals. Most people in our neighborhood used oil-cloth on the kitchen table, but my mother felt that was lower class (in a coldwater flat, which never had any visitors or company!). So each spill became a drama, a tragedy, as did muddied, soiled, or torn clothing.

"What do you care if I rub my knuckles raw on the scrubbing board and then stand over a hot iron for hours?" she'd carry on over a stain. And of course, the clumsiest culprit, the frequent spiller of *every-thing*, was me.

In Maurice Sendak's *Where the Wild Things Are*, I recognized immediately the ultimate term of the angry mother. "WILD THING!" the mother calls Max, and she sends him to bed without supper, the ultimate punishment. WILD THING! The Yiddish *vilde chaya* (wild animal), much stronger than the English, was practically my nickname.

So I resolved that I would be quite a different kind of mother. But I look more and more like my mother each day, and the voice lives on in my head, no matter how hard I work at muffling it. What I learned as a child remains within, and the struggle to modify it is lifelong.

How am I like my mother? I do not think I can count the ways.

My mother had all kinds of disparaging terms for women who wore slippers and were not fully dressed after waking. She dressed the minute she woke, and began her chores. I am unable to lounge about in robe and slippers no matter where I am. In fact, I've never owned a pair of slippers. I rise very early and dress even on vacations or holidays. The very way she said *house slippers* turned them into dirty words.

My mother was a fanatic housekeeper. Her harshest indictment of a woman was that she was not a *balabusta*—her house was a mess, there was a coat on a chair or dust on furniture. Perhaps because keeping the house was how my mother spent her life, she had to make it important. I am a conscientious—if not fastidious—housekeeper. No coats sit on my chairs. I attempt orderliness. But Mama haunts my kitchen. Perri teases me because I never leave anything in the sink, not even a glass or a spoon, and my excuse is the city dweller's fear of roaches. Perfectly legitimate, but when I lived in the bush in Trinidad and India or in a village in Vermont, the pattern did not change. No roaches—still, the sink had to be clear.

One of the ways I knew my mother was getting frailer, in the last years of her life, was the dust, which she could no longer see or reach. This was a woman, after all, who sat outside on the window ledges of her third-floor apartment and washed the windows with cold water and newspapers. City dirt was her sworn enemy. I never wash windows and, indeed, do not notice their condition. My father smoked, and my mother would empty the ashtray each time any ash was dropped in it, making the process agony for the smoker. Garbage in my house goes out immediately, and wastebaskets are emptied before I go to sleep. I can't say why, but the presence of trash bothers me.

My mother was stingy and poor. She neither could nor would ever buy any clothes except as basic coverings. I think she went decades without buying a dress. She cut her own hair. She took no interest or pride in clothes or ornaments. She used powder and lipstick on very rare occasions. She had no friends. She did not seem to like people. I am stingy and not poor. Still, I gravitate to sale racks and merchandise with a reduced price. When I get a great bargain, I am so proud of it that I am eager to show the "damage" that lowered its price. "See the tiny damage?" Mama used to say, and I wondered then why she told, since it was not visible. But I can't resist either. I often resolve to buy "good" things and pay no attention to prices. I can't. Any beautiful clothing I have, Perri has chosen for me, and in fact over the years, it's become an entertainment in the college where I teach. Colleagues commenting on a new piece of apparel say, "I'll bet Perri bought that for you." Since she has sumptuous taste and probably longed for a regal mother, I possess some beautiful things.

I cut my own hair. I do not like people working on me, and the times I've been talked into professional haircuts, I've been disappointed. But my mother cut her own hair to save money! I know, I know.

My mother played no games, and I play none. My mother-in-law loved cards and played poker often, and my father played pinochle. My children play hundreds of games. I've tried to learn, and I can manage a game of "war," though I usually lose, but I'm terrible at Monopoly and the rest, and I learned the rules of chess, but no one who likes the game can bear to play me. Even Scrabble, which I truly enjoy, makes me nervous. It always seems to be taking too long.

All through my children's schooling, I went to their events with my husband, who participated in everything with genuine pleasure. My son, a high school athlete, played every conceivable sport. I loved watching my children, but I had no real interest in the activities. I am game deaf. Watching or playing games, I suppose, will always carry the judgment "Wasting time!"

My mother was terrified of authority—anyone in uniform, a policeman, even a postman—but that might have been the effect poverty had on her. Officials meant trouble: The city marshals evicted us for nonpayment of rent and left our furniture in the street, and the Home Relief investigators (oh, what revulsion that word *investigator* aroused!), she told us over and over, had looked in the pots to see if she was cooking expensive meat.

Did someone really look in her pots? Who knows?

I'm never comfortable with authority, though I'm not terrified by it. Last week, I got a summons to serve on a grand jury, and I felt my heart racing immediately. All my life, encounters with well-dressed people in offices have intimidated me. Each visit to my literary agent is harrowing even though I know she is working for me. The same uncertainty clouds meetings with publishers who are publishing my books, accountants, lawyers, and, of course, doctors.

My mother, who had never had enough money to live on, wanted her children to be safe, to get good jobs, and be secure for life. She and my father fought with me, urging me to take a commercial course in high school, so I could be a secretary and achieve nirvana: a white-collar job. I resisted and took an academic course, and for four years we battled over my impracticality. Remembering those hard years, I wanted my children to be free to dream and follow their dreams. They did: Perri is a pediatrician and writer; David is a screenwriter and novelist; Judy is a college professor, playwright, and poet. I think their grandmother would be proud, but she would have found the choices a horrific gamble. Had it been up to her, they would all have taken commercial courses.

Surely, this mother I have gone on so long about must have given me qualities I should be grateful for. She did. She made sure we got library cards as soon as we were eligible, and she encouraged us to read, because she loved books. As a girl, reading had been her own greatest pleasure, but by the time I got to know her, she had no time for books.

She must at some point really have devoted herself to Shakespeare, particularly the tragedies, because she freely quoted from them all the time. So we had a raging mother regularly interrupting her Yiddish-English tirades to exclaim melodramatically:

> *How sharper than a serpent's tooth it is*
> *To have a thankless child!*

Or she'd glance up at the Unseen Listener to confide:

> *Ingratitude, thou marble-hearted fiend!*
> *More hideous when thou showest thee in a child,*
> *Than the sea monster.*

Sea monster? When I was a kid, I didn't know what this strange language meant, but I knew I had done something so terrible it could not be discussed in normal language.

I may be the only English teacher ever who was introduced to Shakespeare this way.

The few books salvaged from her girlhood traveled with us on our frequent relocations: *The Secret Power* and various other romances by Marie Corelli, *Lorna Doone* by Blackmore, *Ivanhoe* and *The Talisman* by Sir Walter Scott. My mother, who didn't marry till she was thirty, had dreamed all those years of a life filled with gentility and beauty. "A small cottage in the country with roses around it and a white picket fence . . ." Even when she was old, she continued her habit, on Sunday nights, of poring over the real estate section of the newspaper and reading aloud descriptions of country houses. "Listen. 'Three-room bungalow. Wrap-around porch. Catskill, New York . . .'" Her Elysium was a complete cliché, but the cliché gave comfort. It worked, so it was a vision of infinite worth. It may have saved her sanity.

For more than half a century, my mother shopped, cooked, cleaned, and ran a household. Somehow she fed us and kept us healthy. From her, I learned that a mother had to be the first one up in the morning and the last one to bed. I learned one could not start the day without a hot breakfast preceded by orange juice. She'd heard a radio diet expert say that once the juice was poured, the vitamins began to escape, and so once she'd poured juice, we had to come running at her summons. "Quick! Quick! The vitamins are escaping," she'd whisper-shout frantically. Even if you'd just gotten your turn in the bathroom (five people, one bathroom), you had to run out and gulp down your juice.

I learned the absolute dinner-diet rule: a starch, a green vegetable, a protein, and a fruit. And I followed this rule faithfully with my own family. Of course, it was easier for me because I had food money. Basins of soup, intended as fillers, always preceded her dinners; I could buy enough fish or meat for people to fill up.

My mother cared about honesty and truthfulness and loyalty. Morals concerned her mightily, but she had no language for talking about moral issues. She'd somehow been tongue-tied by the worst of Victorianism. The dangerous word *sex* was never directly spoken. She expected us to be "decent" and to figure out how by ourselves. It wasn't easy.

Later, in my own home with my own children, I can trace many echoes, many ways in which we grappled with the same problems. It's never easy to teach morality—but at least we had language. Mort had it more than I, and I think we managed not to make our children feel weird and scared. Nothing was unmentionable. And Shakespeare survived even my mother's handling. Maybe it was a painful way for me to learn the power of his verse, but I learned to love it, and I wanted to bring up my own children to know those lines. Thanks to Joseph Papp and the Public Theater, Shakespeare became a pleasure for my children from the time they could sit still and be quiet, for we all frequented the free Shakespeare performances in Central Park. My youngest child, Judy, when she was five once confounded a visitor by saying, "As Romeo said, 'A rose by any other name would smell as sweet.' "

In her own strange way, my mother gave me Shakespeare, and books, and the power of fantasy, along with the diet rule and the housewifely obsessions. I learned that a mother is responsible and dependable. I learned that a mother cares no matter how sharply she chides, that the bond is unique between mother and child, and marvelous and sometimes terrible, but it holds. I learned that she who gives you life is never completely separated from you.

Finally, I realized that the joy and pride one takes in one's children every single day is the parent's true and most glorious reward for the endless, incredibly difficult job of having and raising them. That pleasure should be savored constantly. It is the grand prize of life. And my mother forfeited it. So afraid was she of taking the future for granted, of summoning the Evil Eye with a *kineahora,* she never allowed herself what was rightfully hers: the pride and pleasure of parenthood.

Often in the mornings as I pour the orange juice, I can hear my mother's voice, and my mind's eye looks for tiny demonic droplets leaping from the glass, trying to elude their function—to nourish.

Mama, they did not get away.

CHAPTER THREE

My Mother's Mother and Mine

✤

Perri: I remember my grandmother, of course, my grandma Virginia, my mother's mother. I remember her cheerless but exceedingly orderly Brooklyn apartment, which always smelled slightly odd to me. Not bad—it just seemed as if the air was different. Later on, when I was old enough to travel, I would sometimes find myself in a foreign house, breathing foreign air that was just slightly, indescribably, different, the amalgam of different products, different cooking, different habits, and I would recall my grandparents' apartment.

To me, my grandmother was a reasonably kind, if dour, lady who fixated on the oddest questions. Take the time we came to visit the day after the Miss America Pageant. It was back in the early seventies, when *everyone* watched the Miss America Pageant. My grandmother was triumphant because the right contestant had won—the girl who sang some refined, operatic number in the talent competition, not the one who did the slightly suggestive Broadway-style song-and-dance. "I think we were all worried," my grandmother announced.

She was relatively willing to praise her grandchildren—certainly more willing than she had ever been to praise her own children—but the praise popped out in peculiar circumstances. Once she saw me eating a cucumber, and she made a tremendous fuss about what a sensible, healthy snack I had chosen, and how most young girls would only eat junk.

What I especially remember, of course, and particularly after reading my mother's memories, is how my grandmother and my mother used to fight. The fights always seemed to me to follow the same pattern: My mother would make some gesture, meant to accommodate or please her mother, and her mother would reject it, completely and absolutely, making a face that suggested disgust and disappointment. My grandmother was strictly kosher and therefore would not eat in our house. I remember her coming to visit, and my mother showing her that she had bought an unopened container of kosher cottage cheese, and plastic utensils. "See, Mama, you'll be able to eat that for lunch," she said, and her mother shook her head, making that very particular grimace. My mother took the lid off the cottage cheese, showing her that the plastic seal was untouched—brought out the new box of plastic cutlery—but her mother continued to purse her lips and shake her head. The unclean unkosher kitchen, she made it clear, contaminated everything. She would not eat in our house.

Or there was the time that my mother discovered a line of thick, soft, cotton flannel overshirts—moleskin, I think they were called. She bought one for her mother, who was always cold and always complaining that woolen and acrylic sweaters itched her. I remember listening as my mother tried to convince her mother to try on the flannel shirt—or even to touch it and see how soft and nonitchy it was—no wool, no acrylic, nothing that could irritate. And again, I remember my grandmother's face of disgust and refusal, as she said, over and over, that she wouldn't try it, it would only itch.

As children, we knew that visits to her mother often upset my mother—as we knew that this grandmother was not "the good cook." (The other grandmother, my father's mother, was secretly acknowledged to be "the nice grandmother," though this could not be said; it was, however, acknowledged that she was a brilliant cook, and that therefore she was the natural one to host seders and other family occasions. My mother's mother, of course, could not eat in her house, either, because she was casual about the dietary laws.)

I was out of the house and away in college during the last years of my grandmother's life, the years during which my mother was shopping for her and schlepping to the doctor with her. According to my mother, the two of them never stopped having those fights, and my grandmother never, not once, let go of her chronic disappointment. She never acknowledged any of what my mother had achieved in life—not the college degrees, the job as a college professor, not the successful marriage and three children, not the comfortable home and the middle-class life. My mother had reason to believe that when she wasn't there, her mother boasted about some of these things, but she never heard as an adult—any more than she had heard as a child—the kind of praise or pride that I would like, as her outraged daughter, to claim for her.

Sheila: My mother's one concession: She was proud of my books, proud that I wrote and got published. She worshipped "culture" and literature. She went to bookstores and moved my first novel, *Come Back on Monday*, so it would be more prominently displayed. She scolded public librarians if the book was not in their collections. Her comment to me about the novel was that it was good, but I shouldn't have so much "sex" in it. (There's almost no sex in it.) She could barely utter the word. She whispered.

Perri: I came home from college for my grandmother's funeral. The eulogy was delivered by some funeral-home rabbi who knew my grandmother only from a quick prefuneral conference with my mother and her sister, and who was probably giving us his formula old-woman eulogy. At one point he praised my grandmother as "A true *yiddishe momma*," and my mother, sitting beside me, her eyes leaking tears, muttered to me, "A *yiddishe momma* who read Delderfield!" Those enormous panoramic novels of English history—*God Is an Englishman, Theirs Was the Kingdom*—were important to my grandmother during her final years. Her strictly kosher brain was living at least partly in the British countryside. It was my mother's way of acknowledging her own mother, I suppose, in all her never-to-be untangled complexity. My mother has never softened her memories of her mother, never forgiven her for the harshness and pain of the home that drove out all its children—but also never simplified her and never lost sight of the crushing burden of poverty under which she struggled.

My mother came so far from her own mother's life that when she thinks about ways they are alike, it's a little hard for me to take it seriously. The air in my mother's apartment smells normal to me: American air, professional, comfortable, middle-class air. The walls do not whisper about money, and it's okay to slam doors and there are no tablecloths to worry about. My mother's need to empty the sink—and the garbage—at insanely frequent intervals is a foible about which she can be teased. I don't think anyone ever teased *her* mother about anything. Life was not for pleasure.

And yet, I can't help reading down that list to see which of the connections extend on to me: I also can't stand to have anyone work on me; I don't actually cut my own hair, but I understand the impulse. And come to think of it, I'm not much of a game-player. I have been persistently unable to learn the rules of bridge, despite at least pretending to try for years. When my nine-year-old learned them, the four other members of my family could play without me, and they have, with some relief, stopped trying to teach me. I can tolerate a single round of Clue or Scrabble, but I get more than a little twitchy. And which connections have I completely escaped or rejected or left, literally, in the dust? Well, that would be the housekeeping impulses, of course—but also the balanced meal rules.

I was brought up by parents who thought I was a joy and a miracle. I cannot understand how my mother could grow up in the household she describes and come away so certain of who she is, so able to laugh at all the jokes in the world—including Shakespeare's. I can see how she formed her own life—and our own family—in reaction to her own childhood, but I still do not understand how she found her way, and how she found her strength.

CHAPTER FOUR

Like and Unlike

I. PERRI'S LISTS

Five ways I am like my mother: external

- I coupled off with a bearded academic guy.
- We have three children.
- I have worked full-time pretty much straight through since finishing my training.
- I write fiction and nonfiction around the edges of my family and my job.
- I very rarely go to the doctor.

Six ways I am different from my mother: external

- I am a physician and she is a professor of English.
- I am fat and she is thin.
- She has a perfectly neat and orderly house, and I live in mess and clutter.
- I spend most of the money I make, and she spends almost nothing.
- I live in Cambridge, Massachusetts, and she lives in Manhattan.
- I know how to drive, and she doesn't.

Five ways I am like my mother: internal

- I tend to get very worried and anxious about vague impending catastrophe, and to stop sleeping.
- I am somewhat prone to depression (and very unwilling to contemplate the idea of medication for it).
- I am easily bored, and impatient when I am bored.
- On some profound level, I am not worried about how I look, and I don't understand women who are.
- I am more relaxed and at home in cities than in the country.

Four ways I am different from my mother: internal

- I can go to sleep if there's a dish in the sink, and she can't.
- I can live with an unanswered letter, and she can't.
- I am not afraid of my agent or my editor, and she is afraid of all agents and all editors.
- I am chronically behind and always missing deadlines, and she is completely caught up.

II. SHEILA'S LISTS

(but Perri had to put the bullets in, because Sheila is afraid of bullets)

Ways I am like my daughter:

- I am a monogamous creature.
- I like men who are sensitive, smart, witty, and who enjoy food.
- I'd rather read than do almost anything else.
- I love travel. I'm insatiably curious about other places, other cuisines, other cultures.
- I have little interest in altering the way I look, so I don't tweeze, massage, cream, or do any of the things that would, no doubt, transform me.

- I do polish my toenails. (I was surprised to find that Perri does too.)
- I have pierced ears.
- I love to eat.
- I love to write.
- I wear comfortable clothing, nothing that pinches, flattens, squeezes me, or takes my heels off the ground.
- I am delighted by small children.
- I have boundless energy for anything except housework (which I do compulsively but hate—wait, maybe it's time to switch to ways I am different from Perri . . .).

Ways I am different from my daughter:

- I eat breakfast.
- I wear shoes in my house.
- I never allow old copies of the *New York Times* to pile up; Perri lives with piles of papers she's going to read someday.
- I try to get a good night's sleep each night because I can't function otherwise; Perri pushes herself until she drops.
- I'm stingy. Credit cards make it easier, but the truth is I've never recovered from the Depression. Perri spends with remarkable ease.
- I suffer anxiety and claustrophobia in taxis, so I use public transportation; Perri would diagnose this as meterphobia.
- I can only work on a single book or story at a time. Perri always has a pile of things due and overdue.
- I have absolutely no self-confidence in any business situation.
- I am terrified of machines and cannot work most of them: cars, VCR, microwave, and, worst of all, the computer on which I write. I distrust them, am afraid I'll break them, and see them as both master and enemy.
- I've found teaching the most wonderful, challenging, and fulfilling profession.

- I like movies, even bad ones; Perri is a highly critical and infrequent moviegoer.
- I put things away as soon as I get home. Perri enters and drops everything in the living room, with good intentions.
- I love corny jokes and bad puns, and they make Perri impatient.

CHAPTER FIVE

Family Stew

Perri: My mother's favorite cookbook when I was growing up was Peg Bracken's *I Hate to Cook Book.* Slightly subversive in the early 1960s, its text offered wit, wisdom, and recipes for women in their unending domestic battles. I read it over and over. Without even looking at the book, I can tell you that early on the author announces that her intended audience is those women who would rather fold their hands around a dry martini than a wet flounder at the end of the day. I was too young for dry martinis, or even dry martini fantasies (and ours was not a martini kind of house, in any case), but I responded to the humor and the tone and the cheerfully irreverent spirit with which Peg Bracken spat into the wind of maternal perfection. Or maybe not. Maybe instead of engaging in a protofeminist rebellion, I was just discovering that I like to read cookbooks, especially cookbooks with a little personality stirred in.

I like to read cookbooks and I like to cook. I clip recipes from the newspaper food section and buy ingredients I've never tried before—though, of course, I also repeat certain weekday meals over and over. And I am very much a creature of my times; unlike my mother, I frequently don't cook at all. My children are accustomed to eating out on a regular basis—which can mean five days a week, when the going gets tough.

My mother was one of the very few working mothers in the New Jersey suburbs in the 1960s and early 1970s. She caught the bus at the corner every weekday morning and went into Manhattan to teach English and writing at a community college. She came home in the afternoon with a briefcase full of student papers to mark, and busily—each and every afternoon—set about preparing a family dinner with a protein main dish, a green vegetable, and a starch. Oh, and some fruit, either before or after. Every damn day.

My mother believed—and still believes—that she hates to cook. She believed that she was fighting against some ideology that prized home cooking, prized anything that took extra time and effort. The world, she thought, was demanding that she produce home-baked cakes to prove a moral point, when anyone could see that bakery goods were actually much better. She invented for herself a rigid kitchen code, of what was doable and what was too much trouble. As with many of my mother's rules and regulations, this code made no particular logical sense; she was happy to deal with whole onions, whole cloves of garlic, whole eggplants—but regarded a whole head of broccoli as a tremendous imposition. Broccoli and cauliflower and green beans could be prepared only from frozen packages, but green peas, in season, could be shelled and eaten as a treat. She would hand-roll dozens of stuffed cabbage rolls, simmer them in tomato sauce—and then serve them over canned potatoes, because peeling potatoes was "trouble." But the rule that never varied, as I grew up, was that there had to be that balanced meal on the table every night—no frozen entrées, no sending out for pizza.

Sheila: I always sensed that I was losing the race in the kitchen. I felt pursued all the time, and very guilty. The only way for me to catch up was with shortcuts, and shortcuts in a race mean cheating. How else to feed the five hungry people who depended on me for at least two and often three meals a day for decades? I was an anomaly, a suburban working mother. Hadn't the school psychologist summoned me to warn me my first-grader was not achieving to capacity? "You should be at home and she should be sitting in your lap," he reproached me as I departed hastily to catch my bus. I wanted to hit him.

Sitting on that 166 bus from the Port Authority bus terminal back to New Jersey in the afternoon, clutching that briefcase full of student papers, I would contemplate dinner not with any sensual or creative pleasure but with a strong feeling of anxiety: Would I be able to do it again tonight, one more time? I was living the life I'd chosen, but I hadn't known it would be so hard. Since I had been away all day, I felt I owed my family a home-cooked dinner; my children sometimes begged for the TV dinners that their friends ate, but TV dinners were anathema to me. A mother owed her family a home-cooked dinner. That must be written somewhere in the Old Testament, because no fundamental truth was more religiously observed in my own parents' home.

The two grandmothers telephoned nightly to be sure, given my errant behavior, that their grandchildren had made it safely through the day. "Who leaves a child with strangers?" my mother-in-law asked rhetorically. While some of my neighbors worked part-time or volunteered a few hours during the week, I, with young children, was the one who had the hubris to accept a full-time job in the city.

When my children look back at their childhoods, they imagine I was a good cook. They think they remember it, but they imagine it. I was not a good cook; I was a captive cook. I knew where my creative impulses were directed: I would rather write than cook. But I thought my obligations included a hot breakfast for everyone every morning, with the obligatory glass of orange juice, and then those protein-starch-vegetable-fruit dinners. So each morning, I set up the Crock-Pot, which turned out eight-hour tetrazzinis and cacciatores and casseroles galore. A particular exotic favorite was Spanish Chicken made with beer and stuffed olives. Oh, and then dessert! Married to a man with a chocolate fixation, whose mother had indulged him with layer cake twice a day, I became an artisan of instant chocolate pudding pies in store-bought graham-cracker piecrusts, an architect of premixed layer cakes lathered together with instant adhesive frosting.

My personal assembly line mass-produced thousands of chocolate-chip and coconut snowball cookies. That was my entire dessert repertoire.

While I admired the glossy beauty of vine-ripened tomatoes and the scent of fresh coriander and thyme, I used frozen-canned-dehydrated-processed everything edible. I followed recipes religiously, deviating only by replacing fresh ingredients with shortcut versions.

I discovered several dishes my family loved: Curried Honey Chicken, Sweet-and-Sour Stuffed Cabbage, and Lamb Riblets. All three have seductive smells. The chicken and lamb dishes were inexpensive (lamb riblets were fifteen cents a pound in the 1960s). Both dishes were easy to prepare, essentially mixing up a sauce, pouring it over the meat, and setting the pot in the oven. The stuffed cabbage was the single aberration, my one great labor-intensive dish. The recipe came indirectly from my grandmother. I'd watched her and estimated the ingredients because she never measured anything. She used handfuls and bowlfuls and pinches of this and that. I'd loved her, and I loved making her stuffed cabbage for my family. The leaves had to be boiled tender and malleable but not mushy; the meat and onions and condiments and eggs required gentle kneading together. Contouring the meat so it was sealed in shapely, symmetrical cabbage rolls (not fastened by toothpicks but self-adhering) was a triumph. To my great pleasure, I recently taught my granddaughter, Josephine, Perri's daughter, to do this. She turned out to be a natural-born cabbage roller.

Over the years, I served these dishes so often that I think the children became addicted. That may account for their inflated view of my culinary skills. I'd conned them into thinking I was a good cook. This got me into trouble in the early seventies, when my fourteen-year-old son volunteered me to provide the chocolate mousse for his French class dinner—to be held at Alan Alda's house, no less. Nineteen students! Up till then, MyTFine instant chocolate pudding was my standby, poured into that store-bought graham-cracker piecrust for special occasions.

I pointed out that any sensible boy would have volunteered me to buy the bread or the Camembert.

"But, Mom," he explained, "I thought—well, you're such a good cook, you'd know how, and it would be fun."

My skill with bottled sauces and canned soups had inflamed his imagination.

What could I say? Can a goddess decline her divinity?

But I didn't own and had never used a double boiler. I'd never melted chocolate. Why would I?

I looked *mousse* up in *Larousse Gastronomique*. The recipe was formidable. Texture—an aspect of cooking I never before had time to consider—was vital. The Chantilly cream—Chantilly cream?—had to be perfect and the egg whites beaten exactly right. I would be multiplying the Larousse recipe by five to feed the banquet. That was five bars of chocolate to melt and fifteen cups of cream to blend perfectly.

My husband called a linguist we knew whose hobby was cooking, and he provided a mousse recipe that didn't call for a double boiler. In fact, there was no cooking involved. This mousse had a secret extra ingredient: one tablespoon of Cointreau for each chocolate bar. I painstakingly whipped up the sweet, and my son carried it away, later reporting his teacher's enthusiastic pronouncement. *"Formidable!"* Madame had declared, eating away.

Bless her. My reputation was intact. I like to think it was the Cointreau that got to her.

When I think back to dusk during those years, I remember the aromas of the cooking luring children in for samples and my great joy at seeing them and being back with them again. At night, after the long day in the city, I had a feeling of contentment that I was at home in the kitchen where I was supposed to be. Mostly, we ate our evening meal around the kitchen table, all together, saving the dining room for state occasions, and that dinner hour was a tumult of everyone's day— for we are all talkers. The food disappeared rapidly. We had no "bad eaters" in our family, and it was always a pleasure to see a dish I'd prepared being appreciatively devoured. So permanent was our family habit of dining together that months after Perri had gone off to college, I found myself still setting her place at the table. But that fond feeling that I was at home in the kitchen where I most belonged was fleeting. After the meal, particularly if I'd drunk a glass of wine, I'd had enough housewifery and would have been happy to flee as quickly as possible. But of course, I could never leave anything unwashed, so my escape was not easy. When I finally turned out the light in the kitchen at night and made my way out, I was a tired mother still running. And then I had all those papers to grade.

Perri: She's wrong, you know. She was a pretty good cook. Even a kind of ambitious, or exotic cook, at least by suburban standards of forty years ago. We were not allowed TV dinners, no matter how much we begged, and we grew up eating a wide variety of curries, because my father was an anthropologist and my parents had lived in Trinidad and India, and both came away with a taste for Indian cooking. Her spice shelf included garam masala, turmeric, cumin, coriander, and cayenne, and her pantry held not only sweet mango chutney but also achar, the spicy mango pickle in mustard oil that my father loved to spoon out alongside his lamb curry or his chicken curry or his potato curry.

But my mother does not believe, and will never believe, that she was a good cook. She will turn this, no matter what I say, into a story about what a good cook *I* am, and any weaknesses I might cite—I often don't cook at all, I bring in pizza or takeout, or just take my family out, when I do cook I make enormous messes in my already disorderly kitchen—she will turn into praise. Praise for me, praise for my skills, and criticism of her own. My mother refuses any suggestion that there may actually be some element of sensuality in her relationship to food, that she may be guided in her choices and her habits by taste and smell and the easy domestic pleasures they bring, rather than by rigid recipe-following and a Victorian sense of duty.

She did have a Victorian sense of duty. When I think of those hot breakfasts, served at the kitchen table on plates—with silverware and napkins—every day of the week, I am torn between admiration and a sense of helpless anger on her behalf. And then of course, there's my own sense of losing my own race, as I hustle my unbreakfasted children out the door in the morning, advising them to grab a handful of nuts to eat in the car.

My mother would probably say that I am a better cook—and certainly a more confident cook—than she ever was. I would probably politicize the discussion by saying that was not because of any innate talent. It's because I don't feel obligated to cook every day. I don't feel it's my responsibility and only mine to put dinner on the table—let alone breakfast!—for my own family of five. I don't think I'm failing as a mother if I come home tired and decide it's a good night for Thai food (as when is it not?), and I don't think it's necessarily my job in the domestic equation to stock the larder and plan the menu. When Larry and I come home at the end of the day, with our assortment of children and bags stuffed with work overflowing into the evening, there's a certain competitive race to ask the question "Is there any food in the house?" It's almost as if we both believe that the one who has to answer "No, I don't think so; maybe we should go out" is the one who has failed to provision the family.

And certainly all that leaves me feeling freer to cook for pleasure—or to take pleasure in my cooking. I have my own repertoire of stock weekday meals as well, of course, and my own list of things that just sound too hard or too much trouble—but food and cooking are also sources of pleasure, fantasy, and adventure for me. I enjoy the preparing of ritual menus on ritual days, from the Thanksgiving turkey to the borscht for the pink dinner we have every Valentine's Day to the macaroni and spareribs dinner that all three children demand on their birthdays. I am, I suppose, a highly egotistical cook: I expect my children to appreciate the culinary effort that goes into these gastronomic observances, to look—and taste—and applaud.

Sheila: I live alone now, and I cook very little. I attribute this inactivity to both the laziness of being a septuagenarian and the lack of company in the kitchen.

How far I've come. When I first married, I thought my husband,

Mort, an intruder in "my" kitchen. I minded him there and tried to keep him out. My father had never been allowed into my mother's kitchen; he would mix up the kosher dishes, he was totally incompetent, and being there was not "manly." Thus instructed, I stupidly followed suit. Stubbornly, insistently, Mort taught me that it was "our" kitchen, and he had his role in it. He had prepared his bachelor meals for years before he met me. He liked to cook, he carved skillfully, and he didn't even mind doing dishes. Mort loved food. His body was somehow mysteriously programmed so that three times a day, no matter what, at rigidly set hours, he had to be fed or he became ravenous and practically irrational. There was a family story that when he was a small boy he'd been sent to bed without supper. He had taken a bite of his baby sister's arm, and when his frantic mother demanded of him, "Why did you do that?" he'd responded, "I thought it was a lamb chop!" That story may well be apocryphal, for we are a family of storytellers—and Mort was a gentle person, but he was transformed by hunger. He was a carnivore with a sweet tooth and no appetite for vegetables until curry changed his life. After field trips to Trinidad and India, he would eat curried anything. And he was terrific company as we worked; I had time with the person I loved most, smart, funny, and interesting. I miss him dreadfully, as I miss the wonderful bright young faces of our children in the late afternoons following the cooking scents to their source.

Recently I've taken to buying TV dinners, which I find generic but acceptable taken with heavy doses of achar or some relish to spice them up. An incalculable advantage to frozen dinners, of course, is that there are no dishes or pots to wash afterward, and that is a continuing pleasure. I am not at present reduced to a plastic wine goblet and disposable cutlery, but I may get there yet. And these days, as I read and eat my Salisbury steak or chicken teriyaki, occasionally I pause to wonder whatever made me so hesitant to serve TV dinners to my family long ago. Could it have been my mother's view of a woman's destiny—fated for the kitchen and the laundry? Was I making myself irreplaceable, preserving the image of the essential homemaker mother? I, who was so eager to be out of the house and having my career? I, who loved teaching and thought it a noble profession? Home-cooked had seemed so important, so vital then.

When I visit Perri and her family, cooking is an indoor sport. Everyone plays. Often the kitchen is a sort of happy bedlam, with Larry baking pies and cakes and the children employed in various preparatory activities: grating, paring, slicing, washing, and, most important, tasting. Perri is the communications center from whom all critical commands flow. Her cooking philosophy requires the use of every utensil possible with abandon and no care as to washing up. There are no bare counters or other surfaces in their kitchen, and where to put hot pans and bubbling cauldrons is a matter of exquisite balance and fine judgment. And yet, and yet, from this maelstrom of mad culinary activity come the most incredible, palatable, indeed beautiful dishes: pasta with glorious complicated sauces, roasted asparagus, gefilte fish, Moroccan peppers, curried pumpkin, delicate risottos, and much more. It is as if one second before eating time, Glinda the Good Witch waves her wand and order and grace descend. Sometimes I get to grate the blocks of Parmesan cheese or cut the bunches of scallions or peel the thirty cloves of garlic. Minimal tasks, which I often do with a grandchild who knows all the house rules.

Then, afterward, comes my real part of the affair. For if I have behaved very well and not been critical or apprehensive of the process and the preparations, usually Perri allows me to wash some of the dishes, which I gladly do, for it seems to me that I, and I alone, can restore Order in the kitchen in the only way I know.

Perri: For years, I tried to stop my mother from doing dishes in my house when she's visiting. I objected, sometimes loudly, to the idea that just when the Thanksgiving dinner was eaten, instead of sitting around the table talking (and digesting), it was necessary to leap up and start stacking and washing. My mother would tell me to sit, rest, enjoy—and I would tell her that it was hard for the hostess to sit and rest while a guest in her seventies was bustling around doing kitchen work. And sometimes I would win, and she would sit restlessly at the table, dreaming of a sink full of hot water, a drainboard full of gleaming plates, and sometimes she would win, and I would resentfully join her in the kitchen.

Mind you, when I visit my mother, she won't let me help at all. She does her best to wait on me—she is the only person in the world who has taken the trouble to learn that I like my tea weak and rather cool, so to that end, she brews me a cup of tea, takes out the tea bag immediately, and then fashions a special little cover for the cup out of tinfoil so that it will cool but not too quickly. But I am not allowed to wash out my own teacup or wrap up a piece of cheese and put it in the refrigerator. She is as fiercely territorial about her kitchen as ever, even if she uses it mostly to heat up TV dinners. But she feels herself entitled to take possession of mine—or perhaps impelled to take possession of mine—whenever there are dirty dishes (and there are almost always dirty dishes). I have tried pressing her on this contradiction, and it gets me nowhere. Why can't I wash my own teacup when I'm visiting her? "Because you're a guest." Why must she wash all the dishes when she visits me? "Because you've worked so hard!" Why doesn't this make sense? "Because I'm your mother."

I believe, against all my mother's protestations, that some of my pleasure in cooking—and in eating—comes directly from her. I believe that she communicated, in the kitchen, a profound—if eccentric—connection to the ingredients she used and all that they evoked, to the Indian spices that called up memories of months lived in distant places, or the cabbage rolls that evoked her own grandparents' origins in Poland and Hungary. I believe that if she'd let herself relax her own rules, she might even admit that there were certain small daily pleasures in providing for her husband and her children—and that some of those pleasures came from her own skill with flavor and texture, and her sense of what was good. I understand that it was probably harder to appreciate those pleasures because of the race she had to run, and because of the stew of guilt and maternal expectations that sloshed around in her cooking pots.

But that in a certain sense is always part of the domestic seasoning; there's always some guilt and some obligation and some tension in there to set off the cinnamon and nutmeg and honey of maternal love.

You need the fiery mustard pickle too, not just the sweet mango. My mother is at least a little bit wrong about not liking to cook, and she's certainly a little bit wrong about what a good cook I am, but in some sense she's right, and she was right all along, about belonging in the kitchen. She belonged in her suburban kitchen, way back when, running her race and feeding her family. She belongs in her solitary—but still fiercely territorially contested—kitchen now, heating up her TV dinners or washing my single soiled teacup. And she even belongs in my kitchen (and can there be some territorial element in my effort to protect my dirty dishes? I am, after all, her daughter!), overpraising what I've cooked, and fanatically filling up my drainboard with carefully washed plates.

Holupchas

Sweet-and-Sour Stuffed Cabbage

This was my grandmother's dish—not recipe. She simply approximated the amounts of the various ingredients by touch and sight, and the result was wonderful, so I talked her into a laboratory situation in which I measured as soon as she guessed. She thought the whole process ridiculous.

1 medium-sized cabbage	¼ cup bread crumbs
1 lb. ground beef	1 no. 2 can of tomatoes (15 oz.)
1 egg	½ cup white vinegar
1 chopped onion	½ cup sugar
1 clove garlic, minced	1½ tb. shortening
2 stalks celery, chopped	1 cup water
Salt and pepper, to taste	

Remove the core of the cabbage, being careful not to cut into the leaves. Place the head of cabbage in a pot of boiling water for 5 to 8 minutes. Remove from the water; drain, cool, and separate each leaf. Mix beef, egg, onion, garlic, celery, salt, pepper, and bread crumbs together. Place a little of the meat mixture on a leaf, roll, and tuck in ends. Arrange in a pot (side by side) and add the tomatoes, their liquid, the vinegar, sugar, shortening, and water. Cover and cook on top of the stove over low heat, or bake in a slow oven (325°F) for about 1 hour.

Serve with peeled boiled potatoes.

Curried Honeyed Chicken

This is the life-sustaining main dish of this working mother. Good hot or cold, in lunch boxes, any meal; the sauce jellies wonderfully.

3 lbs. chicken pieces you prefer   *½ cup honey*
   (with or without skin)   *1 tsp. salt*
4 tbs. butter or oil   *1 tsp. curry powder*
¼ cup mustard

Heat oven to 375°F. Wash and dry chicken. Skin can be removed. Melt butter or heat oil in a shallow baking pan. Add remaining ingredients. Mix and then roll chicken in the sauce. Arrange in single layer in pan. Bake for 45 minutes to 1 hour, basting occasionally.

Note: Often, while the chicken is baking, I make a second batch of sauce—without any butter or oil. This time I caramelize the honey in a saucepan till it is quite dark, then I add the other ingredients, and I pour this on the chicken after 30 minutes or so. The taste and color are richer, and the sauce is always eaten.

Curried Chicken

In a family of curry aficionados, this, of all the many variants, was the favorite curried main dish. Serve it hot or cold with side dishes of fresh coconut, unsalted peanuts, raisins, and cucumber raita (yogurt and cucumber relish).

3 lbs. chicken pieces	1 tsp. ground cumin
3 medium onions	1½ tsp. turmeric
4 cloves garlic	1½ tsp. curry powder
Small piece of ginger, diced	3 tsp. salt
1½ tbs. butter	1 tsp. chili powder
2 tbs. fresh sage	4 large tomatoes
1 tsp. ground coriander	2 tbs. yogurt

Wash chicken, pat dry, and set aside. Mince onions, garlic, and ginger together. Heat the butter in a large saucepan and fry the onion mixture gently for a few minutes. Add herbs, turmeric, curry powder, salt, and chili powder. Stir well and allow to sizzle briefly. Add chicken and fry for several minutes. Then cover pan with a tight lid and cook gently for 1½ hours, adding a little hot water if the chicken gets too dry. After that, add sliced tomatoes and yogurt. Stir well and allow curry to simmer for another 20 minutes. If there's too much gravy, leave lid off for the last 20 minutes of cooking.

Note: Ground coriander and cumin seeds add fragrance and flavor. Add more or less, according to taste.

Lamb Riblets

The cheapest and easiest main dish I ever made. No one can do this badly.

2–3 lbs. breast of lamb,
trimmed and separated
2 cloves garlic, diced
½ cup soy sauce

⅓ cup sugar
Pepper, to taste
Orange juice (½ cup or more,
to taste)

Marinate meat in mixture for 1 hour or more. Roast in a 450°F oven for 24 minutes or so, turning at least once.

PART TWO

Becoming a
Mother, Becoming
a Grandmother

CHAPTER SIX

Labor and Delivery

Sheila: When my first grandchild was a little more than two years old, his mother, Perri, put him on the phone one morning. "It's Grandma," I heard her prompt. "Say hello."

Obediently, Ben chirped, "Hello, Grandma."

"Hello, Ben. How are you?" I asked.

There was a long pause. "Perfect," he said.

And he was. Just the thought of him brought joy to my days.

At his birth, the nurse standing next to me, as she received the wet, sticky baby, said immediately with a smile, "Congratulations, Grandma."

"Thank you. Easiest thing in the world," I replied. And it was.

I had a grandson! First came incredulity, then relief, and then euphoria. I had to clamp my jaw shut to contain a deafening hallelujah. (My resonant voice embarrasses my children—I didn't want my grandson to start out embarrassed as well.) I also smothered the impulse to rise up, grab that nurse, and dance a mad jig around that birthing bed.

I have had few other moments in my lifetime when I knew such elation, such rare exuberance, such distilled joy. This was the big one.

With difficulty, I controlled my excitement and behaved decorously, befitting my new rank. My husband Mort and I, within an hour, were dispatched to buy the birthday dinner, glorious hamburgers from the local legendary Mr. and Mrs. Bartley's Burger Cottage in Harvard Square. We sloshed with joy through the snowy Cambridge streets. "Look who's a grandmother!" I told him. Then I fell back on a refrain he'd heard before: "Look who this is happening to. Me! Most improbable." The last time I'd said that to him, we were standing on the Great Wall of China, and he'd laughed at my awe. This time he didn't laugh; he felt it too. After all, anyone can build a big wall—or fly to China and walk along one. But we were grandparents! It was amazing. We bought the hamburgers—medium rare with mozzarella cheese and mushrooms, and some onion rings for good measure, and hurried back to the hospital with our fragrant, greasy paper bags.

Perri: When I went into labor with my first child, I called my mother. This may be, in some ways, the most old-fashioned thing I have ever done—I'm sure this was standard procedure throughout pioneer times, and it probably wouldn't raise eyebrows in many parts of the world, but it wasn't standard procedure in Cambridge, Massachusetts, in 1984. But I wanted my mother. On some level, I suppose, I wanted someone in the room who had been through what I was going through and had come out fine. My mother, after all, had gone through her own first labor and delivery under much more rustic circumstances—I was born in a small nursing home in rural Trinidad where my father was researching his doctoral dissertation. And maybe my impulses were partly generous—I wanted her to be there to see her first grandchild born, to be part of the experience. But mostly, I think, I just wanted my mother. I was scared of the pain, scared of something going wrong, scared of the way my life was about to change. So I did the obvious thing. "I'm in labor," I said. "Can you come?" She was in New Jersey. "I'll come as fast as I can," she said.

My mother had her babies quickly. The first labor often takes a while, but in her first labor, with me, she popped the baby out so fast they never got her into the delivery room. My brother was similarly speedy—only my sister, who was born breech, took a little time. I felt somewhat entitled to the same speedy delivery—what should be more obviously inherited through the maternal line, after all, than what goes on on the maternity ward? But my own first labor went on, laboriously, all evening, all night, and well into the following day. We walked, endlessly, up and down the hospital corridors. Periodically—regularly—I stopped for a contraction, hung onto Larry or my mother or a door frame, and made appropriate noises. Then we kept walking. My mother and Larry spelled one another—they took turns taking naps. I resented this deeply—but then, after several hours of labor, I had a general chip on my shoulder. My true nature was coming to the fore.

During that first pregnancy, I had met another woman who was also pregnant. She filled that necessary role in my pregnancy, the acquaintance who is doing everything better than you. She ate only organic foods, spent hours on special pregnancy yoga routines, and generally cultivated serenity of mind. I, on the other hand, tried to remember to take my multivitamins occasionally, didn't drink too much alcohol, and thought a lot about horrible diseases, since I was in my second year of medical school, which is all pathophysiology. Anyway, after we had both had our babies—her daughter, my son—this woman and her husband came over to compare infants and compare notes. They told their delivery story—unlike us, they had remembered to play the special soothing music they had taped, and to take those deep, cleansing breaths. "What meant most to me," her husband said, "was this one special moment, in the middle of labor, when she looked into my eyes and said, 'Darling, thank you so much for being here for me.'"

There was a pause. Then Larry said, "Actually, Perri was completely sour and ungrateful right through about all my incredibly sensitive and supportive behavior." At which point, I started in on how he and my mother were always sneaking off to take naps while I had to keep on walking and contracting and moaning. (Because my true spiteful nature has never been suppressed far below the surface, I feel impelled to point out that this same couple, ten years or so later, went through a nasty divorce. And whenever I heard evil-minded gossip about their split, I thought with great satisfaction about that special delivery-room moment they had shared.)

But yes, in spite of my completely reasonable irritability under the circumstances, I was glad to have my mother there. She was cheerful and encouraging and happy to walk and talk and profoundly interested in the whole process. The only thing that made her a somewhat less-than-ideal delivery-room attendant was that every so often she would look at the clock in perplexity and say to me, "Perri, I just don't remember it taking this long! Are you sure you're doing it right?"

Sheila: If becoming a grandmother was easy, getting to Cambridge, Massachusetts, in midwinter to attend the actual event was really hard. Once Perri phoned from home to say her labor pains had started, it was obviously imperative that I be in Cambridge. How could it happen without me? Historically, female relatives have always assisted and comforted mothers-to-be at births. So since this was the birth of my first grandchild, why wasn't I there already? If I cared that much, why was I more than 200 miles away?

I wasn't there because this baby had been planned for the academic winter recess when Harvard Medical School was closed. My own college in New York operated on a different calendar. I was working; our winter term had resumed. My husband drove me over icy roads to Newark airport, to the terminal of the superdiscount airline, People Express. Their business plan was to make air travel as much as possible like bus travel: no frills, no reservations, line up at the gate and buy your ticket and board the plane. First come, first served. I shamelessly crashed a line of standbys, skiers boarding the last and only Boston-bound plane of the night.

"Sold out," I was told, but I pleaded the case of Perri's belly so eloquently, the People Express people found me a seat on the plane. Of course, it was delayed. I willed it to fly with all my being; I cast frequent, reproachful glances at the flight attendants. I squirmed in my seat till at last we took off.

On the flight, my thoughts drifted. *Perri will be a mother. . . . Larry will be a father. . . . The kids are having a baby! . . . How will she manage medical school? . . . Will she really be able to nurse and go to class?* Mostly, of course, I just kept hoping she'd be okay and she'd have a short labor and an easy delivery and the baby would be fine. *After all, a medical student must know all about this,* I comforted myself. I was so incredibly ignorant when my own children were born. *This baby will have a wonderful life. We'll give it everything we missed.*

A young woman across the aisle was knitting a pink bootie. She made me feel guilty. I'd tried, but I'd never been able to learn to knit. *I'll take lessons,* the airborne, heroic me resolved. *A grandmother should be able to knit.* But in my heart I knew I would never be able to learn. My fingers are twigs in the presence of wool and needles. *Okay, so instead, I'll read to the baby!* I made a list in my head of all the wonderful authors I hadn't read in years whose books I would buy again: A. A. Milne, Dr. Seuss, Maurice Sendak, Beatrix Potter. It's never too early to read to a baby. The sounds of the words and the rhythm are like music.

I arrived just as Perri and Larry were leaving for the hospital. Of course, I insisted on carrying the black-cloth overnight bag. I should have lifted it before I insisted. It was unexpectedly heavy. Surprised by its bulk, I said, "I thought you were only going to stay overnight." Perri hates to stay in hospitals as a patient.

"I am," Perri said. "Those are just my nightclothes and some stuff the childbirth course recommended and a few odds and ends."

When I took her bathrobe and gown out so she could be examined, I was impelled to snoop. Surely on the bottom were some enchanted rocks from Stonehenge or Sarnath. Their childbirth course had been a mystery to me; I sought clues. I found a large bottle of champagne, copies of *Little Women* and *Pride and Prejudice,* a Crock-Pot and various soft cloths to be warmed in it, a cassette player and tapes they'd made, potato chips, lingerie, toilet articles, and a small stuffed bear that had long been a member of their family. All the crucial assists needed at a childbirth.

I'd arrived there in fine time, excellent time, excessively good time. Turned out we had the next seven hours to talk and walk nonstop. Round and round we paced the hospital corridors, because walking and talking were what best eased Perri's pain and advanced the labor. The warmed cloths cooked up in the Crock-Pot were soothing, and occasionally, when the pains were bad, Perri and Larry tried out some breathing technique or other they had learned in that birthing course.

None of the breathing techniques seemed particularly effective, but still, I gave the birthing course high marks. Weird but effective.

"Ah, Perri," I comforted her repeatedly. "Soon. Soon!"

Exhilarated by the whole experience, I thought back on Perri's own precipitate entry into the world, in Tunapuna, Trinidad, on a spread of old newspapers during a tropical downpour. It's true—she was born so quickly that we never got past the admitting cottage in the nursing home. Once my labor had begun, there was a flurry of activity and confusion; I rode out the cramps while I rode to the doctor in an old broken-down car on terrible back-country roads. I was excited and astonished and scared. I was far from home. I'd never known such pain. I was committed to having natural childbirth with no anesthesia. And oddly, the whole turmoil served to distract me from my pain—there were too many other things to think about.

How I would have liked to help Perri now! She needed an exotic tropical setting, or a broken car to worry about. But her labor just went on and on in the hygienic comfort of an American hospital. Vainly, I sought to distract her with bad jokes and feeble puns and maudlin reminiscences. It was okay because no one was listening to me anyway.

The baby was born without anesthesia, without any complications, and he was incomparably beautiful. And tiny—I had truly not remembered how small new babies are. My last baby had been born seventeen years earlier, and my memory is a notoriously unreliable reference on emotional occasions.

This was the first birth I'd actually watched. Though I'd had three children, the first without any anesthesia, I'd never seen a child born. It was awesome. In a minute, there was this other person in the world: my grandson.

Suddenly, Perri was asking the doctor for a favor. "Would you allow my mother to hold a mirror?" she wondered.

A mirror? I was surprised at such an unlikely Perri request. It wasn't vanity. It turned out that my daughter had no desire to comb her hair or apply lipstick. She wanted to watch the doctor sew up a small rip in her pelvic floor. (I know, I know, she was in medical school, she was curious, but still . . . Were there no limits? Nope, no limits.) Obediently, I picked up the mirror and held it aloft. Watching her watch the doctor sew was a bit much for me: I'd never want to know anything that much.

Five years after Benjamin, his sister Josephine was born. For her birth, in August, I made sure I was in Cambridge early. She was thirteen days overdue, thirteen blistering days. The only thing worse than a cold Boston is a hot Boston. The Pilgrims made a serious mistake staying there.

Perri: It had worked out pretty well the first time, so when I got pregnant again, I thought the obvious thing to do was to put that same team back together. People Express was no longer in business, and I had high hopes for a more rapid second labor, anyway, one that would move along quickly, as my mother's deliveries had, and therefore not allow time for spur-of-the-moment 200-mile journeys. So I asked my parents to come and stay when the baby was due. My mother would assume her delivery-room duties, I figured, and my father would take charge of his grandson Benjamin—now five and a half years old.

Josephine, unfortunately, was late. I say unfortunately because she was an August baby. I had finished my three-year pediatric residency at the end of June, and toward the end, of course, I had been very visibly pregnant. In fact, for the last week of my residency, I supervised a team of brand-new and profoundly terrified interns, straight out of medical school and onto the wards. They were deeply troubled by my visibly third-trimester status, clearly afraid that at any moment I might go into labor and abandon them to take care of a ward of seriously ill children all by themselves. As we reviewed the list of patients on morning rounds, they encouraged me to lean back and put my feet up. As we went pounding down the hospital corridor in response to an overhead code blue, they worried more about me than about the child who had temporarily stopped breathing.

The truth is, residency was a welcome distraction during pregnancy. Sure, there were the occasional woozy moments, and sure, I surpassed my own unhealthy-diet-during-pregnancy record at certain bad middle-of-the-night moments, chewing on some mixture of heat-lamp cafeteria French fries, vending-machine candy bars, diet soda, and saltine crackers stolen from the patient pantry. The four basic food groups, we used to joke, were: grease, candy, artificial sweeteners, and salt. And then there was the whole joke about trying to tie on drawstring-waist scrub pants over a very pregnant belly—let's just say that the XXL scrubs are designed for very tall surgeons, and after you get done turning up the cuffs, you don't look like anyone's ideal of a sophisticated professional. But on the whole, I was pretty healthy, and I didn't know how lucky I was to be busy, until I found myself, in a sweltering Cambridge summer, waiting out an overdue August baby.

I tried various things to bring on the birth. I went to a local shopping mall and stomped around for hours in the blessed air-conditioning. I ate massive amounts of extemely spicy Mexican food. No baby. So we scheduled an induction and my parents arrived. I am generally quite secretive about medical issues, and I hadn't told anyone else that I was going into the hospital on Wednesday. My father, incurably honest, went to pick Benjamin up at day care on Tuesday and told the teacher that Benjamin would be staying out tomorrow because his mother was going to be induced. The day care teachers sent best wishes, and I squirmed.

The next morning, we all went to the hospital. Larry and my mother were the delivery-room team, while my father and Benjamin wandered in and out. I got an IV—something I hadn't needed during that first medication-free labor. I am a terrible patient, and I hated the IV and I was convinced someone was going to come put the wrong thing into it (a combination of personal paranoia and the occasional bad hospital experience). I got an internal monitor—something I hadn't needed during my first labor. I hated the monitor—I was convinced the doctor and the nurses weren't paying any attention to me at all, weren't the least concerned about how I was feeling, because they were too damn busy looking at the damn tracing. Once again, I was modeling the beauty and unselfishness of motherhood for anyone who cared to look.

Benjamin spent some time in the delivery room, drawing an endless array of rather similar geometric crayon drawings. We hung some of them up and thanked him profusely. We all watched a peculiarly compelling episode of *Divorce Court* in which the man claimed he was divorcing his wife because he had found out that she was a transsexual, and therefore incapable of bearing the children he so deeply desired, while the wife was able to prove that he had known about her surgical history all along. Understandably, Benjamin lost interest, and he and my father headed out to explore the hospital cafeteria and the gift shop. And that was just as well, because after a rather long hanging-around-nothing-doing-okay-let's-up-the-dose period, the pitocin kicked in and labor began in earnest.

I have, it turns out, a reasonably high threshold for pain—and I combine that with an intense paranoia about all medical interventions. Also, I have a long-standing terror about anyone messing with my spine, which dates back to a neck injury I sustained as a child jumping waves, which caused me by far the worst pain I have ever felt and put me in the hospital, in traction, for several days. What I am trying to say is that though during my first labor I felt some strong allegiance to doing things the low-tech and natural way, that had probably been pretty much beaten out of me by three years of pediatric residency, which had included my attendance at many delivery-room disasters of one kind or another. I had no politics left about childbirth; I only wanted the baby to be healthy. I had accumulated too long a list of rare and terrible bad outcomes, from gastroschisis to thanatrophoric dwarfism. But I hated the idea of anyone putting any kind of medication into my spine—hated the idea of an epidural needle and catheter, so I was trying to do this without anesthesia, though I had been warned that the pitocin would make the contractions more intense. And as they got more and more intense, I thought back on that endless first labor, and I began to wonder whether I would make it.

I looked my obstetrician in the eye. I had actually met her when I was a medical student, during my ob-gyn rotation. I had enjoyed watching her at work in the delivery room, and I had responded well to her no-nonsense manner and her efficiency and skill. She was completely un–touchy-feely, and when it comes to my own health, I can't stand touchy-feely. And when I asked her to deliver this baby and started running down my list of requests—no IV, no spinal or epidural anesthesia, I want to go home four hours after the birth—she had laid down the law. "We'll do it your way as long as everything's fine," she said, "but if at any point I decide that something's going wrong, I'm not going to have a discussion with you. I'm the doctor; you're the patient—you trust me or you don't." I trusted her. And I needed to tell her that this was a whole new level of labor pain.

"I don't think I can do this for another ten hours," I confessed between contractions, remembering that endless night that had given me my son.

"I have news for you," she said. "You're going to have a baby in about ten minutes. So this is no time to tell me you've changed your mind about anesthesia."

The conversation paused while I ululated through a contraction. "Ten minutes I can do," I said.

And that's how my daughter Josephine was born, once again with Larry on one side of me and my mother on the other. Each of them, as I recall, was holding one of my legs as I pushed. And as I was holding Josephine (and as Josephine, who had a strong character right from the beginning, was making it clear that she regarded nursing as serious business), in came my father and Benjamin, to share the magic moment.

And once again we sent my father out for those ritual hamburgers from Bartley's. And once again I got my way and made them discharge me and send me home soon after the birth. I actually like the hospital as a work environment; it's an interesting place full of smart and highly trained people doing jobs I deeply respect. But I can't stand being in the hospital as a patient; I can't relax or close my eyes or feel okay until I'm out of there.

A few days later, I decided to be a conscientious mother and review this important day with Benjamin. It would be a project for the two of us, a way to make him feel special now that there was a new baby in the house. I would get him to tell me the story of the day his sister was born, the day he and his grandfather had spent together in the hospital as our family expanded. I would type up the story, he would illustrate it, and we would make a book together. I glowed with motherly radiance at the very idea—Family! Creativity! Writing! Special time! Sibling love!

Benjamin told his story cheerfully. It was quite long and detailed, but if I can collapse it a little, it went like this: "My grandfather took me to the coffee shop and I had a doughnut. My mother was having a baby. Then we went to the gift shop and I got a chocolate bar. Then it was time for lunch, so I had a hot dog. Then we went back to the soda machine and I got a lemonade. My mother was still upstairs having a baby. So then we went back to the gift shop and I got another chocolate bar. . . ." His sister, in the story, was a much more minor character than that climactic Mr. Bartley's hamburger (medium rare with mozzarella and mushrooms for me—I'm a traditionalist).

Sheila: Twenty-one years after Benjamin's birth, fifteen years after Josephine's birth, I'm still trying to deal with the implications of the honorific *grand*. It's not a title I take lightly. I'd heard of grand duchesses and grand dragons and grand masters, but in my whole life I'd never actually been a grand anything till Benjamin Orlando came along.

And he made short work of my grandeur. As soon as he got old enough to feel he should decide things for himself, the *grand* went out the window. He began to call me Sheila in the most friendly, egalitarian way. Nothing personal. After all, he called his mother Perri. He called his father Larry. That was the way he heard adults address each other, and he just followed suit. It made sense. I could accept it. He called me Sheila, but in my heart, I knew I was Grandma.

It was when he started to talk about changing his own name that I really began to worry. The problem was, his parents had picked too popular a name for 1984. There were too many Benjamins in his class.

From the very beginning, he had to learn to identify himself as Ben K. He went along with being Ben K because of the three other Bens in his class, but when a fourth Ben appeared and it turned out he was also Ben K, that was too much. My grandson declared he would not answer to Ben anymore—he wanted a name that would identify him— that would be unique in his class. He would go by his middle name—he was now Orlando. There would be a penny fine for anyone who forgot and called him Ben.

He felt so strongly about it, his parents went along with the idea. They liked his middle name, obviously. My husband and I, on the other hand, were troubled. Benjamin was Benjamin—our Benjamin, our grandson. Orlando seemed exotic in 1984. We'd never met an Orlando. That was not the first name on his birth certificate. All his life, there would be complications on documents if he used this new name. People would wonder what he had done that made him change his name. *That's not something you just go and do casually,* I thought. *It means trouble later on.* Whoever heard of a small boy changing his name on a whim? To us it was a crisis. I expected his parents to put a stop to the whole thing. I expected his school to object. But instead, I paid my penny fines and learned to call him Orlando.

Another five years after Josephine came Anatol, after a labor so short he was reclining gently on Perri's lap, fully dressed, complete with dashing blue knitted cap, when I arrived. Thank goodness he's content with the name Anatol, because *his* middle name is Elvis!

Perri: The third time around, Larry and I made an elaborate plan. Orlando was eleven (and yes, he was Orlando by then) and Josephine was five and a half. Mysteriously, we had managed to space our children perfectly symmetrically. We had a babysitter who carried a beeper—when I went into labor, we planned to page her. She would come running to take the kids—or plan to pick them up from school, as the case might be—and we would go to the hospital. And yes, we would call my parents as well, but after that two-week delay for Josephine, we didn't feel in a rush to have them come up to Cambridge and wait—and anyway, this was April; they were both teaching. August may not be an ideal time to have a baby, but at least all the professors (the father, the grandfather, the grandmother) are on summer vacation and available to rally round.

Well, the third time around I got my wish—I got my mother's labor. "I'm going to have this baby *really* soon," I kept saying to Larry. It was about five in the afternoon. The children were at afterschool and would need to be picked up in half an hour. We paged the babysitter—she was on the other side of town, stuck in terrible rush-hour traffic. I called my parents and told them to start driving. We called the school and asked them to have Orlando and Josephine ready and waiting at the front door. We grabbed our hospital bag and ran out the door, got into Larry's little red Toyota, the first car we had ever bought, and madly drove to the school—well, Larry drove, and I added to the madness by remarking at intervals, "I think I'm going to have this baby *really soon!*"

We collected the children, who sat in the backseat and squabbled. We drove to the hospital. "Do I have time to park?" Larry asked. *"No,"* I said, "just let me out, and *then* you go park." So I wandered alone into the hospital and took the elevator up to that familiar maternity floor. I remember leaning against the wall through a contraction, wondering if anyone had ever had a baby in the elevator, wondering whether I would be the first.

It wasn't quite as quick as that, though it was pretty damn quick. Larry had time to park and bring the children up to maternity, where we explained that no, we weren't one of those family-bed-let-the-children-deliver-the-placenta families, we just had a babysitter who was stuck in traffic, that's all. The nurses, who were quite accustomed to anything anywhere on the spectrum (Cambridge, after all), were very hospitable and set the children up to watch TV and read in the next room. Eventually our babysitter arrived and joined them, and then all three hung out and waited for the baby.

We also had time to set up our cassette player, and Larry put on an Elvis tape—"Blue Hawaii," I think. I wanted to control the cultural influences this time around; no *Divorce Court* for me. When one of the nurses came in to check on me, Larry apologized for the somewhat loud music and asked if we should shut the door. "Oh no," said the nurse, "we like it—it's so much better than those damn whale songs that people keep playing!"

But Elvis had time for only a couple of numbers. Anatol Elvis (and it could so easily have been Anatol Elevator) was born quickly and relatively easily, and by the time my parents arrived, having driven straight through from New York, he was indeed dressed and wrapped and fully among those present.

My parents came and admired him—I was sorry that my mother had missed the birth, though greatly relieved to have finally experienced her brand of quick-and-easy labor. And my father, of course, knew exactly what to do—he had barely admired the baby before people were handing over their hamburger orders. "Medium rare," I said, "with mozzarella cheese and mushrooms."

It seems foolish even to try to write about what it meant—having those children, becoming their mother. Everything sounds like a cliché, and all clichés are true. Life changes in a moment. The earth moves. The constellations shift. Your heart beats differently. Here is what I do know, though: Each time I had a baby, the job of becoming a mother—of becoming this particular child's mother—was connected to seeing my parents become grandparents, and become the grandparents of this particular child. When my first baby was born, after that long, strange night, he became my son and Larry's son and my mother's grandson all in that first wet, bloody moment as the three of us welcomed him. My father's hamburger quests, my older child's thorough exploration of the hospital's culinary possibilities—all these were part and parcel of the way my family grew. I think now that having my mother at my side, especially that first time, helped me believe that I could do it—not just get through the labor but also take on this new job. That I would have help if I needed it, yes, but also that I was born to do this, and that she was there to see me through becoming a mother, even as she was there to see her grandchild born.

Sheila: This being a grandmother is a strange and wonderful avocation. More recently, my son David and his wife, Giselle, have added

Gabriel, who is now four, and Madeleine, who is two. Since they live in New York, their births were a mere subway ride away. No hassle. Glorious grandchildren via MetroCard.

What a pleasure this is from day to day. Maybe it's because I can enjoy my five grandchildren on my own terms without feeling responsible for them. I am once removed from all the crises and decisions. My job is mostly to admire, to sit in the second row and hope and cheer and celebrate. I am shameless about claiming genetic credit for my grandchildren's talents and achievements except in athletics, music, and mathematics—these I exclude because I'd be laughed out of town.

In the early days of grandmotherhood, I witnessed total violation of the "rules" that I'd truly believed governed parenthood.

Children should have early, regular, fixed bedtimes. Real life began in the evening in Perri and Larry's house. It was the best family time of the whole day, the only time both parents were home. So they ate late and they played later.

Never take a baby out in bad weather or at night. When there was some special event, no matter the hour, everyone went—baby too, Massachusetts winter notwithstanding. "You don't catch a cold from cold weather, Ma," Perri would reassure me. I still have my doubts; there are things you don't learn in medical school.

A child should eat a balanced daily diet, including protein, starch, vegetable, and fruit. My grandchildren very early registered strong likes and dislikes, and their parents acquiesced to these preferences. They ate what they liked, and a lot of it, and they flourished.

Strange or exotic foods will upset young children. Chinese, Japanese, Mexican, Indian, the cuisines of the world were offered for sampling, and my grandchildren took to the most unlikely dishes.

Mort and I loved visiting and watching the children grow. Mostly we voiced our own misgivings privately—in the car going back to New York—but we'd been effectively and permanently blindsided. Perri had outsmarted us by becoming a doctor. We would never be able to tell a pediatrician what was best for her babies. Even though we sometimes absolutely knew we were right.

Meanwhile, all around us, our friends were having grandchildren too, of course, and each family was working out its individual accommodation. Our more hardheaded contemporaries persisted in telling their children exactly what to do, no matter how much the advice was resented. They went through some really rough times. Other friends swallowed their words and worried quietly, trying desperately to keep the peace. The whole idea of grandparental wisdom became vestigial once the World Wide Web offered instant access to the world's information. One thing I've come to recognize is how quickly young parents become extremely competent. Looking back, I realize that even we, who started at zero, got to be capable.

Recently, I asked Orlando, college student Orlando, if he still liked being Orlando, and he smiled with pleasure and said, "I love it." So it must have been a wise decision. Funny thing is, these days he looks to me more and more like an Orlando and less and less like a Ben. It was such a neat and simple solution to his problem, and he solved it himself. Such prescience, such good judgment must surely come from his mother's side of the family.

CHAPTER SEVEN

Finding Felicity

Perri: *Trinidad* was a magic word in my growing up. It was my answer to the where-were-you-born question, my own little piece of the family legend. How my parents, fresh out of Brooklyn, adventured to a distant Caribbean island in the late 1950s so my father could spend a year doing anthropological field work for his Ph.D. dissertation. How they lived in Felicity, a small Hindu village, among East Indians. How my Brooklyn-born-and-bred mother made her home in a small wooden house high up on stilts, with a corrugated metal roof, no running water, no refrigerator, outhouse across the yard. How they decided it was time, finally (my father about to conclude the penurious graduate student years), to have a first child—and how I was born in a nursing home in a town with the wonderful name of Tunapuna, born onto old newspapers because my mother's labor went so fast there was no time to get her into the delivery room.

I knew all this because they told it to me, over and over, and also because they wrote it down—which is in some sense what all writer types do with their family legends, or pieces thereof. My father's first book was his doctoral dissertation, his book about the village; my mother published a memoir about that year, *Everyone in This House Makes Babies,* which I read and reread as I grew up, importantly conscious that it was a book about *me,* and the remarkable circumstances of my coming into the world, and that not everyone has a birth worth a book. Her title came from the strong conviction held by the villagers that the house on stilts had magic fertility properties and that this tragically barren, aging (well, thirty-year-old) white woman had been saved by living in their special lucky house.

The three of us left Trinidad when I was a few months old. I always assumed I would go back someday, with my parents, to be shown off and exclaimed over, the baby born to the lucky couple in the magic house. As I got older and had a couple of babies of my own, I began to appreciate more completely what an adventure this must have been, and I thought going back to Trinidad would draw me closer to my parents; they would be showing me how they had become the people they were.

Then my father died. It was sudden and unexpected—he died in the middle of various anthropology projects, in the middle of plans and proposals for further travel—in the midst of life, as the biblical saying goes. And when someone dies, of course, with him die all the projects and plans, everything you were going to do together, some-day, when the right moment came. So instead, two years later, in a kind of vague celebration of my forty-fifth birthday, as a mark of what would have been my parents' fiftieth wedding anniversary, and in trib-ute to my father, my mother and I went to Trinidad. And of course, since we're both writers, we had to do our part, in harmony or in counterpoint, to add to the legend.

Sheila: A promise is a promise. In 1958, my husband, Mort, and I left Trinidad and boarded a plane for New York—he carried Perri, and I, even more carefully, carried his field notes. He had spent the year studying cane cutters whose ancestors had been brought to the island from India as indentured laborers, documenting the persistence of their Indian culture after a century in the Caribbean.

We had promised our East Indian neighbors from Felicity Village that one day we would bring the baby back. She belonged to them too; she was a fellow villager. They had helped me through pregnancy, laughed at my ignorance, provided me with tons of slimy okra, which they believed made the birth canal slippery so the baby would slide out. They had given Perri a lovely Hindu name: Toolsi Devi—the toolsi is a sacred plant.

We pledged to return, and we fully intended to, but careers, new babies, the busyness of life somehow always intervened. "Bring she back, man. Bring she back to she village!" our neighbors had called out as they waved good-bye. And often I had dreamed of walking along Cacandee Road, stepping over burlap sacks spread with rice drying in the sun, and showing Perri off to all the villagers.

Finally we kept the promise, but alas, without Mort.

Back in the 1950s, we had at first felt so visible and so self-conscious in that village—white, Jewish, New Yorkers. And how Mort worried about our affecting Felicity. An anthropologist is not supposed to change the culture he's studying. So we did our best to be circumspect. Still, we walked together side by side and people noticed; women in particular noticed my remarkable boldness. I had opinions. And he didn't get angry! I was educated—in a village where girls were not schooled but kept home to help. And when the baby was born, Mort made formula and changed diapers—and everyone in the village noticed.

By living there, blessed with our first child, learning to care for her, we changed them. And they changed us. Even the young girls had enormous "baby wisdom"; the amount they knew was awesome. We noted the pleasures (and troubles) of family life with three generations in one house, and the great joy everyone took in children. Their frugality, and ingeniousness in making things—a sugar-sack hammock was my favorite luxury. And we adopted their cuisine. Curried *anything* is delicious, and to this day my house, about an hour before suppertime, smells like Cacandee Road. So in a sense my husband and I lived ever afterward in 1957 Trinidad. . . .

At Piarco International Airport in Port of Spain—a gleaming edifice with marble floors, not the dusty airstrip of my memory—the immigration officer challenged me. "Why didn't you bring her back before?" Then she grinned. "I know. You afraid she'd stay." The joke of someone rightly proud of her beautiful country.

I could not imagine what we would find now after forty-five years of industrialization, after the decline of the sugar crop, after the Trinidad oil boom, after political independence and global TV, but I shared my husband's conviction that Felicity would stay much as it was because the culture was deep-rooted and dearly loved. They were so proud to be Indian. I knew that if we went looking, we would find the old Felicity.

Perri: I was less sure that we would find the old village—or old friends—or anything at all, after forty-five years. I knew the house my parents had lived in was gone, so that could not be the object of our visit. I could see that my mother was excited, but I was worried. I thought she would be frustrated, at best, and perhaps deeply disappointed, and I wondered whether I had brought her all this way only to damage a happy memory that would otherwise have stayed pristine and glowing.

I had asked my brother, what kind of hotels should I book? If I ask Mama, she'll tell me she'd rather stay in guesthouses, but maybe I should just book a room at the Hilton. Don't ask her, my brother advised. Book the Hilton. She's seventy-five years old, she's entitled to comfort and air-conditioning.

But somehow I hadn't been able to book the Hilton. I was afraid that my mother would look around and feel that she had not really made it back to *her* Trinidad. So I had booked us into a guesthouse in Port of Spain, which turned out to be comfortable, beautiful, and very hospitable, and over the tropical fruits and eggs and bacon of a massive breakfast the next morning, I listened with some trepidation as my mother explained our errand to the Australian couple who had come halfway around the world to watch a five-day cricket match. True, their journey seemed completely incomprehensible to me, but at least the cricket match was *there*, it would unquestionably take place, all day every day for five days under the blazing Caribbean sun. Would there be anything *there* for my mother and me when we got to Felicity? How on Earth did she propose to go about chasing down remnants of 1957? And if she didn't find them, would the whole trip, at least from her point of view, be a failure and a disappointment and a spoiled dream?

Sheila: Happy and excited by memories, I had no doubt that the closer we came to Felicity, the more at home I would feel. That is, until, riding along the main highway, I noticed that something was missing. The sugar crop! Our driver, Mr. Nizam Azard Mohammed, an articulate and highly knowledgeable Trinidadian, explained, "This was once all sugar. And much more of it will disappear soon." In the global economy, Trinidad sugar is no longer needed.

And when we turned onto a paved Cacandee Road, a road now lined with handsome two-story concrete houses behind wrought-iron grilles, and not a single mud-walled *ajoupa* (hut) with a thatched roof, not a single roadside standpipe for water, I didn't know where to start my search.

"Please take us to the Canadian Mission School," I said. "Our house was in their schoolyard." And he did take us to *a* Canadian mission school, with a schoolyard, but it was not right. "It's not right," I said, helplessly.

The driver got out of the car and walked along the road, looking for someone who might know. He smiled at several passersby but seized upon an elderly gentleman with a white beard who stood just inside a shop (CHICKENS AND DUCKS—FREE CUTTING! said the sign).

"This is not the school," I said, desperately. And I showed him a copy of the book I'd written, which had a photograph of that wooden house on stilts on its back cover.

"In 1957, I was in India. But she will know." He indicated his assistant, who studied the picture, and then said, "That is the other Canadian Mission School, the first one." Then, just as I was about to inquire about our dearest, oldest old friend, she spoke his name. "You want Headmaster Hardeo. He lives right near here."

I hugged her. I would have hugged the chickens. As we drove on, I explained to Perri excitedly, "He's the most important person! He knew everything about the village—whenever Papa needed to know anything, he went to Hardeo! He helped draw the maps, he helped do the statistical studies—and he knew all the secrets of living in Felicity. We would never have made it without him!"

Mr. Mohammed stopped before the designated house, and a distinguished-looking gray-haired gentleman in shorts and a polo shirt walked toward us.

"Good morning. Here is someone you know from a long time ago," said our driver, master of the situation. The headmaster looked at me, first blankly, then incredulously. "You see, he remembers!" said the driver, jubilantly.

"Mistress Sheila!" And he smiled in the same charming shy way he had smiled back in 1957. We shook hands in formal greeting. But I could not contain my joy: "This is *the* baby!" I announced, pointing to Perri. "I have brought her back to Felicity at last!" And I wondered, watching him welcome Perri, in his gracious and completely dignified manner, whether he recalled the uncertain Brooklyn-bred first-time mother, holding a startlingly pale infant, a blond baby so strange looking by Felicity standards that Solomon, one village friend, compared her to a little white rat.

"This is Toolsi Devi," I said urgently. "You remember?"

Of course they remembered.

His wife, Doolarie, appeared, and he challenged her: "You know who this is?" He took my book from me and showed her the photo. "She lived here."

"Mrs. Mort!" Doolarie embraced me. And soon we were all in the living room, grandly furnished—not a sugar-sack hammock in sight—but I knew I was at home again.

I had sad news for them—Mort's death. And they in turn gave me a doleful list of friends, some of them much younger than I, who had died. Others had emigrated. Their own children had grown up and married, and they had stayed in Trinidad, but none lived in the house with their parents—I wondered if the three-generation home was no more.

I asked Doolarie if life was much better now, with plentiful water and with telephone, refrigerator—all the modern conveniences—and she was thoughtful. "It's easier, but it's not better," she said, finally. "The old days were better."

We had dropped in without warning, but Hardeo and Doolarie were the same incredibly hospitable people who had welcomed an itinerant anthropological couple back in 1957. They insisted we come back and spend another day with them before we left the island.

This time they had made some arrangements, and our conversation was punctuated by a series of callers. First one and then another of their grown daughters, each bringing a granddaughter clad in white on her way to an Indian dance class. Then the grown daughter of our friend Solomon, who had made our sugar-sack hammock, and who had learned to play chess from Mort—and then proceeded to beat him. "I had to come—I've heard about you all my life," she said. All these young women were smart, articulate, and charming. All worked as teachers. Just as I was thinking that the women of Felicity had changed beyond all recognition, one of them reminded our hostess that she needed to borrow some pots for a "prayer" later that day. Whereupon five or six heavy metal baby-bathtub-sized metal pots were hauled out of a closet and carefully loaded into a car to be driven away. Clearly, communal cooking was not dead.

We toured the village with Headmaster Hardeo, looking for pieces of the town I had known, and admiring changes. We stopped at Miss Mamit's house; she had made me maternity clothes, which were un-heard of in Felicity, where pregnant women simply opened buttons as they grew larger.

Now she looked at Perri and said, "The face is just the same!" An-other embrace, another little piece of the old Felicity.

We went from one end of Felicity to the other: the new cremation area for Hindu funerals (cremation was banned in Trinidad till the 1970s), the Caroni sugar estate, soon to disappear. We stopped at a handsome house, where Gurdeen, whom I remembered as a nearly blind young man, welcomed us enthusiastically and took us into his cool kitchen, where he fed us sparkling grape juice. I remember wor-rying about what would become of him, since he could hardly see; it turns out he runs a thriving trash-collecting business and has done very well for himself and his family. He gleefully told Perri the story of our entrance into the village and their prediction that I would have a child there: "Every teacher who lived in your house made many babies! We knew your parents go have one!"

Yes, the appearance of the village had changed. In that schoolyard in my mind stood the old house still, and the dry waterpipe in front and the trash pit behind. I looked in vain for the outhouse with its big sign, GIRLS, which served as our facilities for that year. The modern school has indoor plumbing. As I stood looking through the fence into the schoolyard, though, I could see Mort fixing the baby's formula and swatting bugs on the porch while several men sat on a bench nearby, kidding him and marveling. I could hear Perri chortling in her basket on the floor, and the women giggling over my copy of Dr. Spock—"She raise she baby by the book!" one would say, and they would all collapse in laughter. "She tell that the book say baby must sleep in a different room. Man, did you ever hear such nonsense?" I could hear the bicycle bell that announced the fish peddler bringing our dinner, fresh from the Caroni Swamp. And now Perri—grown-up Perri—knew it all a bit too.

Perri: Of course we did other things on our trip to Trinidad. We stayed at a nature preserve, sat on the verandah sipping our afternoon rum punch and watching several species of hummingbird—improbable, iridescent—hover at the feeders filled with sugar water, and listening as the serious birders around us pointed out the cornbirds and the tanagers and the honeycreepers. We spent a night in a Benedictine monastery guesthouse on a mountain high above the little town of Tunapuna where I was born. We dropped in on the University of the West Indies and visited several professors who had known my father. We flew to Tobago, much less developed (and, by tradition, Robinson Crusoe's island), where we breakfasted on brown toast and pineapple jam, poached eggs, and flying-fish fillets, on a teak balcony overlooking the palm trees and white sand of a perfect Caribbean fantasy beach, then strolled down to spend the day alternately soaking in the clear gentle swells and reading under a beach umbrella. We woke at one A.M., when the night watchman banged on our door, and followed him down to the beach to see a giant leatherback sea turtle, all five hundred pounds of her, laboriously bury her newly laid eggs deep in the sand, then slowly inch her way back into the dark waves. We even watched a couple of hours of that famous cricket match and reflected on the peculiar legacies of British imperialism, from cricket to big breakfasts.

We traveled together easily. My mother talked to everyone—to the driver, to the ranger at the nature reserve, to the birders, to the eighty-year-old Irish nun we met at the Benedictine monastery guesthouse. She got their stories—the nun, for example, had left her home in rural Ireland when she was in her twenties, had spent her life teaching English to girls in Trinidad, had gone home to Ireland, finally, and she found it too cold, she missed the Caribbean too much—and so she had come back to live in her order's house in Port of Spain, where she helped with the housework and visited the sick. And Mama told everyone her own stories—the East Indian village, the local midwife whose technique for dealing with a breech birth was to pick the laboring woman up by the feet and shake her until the baby fell back in, the nursing home in Tunapuna (they chickened out on the local midwife). Mama showed her book. The old nun blessed her.

Every so often, as we traveled, a very particular look would come over my mother's face, and she would say, "Papa would have loved this." The cricket match, the hummingbirds, the beach, the giant sea turtle. The news that every sociology student at the university still reads his book and knows his name. The big "buffalypso" steak—from a buffalo herd that has existed on Tobago for 300 years—served on a terrace right over the beach, with the constant noise of the crashing waves. Papa would have loved this.

And he would have. And it seemed right to note it on this trip, which was in part designed as tribute to him. To his scholarly curiosity and sense of adventure that brought my parents to this tiny green spot on the blue ocean of the map in 1957. To his happy energy for experiencing other cultures, other ways of life, and appreciating their beauties. To his enduring passions—my mother, their children and grandchildren, anthropology, travel, talk, food. That's what Mama was missing; that's what she needed to conjure at the happiest, most interesting, most scenic moments. How Papa would have enjoyed this. Papa knew what he loved, and whom he loved. He knew he was lucky, and he made you feel his delight. He and Mama loved their year in Trinidad, loved it then in 1957 and 1958, and loved the memory. If his shadow was with us, with my mother and me on our somewhat sentimental journey, it was a shadow that kept reminding us to glory in being there, in having been so lucky as to return, together, to this lucky place that shaped our family.

PART THREE

No-Man's-Land

CHAPTER EIGHT

My Father's Chair

Sheila: The meals of my childhood and adolescence were eaten with all the members of my family except for my mother. She went back and forth serving and cleaning. No one was allowed to help, my father least of all. He was absolutely forbidden to enter *her* kitchen. We sat on shaky, treacherous chairs around a tottering maple dining-room table. It was necessary to sit gingerly, feet braced for the moment when the chair might give way, or, worse, when a table leg would buckle. There was absolutely no leaning on the table; we knew better than to come into contact with it; still, the furniture was so capricious that each meal was a dangerous game of chance. In addition, my mother had folded a bedspread into an improvised table pad to protect the precious maple finish, so the tabletop under the cloth was soft, and here and there slightly ridged. One had to position a filled cup very carefully when one put it down.

My father's chair was identical to the others, wobbly and unreliable, but it was *his* chair, and that made it different. Only my father sat on that chair. No child ever dared to sit on it. Ever. In my mind it was a kind of ancient throne in disguise, albeit a shaky throne.

"Respect," my mother explained severely. "You need to show respect for your father. Why, to this day, I wouldn't dream of sitting on *my* father's chair. You leave that chair for your father because he is the man of the house." So that chair was how I knew my father was man of the house. It was the single clue.

Over the years, the condition of the furniture worsened, and my mother daily lamented the fact that Papa was "not handy like some women's husbands who could fix everything." He indeed was not handy, and she would never attempt to do what she saw as a man's job. So nobody bought glue.

As a child, I regarded my father's chair with awe. Its rickety self was the single manifestation of my father's exalted place in the household. Otherwise, his position was shadowy. He had been born Abraham Louis Solomonowitz. The judge granting him United States citizenship had said to him affably, "You take the Solomon and leave the rest behind with me." He came to the United States from Hungary in time to go back to Europe as an American soldier in World War I, then came back home and married my mother.

So she married Abraham Louis Solomon. But *Abraham*, shortened, becomes *Abe*, and my mother, though she adored Abe Lincoln, thought the name *Abe Solomon* sounded lower class. Probably she found it too Jewish as well, but she would never have admitted to that. She announced her preference for the more lofty-sounding *Louis,* which, shortened, becomes *Lou.* So he was Lou at home, but he was Abe in the synagogue and among his war veteran friends. He was steady, sober, honest, and hardworking, and though he'd been lucky in the war, he was bereft of luck ever afterward. He worked in the clothing industry as a presser. It was poorly paid unskilled labor—and it disappeared when the Depression came.

Daily, he rose before any of us and disappeared to work or to look for work, brown-bag lunch of egg or cheese sandwiches in hand. I do not remember him ever staying at home on a weekday. Nor was he ever sick in bed. He returned in the evenings, bringing with him, on good nights, the *Journal American,* the *Forward,* the *Daily News,* and the *Daily Mirror,* which he scavenged on BMT subway trains. Those wonderful evenings, we got to read all the comics, while my mother grumbled about how we wouldn't learn anything from *Harold Teen* or *Dick Tracy* or (my favorite) *Terry and the Pirates.* We were so absorbed in our reading, she went unheard. For years it was my dearest dream to grow up looking like the Dragon Lady, cruel and beautiful, in sleek silk slit skirts, wielding a long ivory cigarette holder. Alas, I didn't have the cheekbones for it—and I wore glasses.

To silence Mama's complaints, Papa would say, "What harm can it do? The papers give the children pleasure, and they don't cost me a penny." She couldn't quarrel with that.

We ate dinner together at a quarter to seven, silently for the first fifteen minutes while Papa listened to Lowell Thomas broadcasting the news. Lowell Thomas's broadcast was directly followed by Mama's, as she began to recite the events of the day to Papa while she dished out food. She spoke as she served, allowing no help; she herself ate afterward—and often ate leftovers. Her news, mostly tales of her misfortunes and our misbehavior, invariably upset him. Often these recitals erupted into family fights. Papa was a gentle man, but he had a terrible temper when he was roused. Her talk would bring on paroxysms of rage, during which he shouted and glared over his glasses. When she'd pushed him too far, she'd whisper behind her hand, "Shell shock."

My older sister, who was sensitive, would flee the table. She grew up much skinnier than my brother and I did. He and I learned to hunker down and eat while the battles raged. After dinner, Papa would read the papers and sometimes listen to the radio. Most often he would lie on the couch, his face under the opened newspaper, dozing until it was time to really go to bed.

He was always willing to admire some ambitious homework project or to hear about some teacher's foolishness, but he rarely initiated such conversations. It was almost as if we were Mama's territory, and he was afraid to invade. He was a quiet, thoughtful, religious man beaten down by years of unemployment and poverty.

My mother never went anywhere with my father, nor did we ever go out together as a family. We never had any company except for a rare visit from our maiden aunts, which was no great fun, for they were given to lecturing on self-improvement and grammar and the virtues of whole-wheat bread. While these aunts never disrespected

Papa by sitting in his chair, I knew they looked down on him. He was a "greenie"—an immigrant—and they were American-born. He was a laborer, a clothes-presser, a man who worked with his hands. And, of course, for a long time he was unemployed.

When my mother became pregnant for the fourth time, while we were on Home Relief in the 1930s, my aunts were furious with her and with Papa. In those days, relatives thought they had the right to a big say in your life, particularly if you were a poor relation. Maybe they still do.

My aunts were without mercy. "What are you, animals?" they demanded. Their anger scared me. From my bedroom, I heard them scolding and hissing. They instigated an abortion, and it was accomplished. My mother never discussed it, but she was sad for a long time afterward. The aunts said she was having a nervous breakdown. What my father thought of all this, I don't know. No one asked his opinion. He could not earn a living, and therefore he had lost all rights to opinions. He came home later and later and left earlier and earlier.

School, the public library, the rare movie, and our own imaginations had to provide life's entertainment and pleasures for us. Friday nights and Saturdays, Papa spent in the synagogue. Sundays he often had Jewish War Veterans activities, a parade or a meeting. He spent as much time as he could elsewhere. He had a bottle of schnapps, which he'd take out on holidays for a ceremonial drink, but it was always one drink only, and he'd put the bottle away again immediately. He was a benign presence in the house but not an active one. Yet in a way, he saved us, my sister and me.

The great transforming adventure of his life had been World War I. A newly arrived immigrant, he had volunteered and served loyally in the U.S. infantry. He had a few war stories he loved to tell, and it was a great treat for us to hear them. His favorite, and ours, was about Paris. "During the war, I was in Paris . . ." he would begin.

That was the cue for my mother to try to head him off. She held her ears at off-color comments and never used obscenity, so this story, in particular, offended her. "Lou," she would interrupt in a warning voice. She didn't think he should tell it at all, and certainly not to children.

"It happened to me," he told me emphatically. His war experiences were his territory, and she could not invade. "I was walking on the boulevard," he said, then paused for the marvelous next words—"the Champs-Élysées—when I saw that the lovely young Frenchwoman in front of me was losing her bloomers and seemed not to be noticing it. So I hurried forward and tapped her on the shoulder and whispered to her, 'Pardon me, Mademoiselle, but you are losing your underpants.' She looked down, quickly stepped out of them, kissed my cheek, and said, '*Merci,* Yank!' and went on her way, leaving the underpants as a souvenir.

" 'Three cheers!' my buddies razzed me. 'Abe Solomon takes Paris by the bloomers!' " Papa positively glowed as he finished his story triumphantly. We kids cheered and clapped, and Mama shushed us. His war adventures were the only stories he ever told us, and they were never of combat or death. They were stories of physical discomfort, of trench lice and frostbite and hardtack for dinner.

He remained passionately patriotic all his life, and he was scrupulous about voting. So, when his Jewish War Veterans post started a drum-and-bugle corps, Papa decided that Marilyn and I had to join. Arnold, my brother, was too young to be eligible.

Mama was horrified: It was not refined to go marching through the streets! The aunts agreed with her—but this was one time Papa was adamant. Again, his war record and related activities were not to be trifled with. Refined? Who cared about refined?

We joined the band and paid dues of ten cents each per week for musical instruction. A bass-drummer first, Marilyn then learned to play the glockenspiel and finally became a strutting drum major with a huge silver, tasseled baton. I chose the bugle and practiced it endlessly. I knew Papa was proud of us, and I took it all very seriously. So when the bandmaster, inspecting my bugle, scolded, "You need to use more elbow grease when you polish this horn," I immediately went to several stores trying to buy "elbow grease."

Finally, one kind storekeeper took pity on me. "Girlie," he said, "it's not polish you need for the bugle. You just got to rub it harder with a soft rag so it shines. Elbow"—he pointed to his own elbow—"grease." He moved his arm vigorously.

Papa never missed one of our parades. Dressed up in his suit and shirt and tie and sporting his overseas cap, he marched along jauntily making jokes with the other veterans. He was a different person outside the house: relaxed and sociable. He was always so proud to be stepping out behind us. And we, in blue uniforms, the capes lined with white satin, and snappy peaked caps, marched briskly in every conceivable holiday parade—even on St. Patrick's Day, over Mama's objections. We felt glamorous and important.

I was deeply grateful to Papa, for I became enthralled by this new musical career. I began to earn pocket money playing taps in cemeteries each Armistice Day. All through my adolescence, I bugled in girls' summer camps, and later on in life—in Leonia, New Jersey—I used the bugle to call my own kids to meals with "Mess Call":

Soupy, soupy, soupy, without a single bean;
Porky, porky, porky, without a strip of lean;
Coffee, coffee, coffee, the meanest ever seen!

I'd learned the words from Papa.

Thus his war experiences profoundly altered my life and my sister's life; both of us always remembered the Louis Sobel Drum and Bugle Corps as a major source of pride and escape.

However, in the house, my father was considered absolutely help-less. He could not pour himself a glass of water. He could not boil an egg. He never cooked anything and indeed was barred from our strictly kosher kitchen, because he might drop things or spill things or break things. He would surely mix up the meat dishes and the milk dishes and thus destroy the kashrut.

To hear Mama tell it—and she told it often—he was absolutely inept. If he had not met and married her, God alone knew what would have become of him. He should have been thanking her regularly.

How come he was not doing that, she would wonder, when they quarreled. How come there were no thanks coming her way?

When I was grown and out of the house, I broached the question of a new table and chairs now that there was money for them, but the idea was ruled out. My mother explained to me patiently that they wouldn't think of it because, after all, this set was still perfectly good. "In the old days," she said nostalgically, "they built things to last." She smoothed the tablecloth fondly. "Look how it's lasted all these years. All you need to do is be a little careful with things. Maple is good wood. This dining set was a fine one when we bought it. We didn't go looking for cheap junk."

So my parents lived together for more than fifty years. And when we were all gone, they ate together at that tottering table at last, my father in his special chair, till the ends of their lives.

CHAPTER NINE

My Father's Chicken Shears

Perri: Now that I have three children of my own, I tease my mother all the time about what I choose to call her obsessive-compulsive and overattentive cooking and dishwashing, about bringing up three children while working a full-time job and writing books—and yet without takeout food and pizza. She came home on that bus every day, from Manhattan, out through the Lincoln Tunnel, and along the highways of New Jersey, and she cooked those dinners of protein and starch and green vegetables, and we ate together around a round wooden table in the kitchen. And to tell the truth, she wasn't completely happy with that table either; it was supposed to have a shiny wooden patina that would make tablecloths unnecessary, but the finish turned out to be kind of soft, and if you put your piece of paper down on the table, your pen would leave marks, so you had to use a pad, and we ate with placemats under our plates, and the matching chairs were a little rickety and periodically needed gluing. So maybe my mother just has hereditary bad luck with family dinner tables.

But yes, of course, I do acknowledge that all that time around the family dinner table probably served some important purpose. There are experts out there nowadays proving that eating dinner together strengthens families and helps children grow up sane and healthy. For all my mastery of the local pan-Asian restaurant possibilities in my part of Cambridge, Massachusetts, I also do a considerable amount of cooking, and I expect my children to grow up with around-the-table memories, even if many of them involve little white cartons on the kitchen table, or tables outside the home, perhaps with Korean barbecues inset, or at least Chinese teapots and chopsticks. And yes, I believe that the food you serve and how you serve it gets taken up and built into your children's bodies and brains as well as their memories so that they will never, however long they live, take nourishment without referring it back, just a little bit, to the meals they ate facing their parents, facing one another.

And I did grow up that way. Did I appreciate it at the time? Well, probably not exactly. My goal, as I sat around my own parents' kitchen table, was to grow up and get out—to get out of the New Jersey suburbs, to get out of my fixed daughterly place in the family constellation, to get out of my angry adolescent self. A couple of years ago, I went to my twenty-fifth college reunion, and like most twenty-fifth reunioners, I was astonished to find myself a stodgy middle-aged parental-type adult, shepherding my own children around a college campus that I had once inhabited as a defiant adolescent. I thought back on that defiance and that urgent long-ago need to define myself in opposition to my parents, even around food and eating.

I remember college conversations, usually late at night (as most of my important college conversations tended to be), about the food we had all eaten growing up. The tone, of course, was humorous; my friends and I sat around, late at night, and analyzed the childhoods out of which, we felt, we had just so triumphantly emerged. My mother never cooked pork, even though she would order it in restaurants, like that made it kosher, or something, someone might say, snickering. . . . We used to have meat loaf every single Wednesday night, just like clockwork, someone else would chime in. . . . *My* mother made those square frozen fish filets. . . . *My* mother poured Campbell's soup over things and called that dinner. . . . We were, I suppose, alternately homesick and snottily superior, eager to prove how far we had come in sophistication while still holding on tight to the idea of home, where, right now, someone might be making meat loaf or pouring cream of mushroom soup over chicken breasts. We were, most of my friends thought, quite a different generation from our parents and their peculiarities.

Me, I would acknowledge that my mother's repertory included some exotics—that scored you points with our little circle of critics. I got a certain amount of humorous mileage, however, out of my mother's absolute and unwavering prejudices about what was "trouble" in the kitchen and what was not. My mother would chop onions and garlic, I would explain, but she ruled out most fresh vegetables as too much trouble to prepare (we approved of fresh vegetables). And yet, I would sum up (oh, the ridiculousness of parents!), they bought only whole chickens, my parents, and my father would cut them up with special tools, standing in the kitchen and wielding knives he sharpened himself, and a large and rather menacing pair of poultry shears. And I would shake my head, and we would wonder whether it was time to send someone out of the dormitory and across Harvard Yard to bring back chips and onion dip from the all-night convenience store (we approved of chips and onion dip). I knew, probably, that I owed my father some of those cosmic cool points just for being systematically involved in food preparation; we were pretty rigid, back in 1974 when I started college, about applying feminist checklists to fathers who might, perhaps, have expected to be judged by other standards. But I doubt that the evocation of my father, cutting up chickens in my parents' suburban kitchen, evoked much nostalgic emotion. I had gotten out of the New Jersey suburb I hated; I had left behind high school and childhood and those chicken dinners. I was, as a college freshman, just beginning to forgive my parents for all their trespasses (moving to that suburb chief among them), but I had no desire to be back there.

Now, of course, though I have no desire at all to return to the suburbs (or to my early adolescence, and, to be fair, I may have come to associate the two so strongly that I will never judge northern New Jersey fairly), I think of my father cutting up the chickens and I feel a rush of sentiment. There he is, wearing dark pants and a clean white T-shirt, stripped for action, a clean dish towel slung over his shoulder.

He is fully bearded, of course, and his stomach is prominent—he was overweight during those years in the suburbs, though he became much thinner and fitter later on. He is hovering over a thick wooden cutting board, dealing chicken pieces into several baking pans.

My father believed, of course, that it was better to buy the chickens whole and cut them up. Better prices, sure, for a family that ate a lot of chicken, but also better butchering. Buy cut-up chicken parts, he once told me darkly, and you never knew; the parts might come from a diseased chicken, with the bad parts discarded. According to one of his stories—which is to say, according to a story he told many times—my father had put in a brief stint, in his adolescence, on a chicken farm, bought by his own father. Perhaps it was from there that he drew his poultry authority. Certainly, he could expertly butcher a chicken, just as he could carve a turkey, or, for that matter, carve a roast. And certainly also, to make a point that women often make, usually with complete fairness, about men in the kitchen, he made a big deal out of it.

I was surprised, though, to learn that my mother felt she pushed against having my father in the kitchen. I don't remember noticing that as a child—probably because I cheerfully took for granted any and all activities that resulted in satisfying my own daily needs. I don't remember particularly thinking of the kitchen as hers, though I certainly associated my father with certain very specific tasks, most of them involving animal protein in large pieces. But he also did the dishes after dinner, he did the shopping—what I can't quite conjure, looking back, is whether he hung out in the kitchen, talking to my mother while she cooked, whether he talked menus and choices with her—I just wasn't aware enough of the texture of their domesticity, I guess.

I think about my own son, now off at college. I wonder if he sits around, late at night with friends, and talks about the food back home and his parents' peculiarities. He thinks of himself as quite an epicure, I know, and he laments the dining-hall food as loudly as I ever did—and doesn't want to hear how much better the choices are today than they were thirty years ago. I also know that he thinks he grew up in a house where food was important and where parental cooking skills were more adventurous and more to his taste than they were in many other homes—I used to get a shameful charge of pride whenever he told us contemptuously about some friend's family that *ate spaghetti with sauce out of a jar,* as if he was signaling wholesale approval of all our own arrangements. And I guess I would like to think that even in the midst of his emergent sophistication and superiority, he's speaking kindly of his memories of his parents in the kitchen—yearning after his favorite dishes—demonstrating that he has taken note of our cooking habits and our domestic efforts. But I'm also happy to imagine him making fun of me, and pointing out, no doubt, quirks and compulsions that I can't even see when I think of myself in the kitchen.

And there is my father, standing in his white T-shirt, established at his butchering station, attending to his knives and his shears with surgical self-importance. And at the end of all that ritual, what you have are pieces of chicken. And my mother will make those pieces of chicken into dinner, and we will eat the dinner around the table, looking at one another, and the chickens that my father cut up and my mother cooked will end up being part of us all.

CHAPTER TEN

The Man Who Came to Dinner

Sheila: "It is a truth universally acknowledged, that a single man in possession of a good fortune must be in want of a wife." So wrote Jane Austen, at the beginning of *Pride and Prejudice,* so thought Mrs. Bennet, and she lectured her five daughters early and often about men and marriage. For her, a woman who remained unmarried was a tragedy and a failure. Though men in possession of good fortunes were irrelevant in our lives in Williamsburg, my mother absolutely agreed with Mrs. Bennet. Mama delivered a similar message daily, loud and clear. Yes, for Mama, spinsterhood was a tragedy.

This was odd, because she thought all men incompetents, doomed to empty, disastrous lives—except for those lucky few who married good women like herself, who saved them. Along with her lectures on the importance of finding a man, I heard constant complaints about how useless men were, once you found them—most especially her own husband. Papa, like Mr. Bennet, had developed the ability to tune his wife out on certain subjects. I don't think he ever listened to a word on this topic, though she addressed it often and thoroughly. That was probably a good thing because, had he listened, he might have taken it personally. Did it ever occur to her that the terrible things she said about men cut him down? Of course, it must have; that was probably why she said them. Among other defects, Mama was convinced that men were idiots around stoves and sinks, congenitally unable to cook, mystified by housework and child care, and surviving only as a result of first their mothers' and then their wives' brilliant resourcefulness. Men had to be kept away from infants because, horrified and revolted by body wastes and diaper changing, they were dangerous. Only God knew how many innocent babies had been stabbed by pins held in the wrong, clumsy male fingers. Men totally lacked the desire and the skill to play with children. Men were boors; they had no patience for the small civilities of life like walking right alongside their wives instead of two paces ahead. (Papa did always walk several paces ahead of her, but I think he did not want to hear what she was saying. When he walked with my sister or with me, he stayed right in step.) I think my mother sincerely believed her mythology of the maladroit male, and I, innocently, became a convert.

But whom would I marry? That was the weighty question I spent many happy hours pondering in the late 1930s and the early 1940s, most often after a double-feature matinee. I would amble along the sidewalk slowly, trying not to step on the cracks as I decided between the two leading men: Errol Flynn or Tyrone Power, James Stewart or Gary Cooper? Though I liked Mickey Rooney, who was funny, he wasn't handsome enough. Fred Astaire was a marvelous dancer, but I wouldn't consider him for the same reason. Johnny Weissmuller was somehow not my type. *What do looks matter?* I would ask myself. A phony question. Looks mattered. When Laurence Olivier was Heathcliff, and then again when he was Mr. Darcy, I was his till I got inside our front door. Then I was nobody's.

I didn't brood about the problem, but I understood that getting married was major. My mother had four siblings who hadn't married. The two women, my aunts, were never mentioned without an allusion to their unwed condition. When I was very small, I'd thought that their actual names were Poor Frieda and Poor Lena. While my two unmarried uncles were considered unfortunate, no great fuss was made over them. After all, a man could always marry. But a woman had only this little age window, which I understood extended from about seventeen to her early twenties. After that, poverty, dependency, bleak nights, and desperate years. All was lost. Men weren't worth much as companions, but finding one of your own counted for everything on some grander scale; life without a man was worth nothing at all.

Perri: The first thing that I cooked after my father died was a pan of scrambled eggs. It was the second morning after his death, and I woke up very early in my parents' Washington Heights apartment, after a night of sleeping very little, into what I was discovering was the regular morning pain of opening my eyes to a world that no longer held my papa. I got out of bed and tiptoed out into the hall, and I could hear my mother moving quietly around inside her bedroom, unwilling to come out into her own apartment for fear of waking one of the sleeping grandchildren. So I went in to her, to my mother, who had slept almost not at all in the bedroom that by rights belonged to her and Papa together, the same room in which he had quite suddenly, after their usual peaceful lunch, collapsed and died two days earlier. They had been married almost forty-eight years. How could she bear to lie down in their bed, how could she bear to open her eyes and face the morning? I hugged her, my mama, in her soft blue nightgown.

"I'm worried," she said. "I feel I haven't been giving people proper meals—your children, they need a real breakfast."

I thought of the breakfasts that my parents usually provided when my family came to visit: smoked whitefish from the Russian appetizer store on 181st Street, New York bagels that they devoutly believed were superior to whatever the children were used to at home in Boston, bialys, lox, kippered herrings. My father was an expert in choosing and deboning smoked fish, and my own children, accustomed to the rather haphazard and cold-cereal-based breakfasts usually served at our house, would make appropriate noises of approval and consume an enormous amount.

"Let's go out and get the things we need to make them a real breakfast," I said.

After we were dressed, we tiptoed together out through the living room, so as not to wake the two children sleeping on the fold-out couch and the improvised mattress made of sofa cushions. But my daughter Josephine sat up as we passed, so I told her to get dressed and come out with us. Josephine had just passed through two days unlike any others in her life. I mean, we all had, of course, but for a seventh-grader the seesawing between adult understanding and childlike emotions must have been particularly potent—to hear suddenly that her grandfather had died, to drive down from Boston with her father and brothers and come in late in the evening to a house of grief and desolation. Before they left Boston, Josephine, on her own initiative, had sorted through piles of family photos and put together an album of pictures of my father. Into my mother's apartment, she had brought images of Papa, had brought the travel journal we had all four kept, Josephine, her brother Orlando, my father, and I, when we spent a week in London together. The day before, Josephine had stood up in front of more than a hundred people at Papa's memorial service and spoken, a seventh-grade girl in a black shirt with a filmy pale pink scarf tied around her neck, grown-up and eloquent and beautiful and sure. And then later she had come back to Mama's apartment and cried her heart out. She sat up now on the fold-out couch, her curly dark hair braided back for the night—the hair that is also my hair, and was my father's as well. I told her to get dressed and come out with us.

So the three of us went out into the beautiful spring New York City morning, like some tableau of the three generations of womanhood, left standing after the death and departure of the men, setting out, as is their eternal wont, to provision hearth and home. And it was a beautiful morning. That whole terrible week of my father's death was unimaginably beautiful, a final definitive week of spring after a March and an April of cold rainy days. The trees were finally green and the flowering trees were riotously covering the distance from tiny buds to full flowers—cherry blossom, apple blossom, dogwood, everywhere you looked. The day before, the day of Papa's memorial service, the *New York Times* had carried a photo of pleasure-seekers in Central Park beneath a flowering bough under the headline "Sunday in the Park with Everyone."

At 189th Street we bought bagels, cream cheese, lox, and what my father always referred to as "fancy cheese." Mama wanted to know what would be a treat for my children, and she kept asking Josephine to choose things she particularly liked, so we bought grape tomatoes and smoked trout and spicy eggplant salad. Mama found the right orange juice—Original Style—and the cashier told her there was a sale on, so she could get a second container of it for half price, and then the cashier insisted on searching the store to find that second container. We went into the local supermarket, the Associated Foods, and bought eggs, and at the checkout, as Josephine handed the egg carton to Mama, it slipped between them and fell to the floor. At least seven of the dozen eggs were smashed or cracked, so Mama sent Josephine back to get another carton, and paid for both. Mama couldn't believe she had dropped the eggs like that: "I'm not seeing straight," she kept saying. "I'm just not seeing straight."

When we got back to her apartment, Mama opened the carton of cracked eggs and skillfully extracted them, one by one, into a bowl, carefully picking out the pieces of shell. "Someone ought to be able to do something with those eggs," she said, as she cut bagels and laid out smoked fish and opened cream cheese, as she set plates and cups out on the little round table at which she and Papa ate breakfast every morning of their lives.

So I made scrambled eggs. I had eaten almost nothing since Papa died, although I was constantly drinking seltzer or Diet Coke or ice water, because my mouth was so constantly and terribly dry. I wasn't sure I would be able to eat the eggs now—or anything else, for that matter. But I put butter in a pan—or actually, it was Promise margarine, I remember that because as I put it in the pan, I thought about how faithfully Papa followed every piece of advice his doctor ever gave him, battling to keep his blood pressure under control, taking up artificially sweetened cakes and cookies when his blood sugar got a little out of order, monitoring his cholesterol—I thought about how Papa did all that because he so wanted to stay alive forever, to finish his book and write more books and eat more meals and travel and go to the theater and watch his children and grandchildren grow up—and of course I started to cry yet again as the Promise margarine sizzled in the pan, and I stirred low-fat milk into the bowl of eggs and beat them as hard as I could.

I poured the eggs into the pan. As the eggs began to cook, I grabbed a handful of the grape tomatoes and sliced them into halves, dropping them into the egg mixture. Then as Josephine passed me with the smoked trout filets laid out on a plate, I took a chunk of fish and flaked off little oily pieces into the pan. I thought briefly and dizzily about what else could go in—chives, I thought, which would be unlikely to turn up in Mama's kitchen. Maybe a chopped onion, I thought, but that should have gone in first, before the eggs. And anyway, I was already in tears.

Through my tears, with some faint surprise, I watched the cooking process work: *My Papa is dead and I will never see him again, and yet the heat of the burner still makes a film of egg congeal and harden on the bottom of the pan. And yet my fork still slices through it, dividing it into furrows and runnels of pale yellow, and making way for more liquid egg to coat the pan and cook it in turn.* I stirred the eggs, tumbling the red hemispheres of tomato and the flakes of smoked fish and watching the pan of liquid cook into a pan of soft egg hills and valleys, egg lake into egg landscape. The however many billionth pan of scrambled eggs cooked on Earth. I spooned them into one of Mama's big white bowls and put them out on the table that she and Josephine had set with all the other parts of the breakfast. My six-year-old was already waiting expectantly at his plate, giving his grandmother directions about exactly what he wanted; my older son had materialized, still in pajamas, and was circling intently. Their father, Larry, whom I had abandoned a couple of hours earlier, as he slept, was in the bathroom, washing up. Mama had toasted bagels. She had made me tea and anxiously taken out the tea bag after what she hoped was the exact right interval, not too strong, not too light. I made her sit down at the table, even though she hadn't set a place for herself, because she was worried the table was too small. "I'll eat later," she said. "After the children."

But the children made room and we set another plate, and I insisted, with a slightly wounded tone in my voice, that my special scrambled eggs would be spoiled if she didn't eat them while they were hot, and she finally sat down. The children took warm bagel halves and cream cheese and lox and eggplant salad, and I passed the scrambled eggs around the table. When the bowl came back to me, I spooned a portion onto my mother's plate and then, after a second's hesitation, onto my own. We all started eating. The eggs were hot and the tomatoes only very slightly cooked, warm and sweet, and the smoked fish was rich and oily and a little bit exotic. "And all from a box of broken eggs," said my mother.

Sheila: Every novel I read during adolescence seemed to deal with the heroine choosing a suitable mate. How I worried over these women, as they did or didn't marry: Catherine Earnshaw, Jo March, Jane Eyre, Kitty Foyle, Miss Havisham, Alice Adams, Elizabeth Bennet, and then, of course, there was always Juliet.

My parents had the problem on their minds too from the time I reached puberty. I was about thirteen when I first began to notice that the admonitory clause "No man will want to marry a girl who . . ." started every sentence about my personal indiscretions. I whistled, I laughed raucously, I read so much that I needed to wear glasses all the time, I wore too much makeup, I was too smart for my own good, and I had a big mouth.

My mother would stand in the middle of the living room and demand of the cracked ceiling, "What man will want to marry her? He'd have to be crazy." Part of me was convinced that she was right. Another smaller part of me—the braver part—dismissed my mother's vision of those potential suitors, the ones who would be disgusted by my reading—or my whistling. They were morons who didn't recognize true worth; in my braver moments, I wondered where I could possibly find a man whom *I* would want to marry. My father was the only adult male I knew personally during those years in my parental home, but I heard constantly from Mama how useless he was. He couldn't even pour his own glass of water. He couldn't boil an egg. He would not do as a real-life model for the kind of marriage I thought I wanted. And Laurence Olivier was not available.

By the time I was seventeen, I'd escaped from all that. I moved out;

I went to college; I made a different sort of life for myself. I met a variety of men—in college, in graduate school, in my life as a teacher, living alone in Greenwich Village. I had boyfriends, but never a Jewish boyfriend, and my mother, somehow, never took those boyfriends seriously. Obviously, she felt, they were not really possible husbands. And while I wasted my time with these impossible men, I was outgrowing my young and nubile years. I was halfway through my twenties. Who would ever want to marry me, loud and whistling and living away from home—and now aging? And then I was lucky; I met a man who was kind and smart and funny and romantic—and Jewish, as well. My parents were ecstatic—my first Jewish boyfriend after all those years of thwarting their will.

We married. He was a scholar, so he studied; I supported the household. No big thing. Jewish women, historically, had supported scholarly husbands. Mort was just out of the Merchant Marines, where he spent the last years of World War II, and he was going to college on the GI Bill. He didn't study the Talmud; he studied anthropology, and our plan was that he would get his B.A. then his Ph.D. so he could teach and do research. No prenuptial agreement was necessary since neither of us possessed anything of value. Even if we'd had wealth, it wouldn't have mattered. We trusted each other. We were in this together.

So I supported us, but at home, the division of labor in our household was mostly traditional. I did the cooking and felt responsible for the kitchen and the laundry, the domestic chores. I was supposed to "keep the house," but I hated housework, so I avoided it. Luckily, in the great tradition of scholars, he was so busy thinking about other things, he never noticed. We shopped together. He drove; I was too cowardly to learn, so he did many of the errands. He kept the books and handled all the business of dealing with the outside commercial world.

The 1950s was a time of sorting out new ways to live, more equal ways. I don't know about others, but I had no idea of the complex tangle we were enmeshed in, the tangle of our personal histories. I was in love, newly married and happy, teaching in the New York school system, which paid men and women equally. I had no problem.

My husband had the problem—and it was me. From the first, he rebelled. "It's not your kitchen," he said grimly, forcibly taking the chuck steak out of my hands and insisting that he would broil it. (Chuck was the cheapest cut, so we were convinced it was the best. We were young, in love, and we had good teeth.) He grilled the salmon and cut the chickens. (He was surgically gifted at that, so much so that once when we were visiting Los Angeles and we saw a Rodeo Drive storefront for rent, our son, the screenwriter, offered to bankroll a chicken business there, my husband performing his magic with the poultry shears in the window.)

I tried to drive him out of the kitchen—my kitchen. "You make me nervous when you're in here," I explained.

He wasn't going. "Well, you have to get used to me," he said. He wouldn't budge. For almost fifty years, he grilled the meat and fish, and he often washed the dishes, and I did get used to it. But I always had the small uneasiness that what he was doing was somehow not manly, not appropriate. It was a vestigial idiocy, one of many, and it was our ability to joke about it that saved us.

Petti: My mother has been known to quote the epitaph that Keats wrote, and that is carved on his tombstone in the cemetery in Rome: "Here lies one whose name was writ in water." She thinks of it as very sad, my mother, who has dreamed all through her own adult life of writing success and literary immortality. Me, in the adolescent cynicism that perhaps I should have outgrown by now, I wonder if Keats was not perhaps protesting a bit too much, leaving something to be carved on his tombstone in the precise hope that perhaps for generations, visitors would shake their heads and cluck over just how completely he had gotten it wrong: Imagine *this* man thinking he would not be remembered! In any case, I have tried to decide what the appropriate epitaph would be for my father, a man who loved to eat, who measured out his life in meals and mealtimes, and who told stories of himself as a great, a prodigious, a prize-winning eater. *Here lies one whose name was writ in gravy,* perhaps. *Whose name was writ in chocolate.*

For years we joked—and teased my father—about the regularity with which his stomach alarm went off. When he got up in the morning, my father needed to eat breakfast immediately—and not just a cup of coffee, either. In his soul, I think, he yearned always after a full cooked hot breakfast, and certainly during the week I spent with him in London a couple of years before his death, he did full justice every morning to the eggs, bacon and sausage, fried tomato, toast, fruit compote, and coffee served in the dining room at St. Margaret's Hotel in Bloomsbury. But over the years he learned to respect the rules of late-twentieth-century dietary political and medical correctness. He adapted to a toasted bagel, a little low-fat cream cheese or cottage cheese, a glass of orange juice—as long as he could eat within twenty minutes of opening his eyes. At noon the clock went off again, and in fact by eleven or so he would be making nervous inquiries, if he happened to be anywhere where the punctuality and the nature of lunch might be in any doubt at all—if he happened, for example, to be visiting my notoriously disordered and irregular household. And then, no matter how much he had eaten at lunch, at six PM, there was Tummy again, rumbling and complaining and asking to be fed. And the result was that soon after breakfast, he would start to check on plans for lunch, and similarly, soon after lunch, he would ask about supper. We teased him about it—but it drove my mother crazy.

"But you just finished lunch!" she would yell.

"I was just asking," Papa would say, mildly but undiverted. "Perri, were you thinking we would eat in a restaurant tonight, or were you going to cook at home?"

In recent years, Papa used to apologize for not being able to eat as much as he had once been able to. In a Chinese restaurant, he would look at any food left on the serving platters and say, ruefully, "Ah, in my youth . . ." I grew up on stories of the mammoth feasts of his adolescence, of especially his years in the Merchant Marines, of his first visit to Durgin Park in Boston, where famously, the prime rib hung over the side of the plate and no one could finish the portion—except Papa, of course. Once at a Thanksgiving dinner, where Papa had told some of his eating stories, one of my children, then maybe four years old, overindulged and paid the terrible price of conspicuous consumption, and Mama got angry at Papa: "Eating contests!" she said to him. "What kind of fool tells a child stories about eating contests?"

But my children loved Papa's stories about eating, perhaps because they allowed them to invest their grandfather with their own feelings of eager childish greediness, or perhaps just because they made him out to be a kind of Paul Bunyan figure of happy tall-tale glory. At Papa's memorial service, my older son, Orlando, told two of the stories of Papa's days in the Merchant Marines. In one story, Papa was standing watch one night with another merchant seaman, and the two of them got hungry. So Papa crawled into the galley through a window and found an enormous roast of lamb, and made sandwiches for them both, and they continued standing watch. A little later on in the night, they got hungry again, and he went back through the window for more sandwiches—and then again, on toward morning. And in the morning, the ship's cook came rushing out of the galley, crying out that a gang had broken in and eaten the entire crew's lunch.

But Papa's favorite story of all was the second story, the story of the steak-eating contest. It seems that he was challenged by a shipmate to a competition: Who could eat more steak? With the other sailors watching (and placing bets), Papa and his challenger each ate one steak—then another—and then a third. Papa liked to draw the story out, of course, describing the other man chewing slower, finally coming to a stop and conceding. And so Papa, victorious, went about his evening chores. "Toward midnight," Papa would say, "I started to get a little hungry." He would pause for the laugh. "So I went back down to the galley, and there was a pile of cold leftover steaks. So I sat down and had a snack. And there was one sailor who had gone out on shore leave, earlier in the evening, while we were having the contest, so he didn't know how it had turned out, and he came back to the ship right then, probably a little bit drunk. He came in and saw me, and he screamed, "Great God, it's been six hours and he's still eating!"

Papa always loved red meat—steak especially, but also ribs and roast beef and prime rib. My son Orlando, who was seventeen at the time, also spoke at the memorial service about his earliest memories of my father, which turned out to date to a certain Korean restaurant in Cambridge, the wonderful New Korea in Inman Square, where we often took my parents when they came to visit. Back in the 1980s, Korean food was new to us all, and my son remembered my father's intense excitement at the new tastes. He recalled his grandfather eating huge quantities of *bibim naing myung,* the cold cellophane noodles served in an incendiary red pepper broth and ornamented with sliced cold meat, but I also remember Papa, in that same restaurant, discovering *galbi gui,* the succulent Korean barbecued ribs.

He loved almost every cuisine he encountered—as a young anthropology graduate student from Brooklyn, he had fallen in love with Indian food, as had my mother—curried vegetables, curried mutton, curried goat—and with the tastes of the Caribbean—tropical fruits, sugar cane juice, rum. He took an anthropologist's delight in the variety and complexity of human inventiveness around food, from Mexican mole sauce, which allowed him to eat chocolate with his main course, as well as with his dessert, to Vietnamese fresh spring rolls. He embraced each new learning adventure as Chinese food in New York got more and more sophisticated—the Szechuanese food of the 1970s thrilled him, since he liked spice and heat, but he was happy to inform me in the 1980s, after the trip that he and Mama took to China, that Cantonese cooking was nothing like the American Chinese food we had eaten in New York when I was small. "Cantonese cooking is considered to be the best Chinese cooking of all," he explained, delicious, simple, sophisticated, indescribable. In the years before he died, he had also become enamored of Shanghai cuisine, both the soup dumplings and the rich lion's head meatballs, and also the cold smoked appetizers, so unexpectedly similar to Jewish tastes and textures. And of course, all his life, he loved the Jewish foods of his childhood, pickled herring and smoked sturgeon, stuffed derma and gefilte fish, borscht and roast chicken. The one food from his childhood that he could not abide, the one bad memory, was lima beans, and he often claimed to be worried that people were going to try to sneak lima beans into other dishes.

Papa always said that he had taught Mama how to cook, that when he met her, she thought that cooking was putting ketchup on spaghetti ("That was how everyone ate spaghetti in Williamsburg in the 1930s," Mama said), and that left to herself, she would still over-cook the roast beef ("Some of us *like* it well done," Mama said). But aside from those certain ritualized male prerogatives—the big hunks of meat, the barbecue—Mama did most of the cooking. But Papa shopped with her—in fact, he took her shopping, since despite twenty years in the New Jersey suburbs, Mama stayed a girl from Williams-burg, Brooklyn, and did not learn to drive. ("Who had a car in Williamsburg?" Mama said.)

But what was definitely clear to me, I think, then and now and for-ever, was that food was love. That the choosing and preparing and eat-ing of food was something that they did together because they loved each other and because they loved us; that it was not something to get out of the way and minimize, but the stuff of daily life and nourish-ment in every sense. And that dinner every night around that kitchen table was part of the framework on which a family was built.

I think about all my father's meals, over the years, each one antici-pated, even worried over, and almost all enjoyed. Just as his appetite came back to him on a regular, even compulsive schedule, so did his joy in the taste of what he ate. I think of meals he served to me—those ritual breakfasts in their apartment in Washington Heights, after they left the suburbs and moved back to the city, my father standing over the toaster oven, superintending my bagel. I think of meals we ate to-gether, in obscure street-food joints in Cairo (where a student who had taken his classes at Barnard years earlier recognized him, and began yelling, "Professor Klass!") and in intimidatingly elegant New York restaurants (my brother has a taste for elegance). And, of course, I think of meals I served him, around my own family table, the last one just a week before he died. We had made pasta with chicken and asparagus, and of course we served it late, by his standards, because everyone had had a big lunch and the six o'clock dinner hour is not as rigidly observed in the wild bohemian precincts of Cambridge. But Papa was a good sport, especially with drinks and hors d'oeuvres to keep him busy till the food came, and when the food did come, he did his part. He ate two helpings, and then wished aloud that he could eat more—in his youth, he said, he would have been able to. And I know he saw, when he looked around the table at his grandchildren eating, that all his own ideas were correct, that food *is* love, and that when you prepare it and serve it and eat it right, you nourish your family, day by day.

Sheila: We'd received a copy of *Larousse Gastronomique* as a wedding present. I was a Crock-Pot and meat loaf kind of cook, but my husband loved to eat and was intrepid about experimenting. Sometimes he felt like cooking up some wonderfully exotic dish like entrecôte Mirabeau—steak with tarragon, anchovies, and olives—and when he did it successfully, I was always so surprised. Why? He was smart, he was handy, he could follow a recipe. He'd been a bachelor and cooked for himself for years. So he was a good cook. But apparently, in my mother's daughter's house (which also happened to be his house) there could be only one cook, and that was me. I'd absorbed the propaganda I grew up with.

The mind-set never quite went away. But it got a good hard shove in 1958, when Perri was born and we were living in that house on stilts in Felicity. All went well until the baby was born, but suddenly we had a problem. I had planned to nurse, but I did not have sufficient milk, so we had a hungry, crying baby and the only answer was powdered milk and glucose imported from England.

Infant diarrhea was not uncommon in Felicity, and two of our friends had lost babies during the year. Babies in our village who could not breast-feed often died. Some mothers were so poor that they could not afford milk, so they whitened water for their infants with arrowroot so it looked like milk; those babies died of malnutrition, killed by poverty, not by lack of care. Still, there I was, looking at my new baby and thinking about those deaths. I was terrified, but Mort stayed calm. He made a list. We went looking for a huge Thermos to keep sterile water in and a great pot to use as sterilizer on our two-burner kerosene stove. We put in a big supply of nipples and nursing bottles. These last were a curiosity in the village, where women used sweet drink bottles with nipples fitted on them; the hourglass-shaped Coke bottles were favorites. Infants loved holding them. Someone should tell the Coca-Cola people.

I wanted to feed the baby on a demand-feeding schedule; I was, after all, a devotee of Dr. Spock. This meant that when she cried to signal she was hungry, we had to spring into action. Six times a day, we needed boiled water into which the proper amount of powder and glucose had to be dissolved. Absolutely dissolved, or the nipple would clog. Bottles and nipples had to be carefully sterilized. What was most crucial during the formula-making was that there be no contamination. The air was so thick with flies and other insects that sometimes as we ate we fished drowned bugs out of our soup. Nothing could be put down safely for a minute.

Mort opted to be the formula-maker. He seriously and systematically undertook the job, spending long hours in that tropical ninety-degree kitchen, concentrating on keeping his implements and ingredients sterile. And so the village men would come at dusk and sit on our gallery and watch Mort and tease him. The women, too, marveled at his skill and, more so, at his willingness to do what they called petticoat work alongside me. Indian women were considered unclean after childbirth and were isolated for twelve days. Their husbands didn't go anywhere near them.

The baby flourished. Her father, born into a gender that couldn't pour water, had become an alchemist. Not only could he pour and boil water, he transmuted it into life-sustaining milk. I couldn't wait to get home and describe it all to my mother.

Perri: Holidays suited Papa. Papa thrived on family occasions. He himself would probably have said that as a cultural anthropologist, it well behooved him to appreciate the importance of kinship rituals and

other tribal epochs, but the truth is, I think, he loved the role of patri-
arch, paterfamilias, founder of the feast. He was a white-bearded sage,
a raconteur, a professor with a tendency to lecture at any opportunity,
and holidays suited him well.

On Thanksgiving, of course, Papa always carved the turkey. Thanksgiving has been at my house for at least twenty-one years now, ever
since I had my first baby and refused to travel on the holiday. We make
too much food, of course, and we go through various family rituals, of
course, ranging from what we refer to as our "Kennedy-esque touch
football game" before dinner with another family to the after-dinner
flurry in which both grandmothers compete to clear and do dishes,
while I beg them to sit a while and relax, so I can sit and relax as well.

As the turkey roasted, Papa would make anxious inquiries about
when we thought it would be done, bringing together the ticking of
his stomach clock with his anxiety about his own moment in the spotlight. He would assemble my best knife and sharpen it carefully, position a cutting board and a platter and a bowl for the stuffing. He
would take off his good shirt and tuck a dish towel into his belt. And
finally, when the turkey was judged perfectly cooked and had been
carefully lifted to the cutting board, he would begin. He liked silence
while he carved, but he also liked an audience, and would ask ner-
vously every now and then if this was enough, if he should cut more,
if it wouldn't dry out if he cut too much. And he would create a beautiful, perfect platter, thin slices of white meat, dark meat, pieces of
turkey skin, wings, and drumsticks, all fanned out in a holiday
arrangement, stuffing spooned out of the cavity and heaped in a bowl.

We cooked other things on Thanksgiving, of course, an enormous
array of vegetables and noodle dishes and whatever came to mind—
certain things the same every year, certain things new inspirations.
Curried pumpkin as a nod to the time my parents spent in Trinidad
and India, spinach with jalapeño peppers because everyone likes hot
food, mashed potatoes with basil and garlic because my older son
loves them so much. But the turkey was the center, and the one thing
that everybody always ate, and exclaimed over, while Papa stood happily by and reminded us, over and over, that he would be happy to

carve more as soon as we had finished what was there. And so I guess he was right yet once again: that the ritual roasting of the great bird on its ritual day was our tribal rite, both as a family tribe and as members of our national tribe, and that the carving demanded special tools and special garments and special very close attention, a once-a-year kinship ceremony starring a cultural anthropologist and his kin.

Sheila: "We need a chapter in this book about Papa and you. Early Papa and you," Perri reminds me. I haven't forgotten, Perr. I've tried a dozen times, but nothing I come up with seems right. I think that's because this whole book is really about lives so blended as to be inseparable. I can't distill the essence of fifty years into such a small decanter.

"Try," she urges. "Think of a few things that really represent your relationship."

Well, of course, you know, Perr, first has to be the matter of the roach. We'd had that battle on our first date, and neither of us ever acknowledged defeat. There I was with two graduate degrees in English, and this guy starts telling me nonsense about Kafka, a writer I adored. (So did this guy, he said. But I adored him better.) Our disagreement over why Gregor Samsa was turned into a roach was vital. Why a roach? Now, there are those translators and partisans who use *bug* or even *vermin*, but that's another argument. Our dispute was over *roach.*

"Because it's the most universally detested creature," I said positively. "Kafka carefully calculated this choice. The roach is the perfect symbol. Don't you see? It's the way Gregor thinks of himself."

"Nonsense," Mort said, dismissing that. "You're making too much of it. Look—it's late at night in Prague. There's Franz sitting in his parents' middle-European kitchen. You know what those crummy apartments were like. A towel is wrapped around his head because he has one of his damned headaches. He wants to write his story. He's got the perfect name for it already: "The Metamorphosis." All he needs is a symbol. He looks up at the wall. Crawling down the wall toward him is a huge roach. That's it."

I was outraged. I took the offensive, mustering my many literature courses and my deep thoughts about symbolism. I couldn't shake him. He stayed with that roach-on-the-wall theory. It was very late when we finally called it a draw, neither of us conceding a millimeter. The silliness and ferocity of the disagreement had exhausted us, so we walked together quietly.

"I'll call you tomorrow," he said, as he left me at my door. The funny thing was that I wanted him to call. I was already summoning up new arguments to prove that I was right.

I couldn't convince him. He stayed with that roach-on-the-wall theory even after we were married. If we discount that roach, there were many aspects of living that Papa had worked out for himself, and he passed them on to me; he knew how to laugh at himself, at his huge appetite, at his lack of athletic skill, at his childish sweet tooth. When we dined together, he always finished way before me. "If the end of the world comes, I want to have had my dessert," he explained, unabashed.

He made me recognize my own peculiarities, such as my stinginess. "You don't think you're worth it," he'd tease me, a bit sadly, when I turned away from little luxuries. He was profligate compared to me, but who wouldn't be? He just liked nice things. He was aware of his own shyness, and his compulsive talking-too-much to conceal it. He recognized my lack of self-confidence and tried to reassure me. We laughed together at our difficult parents and mutual poverty, at our joint inability to carry any tune. I'd always been upset by obnoxious relatives, but he taught me to care less about what peripheral people said. Take his cousin, who came to our wedding and told me she never gave a wedding present till after she met the bride and knew what kind of person she was. That cousin never sent anything. I learned from Mort how to dismiss petty, unfair colleagues and grasping landlords, dishonest merchants and the bigoted bureaucrats for whom I worked, in the New York public school system. I learned to get on with my life.

When I repeated to him my mother's continuous rhetorical reproach to her children—"You think you were put on this earth to enjoy yourselves?"—he was amazed. "You should've answered, '*Yes*. That's why we're here.' " When a child, I'd never even dared to think *yes*.

He rejoiced in the marvels of anthropology. Remember how he loved to tell the story of how, when he was eighteen years old and a merchant seaman, aboard ship, he came upon the paperback Armed Services edition of Margaret Mead's *Coming of Age in Samoa,* read it, and recognized his vocation? He'd truly had an epiphany.

He reveled in his discipline, both the field work and the teaching. And he was vastly entertained by his noisy, proud mother, who could not get his academic field straight and referred to him as "my son, the anthologist."

You cannot imagine how concerned he was, Perr, in Trinidad, because you'd lose eligibility to run for president of the United States by being born outside the territorial United States. I never would have worried about my child's presidential aspirations. When David was born in Vermont, his presidential eligibility was pristine. No stress for Papa. Again, when Judy, the most political of you three, was born in New York City practically on the doorstep of Columbia, Papa breathed freely. She was eminently eligible.

Nothing you children did was uninteresting to him. Reading aloud to you each evening after dinner was his great pleasure: Collodi, Milne, Wodehouse, Tolkien, London, Renault, hundreds of authors. It was my entertainment too, as I washed dishes. Those evening reading sessions are probably responsible for all three of you becoming devout readers and then professional writers, with incredibly eclectic tastes. Hyperliteracy was Papa's singular gift to each of you.

Perri: For New Year's Eve, 2000, we gave a small party at our house in Cambridge, my own immediate family, both sets of grandparents, my sister. We decided to orient it a little toward the foods and party games of the 1950s, so we served martinis and onion-soup dip, and we played charades. We also read aloud the second act of the Kaufman and Hart play, *The Man Who Came to Dinner,* the play about Sheridan Whiteside, the acerbic critic and radio commentator modeled on Alexander Woollcott, who falls down and injures himself on the doorstep of a Midwestern couple after having dinner at their house, and moves in with them to recuperate over the course of weeks. I had first come across this play as a child, when my father read it aloud to us, as he did *You Can't Take It with You* and *Once in a Lifetime,* and though I know there have been other great Sheridan Whitesides (Monte Woolley onstage in the original production, and in the movie, and, most recently, Nathan Lane on Broadway), to me, Sheridan Whiteside will always and only be Papa, bearded, scene-stealing, and thunderous of voice.

And so, on the last night of 1999, with the rest of us taking the other parts—the promiscuous starlet, the songwriter who is clearly meant to be Noël Coward, the Harpo Marx–like Banjo, and the various bewildered members of the Stanley family, who are unwillingly hosting this drama, Papa was Sheridan Whiteside. He stormed and he scoffed and he blistered with sarcasm. And then, at the end of the act, with chaos swarming around him and every single other character furious, with penguins loose in the living room and his host about to murder him, the moment came for Sheridan Whiteside to broadcast his Christmas Eve message to America. And Papa delivered the Christmas Eve broadcast of love and peace, and you could imagine his honeyed tones going out over the radio to listening Americans everywhere.

Sheila: When we got married, I was greedy with the possibilities the 1950s offered women, and Papa was eager that I should sample them. I was already happily teaching, but he believed in me as a writer, as well. From that very first roach argument, he believed I was a professional writer. And when we married, he insisted that a professional writer required a desk of her own. We had little money for furniture, so I tried to talk him into sharing a desk, but he wouldn't hear of it. We ended up in that two-room apartment, over the Squeeze Inn bar on East 4th Street, our home divided into one living-dining-cooking room with an oversized couch-bed crammed in, and one brave office with two massive (secondhand) rolltop desks. And one of those desks was mine! Papa loved life and knew how to live honorably and enjoy it. His imagination was brilliant and unbounded, and he led the way for us all. This brief note acknowledges that our book is by way of a fond elegy.

PART FOUR

Domestic Bliss

CHAPTER ELEVEN

Nothing but a Hound Dog

Sheila: The one thing a family should not do when they buy a house in the suburbs is buy a new rug! This advice comes of bitter practical experience. In the late 1960s, we moved to a house in Leonia, New Jersey, just over the George Washington Bridge, a stone's throw from Manhattan. I'd be willing to throw the stone.

Why did we go? Well, we had three young children, Judy, who was still a baby, and Perri and David in elementary school. Mort and I both worked, and it was a strange time in the city; New York's streets seethed with anger and with antiwar demonstrations. Up near Columbia University where we lived, the people of Harlem were marching in the streets to protest Columbia's plan to take over their Morningside Park and build a university gym. The city, much as I loved it, seemed unfriendly and unpredictable.

Fresh air, my husband said. Trees. Gardens. No traffic. Safe streets. Good schools. The university would help with our mortgage. It was all true. But he could have lived anywhere happily. He knew how to inhabit a culture and sense its values. That's why he was such a good anthropologist. Not me. While I too thought I could live anywhere happily, even for years, I had to know that, ultimately, Manhattan was my home.

I had never dreamed of owning a house. In fact, the very idea of a house was overwhelming for me. I did all my own housework. The extra rooms meant much more work. I'd had a housekeeper for a year in Trinidad and discovered I couldn't bear having a stranger do my dirty work. It was a moot point anyway in Leonia, because we didn't have money to hire domestic help. We had to pay for the house. The garden was a totally alien concept. I would never go near it. I was a writer. What I wanted to do was write. For these and many other good reasons, I tried to hold out—but it was clear that for the children, for the family's general good, the move was necessary. And so I was suckered into the Leonia mirage, and we surrendered our Columbia apartment.

So I was stuck. Literally. I couldn't drive. I'd had lessons years before, in 1960, when Mort got his first job in Bennington, Vermont (now, that was real exile—don't get me started on what it was like for me in Vermont, without a job, watching the leaves turn color), but I'd been too terrified ever to take the driving test. My fault: cowardice.

So we moved to New Jersey. We did our own painting of walls and ceilings, and Mort, who was a good carpenter, built great bookshelves on any available wall. David, who played every possible sport, liked his shelves until he began winning trophies. Then he developed a peculiar phobia; he was convinced that one night when he was fast asleep suddenly he would be buried alive by the trophies falling from the shelves his father had built for him. Poor Mort! We moved the heavier pieces away from above the headboard. Of course, nothing ever fell.

Our limited money spared us the task of furnishing. That is, we bought minimally what we needed to set up housekeeping. We lived there for more than twenty years, yet we never "decorated." Few things matched; nonetheless, the house was comfortable. It is my guess that we probably had the least decorated house in town, but the children had rooms of their own, the kitchen was large and comfortable with that good round table for family meals, and Mort and I had our tiny attic offices.

Our single large luxury was a huge rug, not a valuable Persian but a durable brown shaggy Sears Roebuck carpet, vaguely modern in its squarish linear pattern, for our living room, which had old, impossibly scarred wood floors.

We would never have bought that rug if we'd had a dog.

No, I did not learn to love the safe green town of Leonia. Not ever. Lest I be thought misanthropic, I need to emphasize that many wonderful things happened during those Leonia years. Our family flourished. The children grew and thrived, Mort and I taught in our colleges and wrote our books, Mort began to act in community theater and proved an astonishingly good actor; an alternative high school started up and we taught classes in our living room. Most important to me were the friends I made in the community, smart, socially conscious, talented women, who are still important in my life. Life was good to us, and I was grateful.

Petti: Just for the record, and to no one's surprise, I would like to state that *I* did not particularly thrive in Leonia, though I unquestionably adolesced. I was ten when we moved, and I was unhappy pretty much immediately. It was supposed to be a good school system, and it wasn't; it was a pedestrian school system run by unimaginative and fundamentally dumbheaded bureaucrats. It was also, which probably had a much more immediate impact on my own life, a school system in which most of the children had known each other since kindergarten, and there were very specific rules about how to dress and how to talk and how to act. I got everything wrong, in my newly imported socially tone-deaf city child weirdness, and they let me know it. I didn't like the schools, I didn't like the other kids, and I didn't like the suburbs. That alternative high school that my mother referred to—for me that was a lifesaver, precisely because it got me the hell out of the supposedly good schools for which my family had crossed the George Washington Bridge. I was an angry, unhappy twelve- . . . and thirteen- . . . and fourteen-year-old, and I blamed it all squarely on Leonia and my parents' foolish decision to move us there.

I am old enough and (barely) mature enough now to recognize that I might have been an unhappy thirteen-year-old in any setting—an unhappy thirteen-year-old in New York or in New Delhi, in New

South Wales or in New Rochelle. An awful lot of it was probably me. Still, I didn't like the suburbs. I still find myself starting to twitch when I visit gracious homes with beautiful green lawns, and communities without sidewalks give me the willies. My own adult life has been partly shaped by an absolute determination never to live in some particular town for the sake of the supposedly good schools, or for the sake of my children having a yard.

And in all this, despite her determination to put a good face on things, I am absolutely and completely my mother's daughter. She hated the suburbs, much as she may have loved individual friends. She never belonged there, in that perfectly nice and perfectly friendly place (see how mature I've gotten?), and somehow, neither did I.

Sheila: I would still argue that the Leonia years were good years, happy and productive, but that was despite the location, not because of it. I sound unappreciative, a malcontent, I know—not as crabby and sour as Perri, perhaps, but she was a sullen child during those Leonia years, while I was supposed to be an adult. My only defense is that I need Manhattan as my living space and cannot live elsewhere, certainly not in a suburb where no one walks except to walk a dog—the worst of all possible reasons.

I commuted to the city, marking papers. Saturdays, Mort drove us to the supermarket and we shopped for the week. I did a lot of cooking weekends and froze the food. I tried to cope with the house, according to my own peculiar standards; housecleaning was haphazard; it got easier when the two older kids didn't want me touching their stuff. I consigned their rooms to oblivion and tried to keep the rest of the place neat.

No one puts things down casually in any space I'm responsible for, even today, not shoes or garments or packages or books or even mail. That compulsive pattern helped to maintain superficial order. (It may also be why my daughters—not David, interestingly—scatter everything everywhere and never hang up a garment if they can drop it.)

When we'd been in Leonia a short while, the pressure for a dog began to build. Apparently, you couldn't live in a suburb with small children and no dog. It seemed to be almost a religious dictum. The neighbors, the sitcoms, the children's fiction, the comics all had pets as integral parts of childhood. It's always been my philosophy that one should never seek extra dependents: I wouldn't have a bird or a fish or a cat or dog or even a plant that needed care. (I do keep some cacti, but they were Mort's.) When I have free time and energy, I write. But like the house propaganda, the dog propaganda was so insidious and powerful, it prevailed. After I exacted sworn oaths that all the dog care would be the responsibility of the others, Mort and the kids brought a cute black-and-white puppy home from the pound and named him Bingo. He began peeing, and it seemed to me as if that and worse were his only skills. I was right.

Petri: Every night, before she went up to bed, my mother would try to protect the living room rug from the dog. Over time, as she and the dog refined their complex and hostile relationship, this evening ritual grew more and more elaborate. She would fold back the edges of the rug, carefully lay out newspapers blanketing the folded-back rug, and then she would position the coffee table strategically. And then she would go up to bed and the dumb dog would do his dumb dog thing, attempting to dig his way through the rug, or through the floor, and in the morning, my mother would be furious.

In the morning, she would also have to walk him. My mother hated that dog, and, as she would have told you anytime, as she would still tell you now, she had never wanted a pet. In fact, this should probably be her story to tell, and it generally has been her story to tell, as family stories go. It points up various sardonic morals—don't trust the children when they promise to feed and care for a pet; don't expect me to grow fond of an animal I never wanted; dumb is dumb (meaning the dog, of course).

My mother may think that she had come a long way from her own parsimonious and old-country-minded mother, but one thing they both had in common, I suspect, was a strong sense that animals are dirty, and perhaps an old-country conviction that the reason to keep animals is, eventually, to eat them—or at least, to drink their milk and eat their eggs. She's certainly right that Bingo was the result of a certain suburban mania that overtook her nearest and dearest, a fond wish to participate in a fantasy of American childhood. My father fell for it. My brother and I were convinced that we wanted a puppy. My father supported it. My mother protested, as she says. And, as she says, we promised, as all children in such circumstances promise, to walk the dog and take care of the dog and feed the dog and clean up after the dog. I don't think my mother was fooled, but neither could she hold out against both children and her husband, all of them dreaming puppy dreams. We got the dog—according to my father's fantasy, we went to the pound, though I had read a couple of Albert Payson Terhune novels and would have been willing to be caught up in kennel romance. We named him Bingo. He started out as a small reasonably cute black furry puppy and grew into a fairly large black dog with a white bib; my father (who perhaps had his own Albert Payson Terhune fantasies) identified him from a dog book as a border collie.

And man, was he dumb. We tried to train him. We took him to obedience school. Eventually he was more or less housebroken, but that was as far as his education went. Never learned to heel—when you walked him, he charged ahead, trying to pull your arm out of its socket. Never learned not to attack strangers coming to the house—Bingo had to be shut in the basement whenever anyone came over, and he would hurl himself repeatedly against the door, barking loudly. As soon as I left for college, he proved generations of sentimental dog authors wrong, from Homer on out, by forgetting me immediately; when I came home on vacation, he had to be shut in the basement. I was just another dangerous stranger. No, clearly that fantasy American childhood was not for us. A boy and his dog, indeed!

It turned out, in the end, to be my mother and the dog. She walked him every day. Grimly, but she walked him. She fed him. She got expert at tackling him and locking him in the basement whenever the doorbell rang. And every night, she tried to protect the living-room rug against his earnest, useless, genetically programmed desire to dig his way down through the floor.

Sheila: The very memory upsets me, so I will sum up quickly. He was a hopeless dog, whom the others enjoyed and whom I despised. But Judy, our youngest, played with him, and he never hurt her. David enjoyed teasing me, saying I did not appreciate the dog's hidden depths. He himself, he claimed, often discussed Wittgenstein with Bingo. Perri's enthusiasm cooled quickly; she had no great interest in him.

I ended up doing most of the work. Mort bathed him and saw to his meals and walked him when he could. But Mort was away a lot, and the kids abdicated all responsibility. The chores fell to me. And I minded. But what I minded most was what he did to our good rug— our only rug. He would spend the nights scratching up the wool as if he were trying to bury a bone, so each morning there were clumps of fibers like wispy dandelion balls. There was no way to shut him out— there were no interior doors on the street level of our house—so I ended up having to roll up the rug every night. And I minded doing this every single night I did it. He lived to be quite old; that was a lot of nights.

While we lived in Leonia, I wrote a series of columns for the *New York Times* about life in the suburbs. One was about Bingo and his special talents, which I had so quickly discerned: One morning, while I was walking him, we encountered a neighbor, all dressed up for a job interview. Bingo urinated on his leg. After the *Times* accepted the article, they sent a photographer to Leonia to take some pictures. During the shoot, I heard my neighbor call to his wife, "You're not going to believe this, but there's a photographer taking pictures of Sheila and that dumb dog, Bingo." His wife came running out in her bathrobe to gape.

The article ran in the *Times* on January 25, 1975. The photograph shows me walking along the curb reading a feminist tract as I hold Bingo's leash and try my best to pretend he's not there. It's emblematic of how I lived my life in the suburbs.

Perri: After I left home to go to college, I have to admit, I kind of forgot about the dog. I felt no great affection for him—it turns out that perhaps I am my mother's daughter—and my grandmother's granddaughter—when it comes to animals in the house. Or maybe I just felt uncomfortable around that dog because he was a furry, noisy, troublesome reminder that my mother had been right—we would not, in fact, feed him and take care of him ourselves. I deserved, I suppose, to be greeted with hostility when I came home to visit. Bingo and I had never really bonded; I had never fulfilled my responsibilities. Pets may help some children mature; Bingo had proved me childish, unreliable, and unable to keep my promises. Or maybe it was nothing so deep; maybe I just resented the way he attacked any friends I brought home. But year after year, there he was, locked into this long relationship with my mother. She fed him, she walked him, she tried to protect the living-room rug. When he was particularly difficult, or the weather was particularly bad, she dropped the occasional remark about how she had never wanted a dog in the first place. But then she hooked up his leash and out they went. It was, I suppose, some kind of object lesson in how real adults with real responsibilities behave.

So I don't know what the moral is. No one who watched my mother with that dog, or listened to her talk about him, could believe for even a minute that this was really the heartwarming story of a deep affection that grew up between a dog whose child owners had grown up and left him and a woman who grew to appreciate the nobility of canine friendship. Not in a million years. Maybe there is a moral about responsibility and duty and consistency. Or maybe, when I listen to my mother talk about her own childhood, I recognize something else—my mother tended that dog with a kind of grim, sour devotion to duty, as she describes her own mother bringing up children. My mother makes every honest criticism I might offer of myself into a backhanded way of praising me and celebrating my achievements, but when it came to the dog, she was a flinty realist. She never made his antics out to be anything other than conclusive evidence that he was stupid, untrainable, and a great burden. Maybe that was the stage on which she acted out the lesson she had learned as a child—the absolutely reliable but joyless acceptance of obligation.

The dog died right as I was starting medical school. I had had a bad day—back in Boston after living in California and Italy, temporarily in the medical school dorm, looking for a place to live, unsure about the return to Boston, unsure about the medical school decision. I called my parents, looking for comfort and a pep talk. Instead, my mother was sad. "Bingo died," she said. In the morning when she came downstairs, she had found him dead. "Boy," she said, with tears in her voice, "boy, was he dumb. But we knew each other for a long time."

CHAPTER TWELVE

Coming of Age in Suburbia

Perri: My mother knew what marijuana smelled like. In suburban New Jersey, in the early 1970s, that was one of the great divides. There was a certain adolescent arrogance way back then—well, perhaps there is always a certain adolescent arrogance, but surely my adolescent children and their contemporaries can't actually believe that they *invented* sex, drugs, and rock and roll. I mean, I have a college-age son who downloads old Rolling Stones music; surely he isn't surprised when his father and I turn out to know the words.

But in the early 1970s, we believed smugly that our parents were, and always had been, completely clueless. And many of my friends had parents who obliged. Oh, how we hooted at their simple credulousness: They came to pick me up at the party and they asked what was that funny burning smell! But *my* parents were college professors, and they spent a great deal of time around college students, who were, after all, even cooler than high school students, and I knew that they knew what marijuana smelled like. It even occurred to me to wonder whether they occasionally encountered it at the academic parties they frequented, and whether, perhaps . . . but I didn't pursue the question.

When *Hair* opened on Broadway, my parents took me to see it as a birthday present. The famous nude scene, we were all expecting, of course; my mother, sitting next to me, was mildly surprised when, in the early minutes of the show, a tall and hairy (of course) actor, wearing only a kind of loincloth, went leaping out into the audience and chose to perch precariously on the armrests of a nearby lady's seat, dangling his near-naked self above her. He chose, of course, a suburban matron type, and he taunted her, "Didn't think you'd see it this early in the show?" It occurred to me, sitting safe in my own seat and laughing my head off, to be grateful that I had not myself been singled out for any such demonstration. It also occurred to me, as my mother, beside me, howled with laughter, that suburban matron though she was, she might have been able to handle it with perfect good humor, that she would have been less thrown by it than I.

I knew, as a resentful and rebellious adolescent, in suburban New Jersey in the 1970s, that my parents were somewhat problematic. They did not, by and large, set arbitrary harsh rules restricting my life. They did not seem shocked at the idea of marijuana or adolescent drinking—in fact, when they had wine with dinner, which was not all that often, they always offered me a glass. They weren't foul-mouthed, but I had heard them use pretty much every bad word I knew at some point or other. My mother taught a writing course in my alternative high school and listened, apparently unsurprised, to everyone's outpourings. Well, after all, it occurred to me, she taught writing courses to college students. My parents' politics were academically left wing— they marched against the war in Vietnam, they supported the liberals in every local school board election, they mourned the election—and reelection—of Richard Nixon, they enjoyed Watergate to the hilt. Hell, they took me to see *Hair* as a birthday present, and they didn't have a problem with the onstage nudity.

And all this was problematic because it was perfectly clear, in suburban New Jersey in the early 1970s, that the role of parents was to be pointlessly strict, reliably shockable, and above all, hopelessly out of it. It was supposed to be outside their imaginings that their children might break rules, might smoke dope, might have sex. Part of the joy of doing anything slightly over the line was that if-my-parents-only-knew jolt, that happy frisson that comes from knowing you're naughty.

So, like many other children of reasonably liberal and reasonably honest parents, I lied. I moaned and groaned in public about my unreasonable mother, about how shocked she would be, about if-my-parents-only-knew. I tried hard to present them as constant thorns in my side, as parents firmly on the other shore of that great unbridgeable divide. And sometimes I think I persuaded myself. The early 1970s, as I remember them, were a time of pretty diffuse free-floating hostility toward the adult world (am I remembering an era or just my own early adolescence?). My goal was to read angry books about clueless, insensitive adults and identify with the anger, to listen to the songs and feel they were somehow mine. "She's leaving home after living alone for so many years . . ."

Or is this really true? Yes, I was an angry, resentful adolescent. I was furious with my parents for moving us to the New Jersey suburbs in the first place, depriving me of the complex Manhattan adolescence that I was sure would otherwise have come my way and forcing me instead into attending a stupid suburban school full of stupid suburban kids and stupid suburban teachers who somehow failed to appreciate me. I was suffering from a common delusion of fourteen- and fifteen-year-old girls, the conviction that I was a fully mature adult, and if my parents would only get out of the way, I was ready to make all my own decisions and conduct my life in a style far more admirable and cooler in every way than anything they could ever achieve. And yes, those were politically tense and generationally polarized and profoundly druggy times. On the other hand, I had plenty of interludes of reasonable coherence. My mother is boasting when she tells stories of her children as Shakespeare-quoting prodigies, but she is perfectly right that all through my cantankerous adolescence, we went regularly to two Shakespeare plays a summer in Central Park. What I mean is that I know I sometimes complained about my parents because you were supposed to complain about your parents, and I know I sometimes worked myself up into introspective fits of mother–daughter hostility, but I also know that mostly, I thought they were okay. In fact, looking back, I wonder whether one of the forces tying me up in knots was the strong feeling—which was absolutely *not* the feeling you were supposed to have, not if you were in any way cool—that I might grow up to lead a life not so unlike my mother's life.

CHAPTER THIRTEEN

The Shoes on the Staircase

❦

Perri: So I asked my mother to write about my house and my household. I know that whatever I say, she is going to turn this into a cheerful self-deprecating account in which every single thing that worries her or bothers her turns out to be just part of my domestic triumph. And I'm going to have to read it and resist the urge to cut and trim and rewrite. She can't help it.

Sheila: I'm headed for a party at Perri and Larry's little lavender house on the quiet cul-de-sac in Cambridge, Massachusetts. I have just arrived at South Station from New York on a Greyhound bus (fare: $30), disdaining the Chinatown bus (fare: $10) as well as the various air shuttles (fare: $150). As far as I'm concerned, I've traveled in high-middle-class style. My children find this hilarious. My cheapness is family legend. Who cares?

I board the subway's Red Line to Harvard Square. I am in very good time. It is more than four hours before the huge party they are hosting. I do not know how many people are coming tonight, thirty or forty or sometimes more. They love to entertain, and they do it often and handsomely. I enjoy these parties immensely, though I am always a total wreck by the appointed hour. Then Larry mixes the first martinis of the evening and all suffering is assuaged.

For twenty years, we have maintained this pattern: They send an invitation. I accept. On arrival, I am appalled at the lack of readiness there, and I suffer exquisite anxiety. I volunteer my services and eagerly work hard; then I have a wonderful time. I depart with luggage loaded with edible loot.

Since Perri is my first child, I had time to focus on her early upbringing. I stayed home to raise her for the first seven years of her life. As her brother and sister came along, my energies were dispersed and my influence weakened, but Perri—Perri is surely the prime product of the virtues and qualities I so strongly endorse: systematic housekeeping, putting things where they belong so there is neatness and order; keeping a meticulous social calendar as well as precise lists of groceries to be bought, tasks to be performed, and medical appointments to be kept. My refrigerator door with its montage of lists was itself worthy of the Good Housekeeping Award. I stopped teaching other people's children so that I might stay at home and teach Perri how to live a happy, orderly, organized life.

Perri: What a setup, right? I mean, come on! She was a much better mother than that; she showed no interest at all in teaching me to be either orderly or organized. And in any case, she did not at all like staying home with young children. And I can't say I blame her—I never wanted to do it, either. But do you notice how, when it suits her, she talks about her own lackadaisical suburban housewife style (because she was busy with more important things), and then, when she wants to spotlight my own far more haphazard and disorderly ways, suddenly she's winning the Good Housekeeping Award? Keep your eye on her—she's kind of slippery.

Sheila: At last, I am right outside their house. I pause, but I don't click my tongue in dismay, for I am not that old. I do note leaves and small branches scattered on the steps and the porch. A party in four hours, and no one has swept outside. I shake my head and I enter.

My daughter's family is surprisingly Japanese. Not in their spare, elegant aesthetic, but in the twenty or more pair of shoes that line the staircase leading up into the living room. Since there are no very young children in the household anymore, and some of the shoes are rather tiny with lights and bells on them, I guess there has been no sorting and discarding for some time. I understand that it's hard to throw away outgrown clothes, but one must make an effort. Still, here are all these shoes!

My parents taught me to put my shoes on in the morning and re-move them at bedtime, and that's what I taught Perri to do and what I still do today. I climb up past the array of shoes and, though my feet are tired, I keep my own shoes on, firmly laced.

I look around. I have entered their charming Victorian living room, which is, at the moment, crammed with piles of books, newspapers, clothes, CDs, mail, towels, toys, and packages. Two glorious bouquets of spring flowers bloom in vases amid the disorder. I thread my way carefully. I am suddenly unsure I have the date of this fete right or, at least, the time. The festive flowers seem to signal that I've come on the right day.

However, it is inconceivable that a party will take place here tonight. First, there must be at least a week of vigorous housecleaning: sorting and shelving books, discarding shoes, clearing away the debris, straight-ening up the rooms, dusting, then vacuuming and rearranging the furniture. The windows need a good washing, and the sidewalk and porch must be swept.

I stumble over a suitcase overflowing with Hawaiian shirts—or it could be Polish vodka or Italian ceramics—depending on who trav-eled where recently. Last time, there was a fanciful collection of minia-ture religious art, candleholders, lamps, and altars fashioned from tiny delicate seashells. The suitcase is always open but not yet unpacked.

Mozart sits on the music rack of the piano, while somebody's lunch box rests on the bench alongside a baseball mitt, a bat, and a Boston Red Sox jacket. A pile of *New York Times Book Review*s, along with three Harry Potter novels, crowd the baseball stuff.

Perri: So far, so good. I mean, you can probably tell where she's going with all this stuff about how there can never be a party here, you need a week's cleaning, but still, this is reasonably accurate. Not exaggerated, not made ridiculous—unless you think twenty or thirty pairs of shoes lining the stairway is ridiculous, or a couple of suitcases in the middle of the living room, waiting to be unpacked.

My daughter, who has apparently inherited my mother's orderly genes, thinks *all* of this is ridiculous. As the adolescent daughter that I fully deserve, she is less polite than my mother. "Nobody lives like this," she said to me furiously, not long ago. "Laundry on the chairs in the living room! Piles of papers all over the dining-room table! No wonder things get lost! No wonder no one can ever find anything. Nobody else lives this way."

I pretended to laugh it off, like the free spirit I am, but I needed to call a friend, also a doctor with three children, and check with her that indeed, other people do live like this. In fact, my friend was able to prep me with a few comebacks, things she had let slip in her own life that I, at least so far, haven't let slip in mine. "At least I've never lost my cell phone," I reported, virtuously, to Josephine. "People do that all the time. At least I've never let the life insurance lapse." (Well, once I almost did, but I caught it just in time—and there was no need to tell her how close I had come.)

But my mother is being reasonably accurate. Yes on the shoes, suitcases, religious shell art, piles of old newspapers and old mail, nowhere to sit. Let's not talk about dusting. Sometimes I tell myself that really, I am a compulsively neat person fighting her destiny. When I do things, I tend to do them somewhat obsessionally. I am someone who needs to read two newspapers cover to cover every night before bed, no matter how late it is and how tired I am (that's why those piles of newspaper sit in my living room—I have to save the papers when I'm out of town and then go through them before I recycle them). *Once I started cleaning and straightening*, I tell myself, *who knows if I would ever do anything else?* Let's just say that I have been unwilling to take the risk. And once again, I am my mother's daughter: I have never been able to hire help, never been able to stand the idea of strangers in my house, touching—and cleaning—my stuff. I stand—or fall—by more homegrown assistance.

Sheila: "I'm here," I call.

"Mama. Just in time," Perri answers, and comes out of the kitchen to kiss me. "Come and kibitz in the kitchen."

I'm delighted to join them.

Now, I am a person who washes each pot or implement after I use it and puts it away. That way there's no accumulation. Their kitchen has suffered a massive bombardment of dirty pots and cooking utensils. The sink is gone; it has vanished under its contents. Every other surface is in use. Electric machines whip and chop.

Larry is at the stove, where he is monitoring the baking of six different pies. Six different lovely aromas.

It is four hours to party time!

Be quiet, Sheila, I tell myself. *Don't make them anxious. They know what they're doing.* I don't really believe that in my heart, but I keep quiet.

My own kitchen ventures have always been small-scale operations. Our occasional dinner parties for six or eight seemed major undertakings, a necessary part of academic life, always undertaken with great nervousness and little skill. After all, my own parents never entertained anyone. *Never.* Nor were we children ever allowed to bring home any friends.

I understand generational differences, and I love Perri's sociability and the freedom of her house. But it is three and a half hours to party time! They kibitz, and Larry begins to whip cream. They discuss whether to add the Moroccan pepper dish to their menu. "There's plenty of time," says Perri.

No, no, no! my mind screams. *Not another dish!*

"We have the peppers, so let's do it," Larry says decisively.

"Let me help." I weakly offer, aching to attack the dishes and pots that threaten to engulf us. The sink is now a no-man's-land, so the cooks are reduced to going to the bathroom basin for tap water.

"Oh, sure," says Perri. "You can sort and trim the asparagus." She takes out six gorgeous pound-bunches of asparagus, thin and green and garden fresh. Beautiful to contemplate, granted. But if I were giving a big party, I'd do a simple vegetable like green peas with mushrooms. Birds Eye frozen green peas. With luck, Mrs. Birds Eye will already have added the mushrooms.

"Here, Mama. We're going to roast them," she tells me. I don't say I've never even heard of such a thing. Turkeys, you roast—not asparagus. I don't offer the wisdom that a vegetable is a side dish; it need not be the star of the meal.

"After that, you can work on the peppers," she says contentedly.

I wash the asparagus in the bathroom sink. Other times I wash strawberries or cilantro or I chop onions or garlic. I'm useful, though it's a challenge to wash long, delicate asparagus in a tiny, round basin. I break only a few.

I join the conversation, and we handle the great political and social issues of the day with wit and imagination, solving nothing. I keep my eyes on the clock.

After the peppers (there seem to be hundreds), I ask Perri, timidly, if I might wash a few pots. It's my specialty. She graciously assents, and I go at it. This I can do! Better than asparagus. Better than peppers. I'm cleaning up! I press my grandchildren into service drying and putting away. "But we never dry, Grandma. We let them drain."

"Today you dry. It's D-day in the kitchen. I'm liberating the sink!" While I am safely deployed, scrubbing away with my steel-wool weapon, the others have all drifted out of the kitchen and disappeared. Somehow, mysteriously, magic is being wrought elsewhere.

Perri: Well, the truth is that if I were telling this story, the Perri character would be a lot more irritable and tense. In the scenario my mother is describing, I am actually filled with anxiety, wondering how the hell my life got into this irredeemable mess—or else wondering why, with my life in this irredeemable mess, I ever give parties. I snap at people, I order them around, I get frantic—and all the while, as my mother says, I keep adding new challenges and deciding to make the Moroccan peppers after all. And all the while, some internal calculating clock is ticking—things usually *do* get done, more or less, with enormous piles of newspapers shoved into bedrooms, shopping bags full of unexamined mail stored in a back room, possibly never to be seen again, armloads of unsorted shoes flung into closets. Every so often, when I visit someone else's house and go in search of a bathroom, I pass an open bedroom door, and I see order and harmony—and I feel just terrible. When I give a party, the bedroom doors are shut as tightly as possible—the living room is, we hope, presentable (though God help us if someone gets the time wrong and shows up half an hour early), but the rest of the house has to absorb the overflow.

This is not cute and quaint and lovable. This is not high style. My daughter is right: This is not the way you would choose to live. This is the way we live as a consequence of who we are and what we do—and what we don't do.

I would like to live a life, really I would, in which my house was always reasonably clean and neat. When my oldest child was three or four, he once saw me vacuuming the living room, and asked casually, "Oh, are we having company?" And you know what? We were. Well, I could certainly aspire to living in a way that gave my children—and my mother—a different impression. But I don't seem to have the temperament to make it happen, and I'm not willing to give up any of the various things I grab at in my greed—including giving the occasional party.

Sheila: This prologue is really a history of twenty years of parties. Entering chaos, I am always anxious—near frantic. Then, about an hour before the party, Perri strategically deploys her troops. Someone vacuums, someone picks up shoes, the living-room clutter disappears, and order is restored. Everyone works with unbelievable rapidity and ingenuity because what cannot be easily put away must be artfully concealed. It always is. I have wondered where the junk goes. I hate to admit this—it really doesn't matter. What matters is it's gone and the house is in tiptop shape.

Party time. The family is nicely dressed and the food all done. Lovely wildflowers grace either end of the long table. Martinis supply instant bliss. Talk abounds and guests arrive and begin to eat and they marvel at the variety and the delicacy of the food, particularly the Moroccan peppers and the roasted asparagus. For hours and hours, they talk and they laugh and they eat.

Nobody in that crowd ever notices that the porch wasn't swept or the windows washed. Even I forget. I am so pleased that my children know how to entertain beautifully and graciously. When I go home, my suitcase is crammed with delicacies, which I immediately store carefully in my refrigerator. For the next week I live on memories and brie, fois gras, parmigiano, Gorgonzola, feta, tiny meatballs stuffed with pine nuts, curried squash, Moroccan peppers. The roasted asparagus were all gone, but I do have chocolate pie or peach or apple-walnut or some other variant. I never leave empty-suitcased.

The next time they invite me, it'll be the same story. I'll come, with alacrity, bearing my usual luggage: all the old uptight bugaboos, which will never disappear.

CHAPTER FOURTEEN

Teaching My Son to Cook, Or, The Meaning of Life

❧

Perri: The summer before high school, my son was nervous. The school has a time-honored tradition of beginning ninth grade by busing all the ninth-graders up to the wilds of New Hampshire, where they live in tents for two weeks, divided into squads of eight boys or eight girls, digging their own latrines, chopping wood for fires, bathing in a lake. The idea is that they come back individually more grown up and mature, and collectively bonded together into a class. And everybody has to go; no excuses, no doctor's notes, no chickening out—that's a time-honored tradition for you.

I ran into one of his teachers from middle school, one day at the movies, and she asked me whether Orlando was nervous. "Well, maybe a little," I admitted. "He's not exactly an outdoorsman."

"Teach him to cook," she said. "In the boys' squads, a kid who knows how to cook is king. Some of those all-male squads go the whole two weeks and never have anything edible to eat because most of the boys don't know you have to cook spaghetti in boiling water before you put sauce on it. If Orlando can cook, he'll never have to split kindling or dig latrines, and he'll be an instant social success."

So we concentrated on cooking. Orlando had already had a certain amount of somewhat ceremonial cooking experience—mixing in the chocolate chips or dolloping out the dough onto the cookie sheet—

and as a child, he had a very particular pièce de résistance, frozen bananoids, a recipe out of a cookbook for children that involved dipping
bananas in melted chocolate, rolling them in nuts, and freezing them.
But man does not live by frozen bananoids alone—even he could only
eat one of the things, at most—and he had never really looked the
world in the eye and demanded, *How do you make the things I like to
eat?* Of course, many of the things he liked to eat were not practical for
outdoor cooking over a bonfire or involved ingredients unlikely to be
found in the school's provisioning—pasta with pancetta and fresh
mozzarella, say, or that spicy beef with watercress dish they make at his
favorite restaurant in Boston's Chinatown. . . . Still, there was plenty
to learn. The art of the grilled cheese sandwich, and the importance of
a slice of tomato. Eggs, and how to scramble them so they come out
with the desired texture, and how to add some other things—chopped
onions or red peppers or cheese or ham—to make the scramble more
interesting. Omelets and their mysteries. Frying bacon—surely important for that North Woods lumberjack breakfast experience. Beef
stew—basics of the one-pot dinner. Baked potatoes.

He learned how to cook spaghetti, and how to tell when it's done,
burning his fingers over and over as he handled noodles plucked from
the boiling water. But spaghetti alone, no matter how perfectly al
dente, does not a dinner make. So his father demonstrated how to
make a basic tomato sauce, and Orlando hung over the stove, fascinated by the simple alchemy of sautéing onions in olive oil. He says
now, looking back, that that was a revelation to him: so easy to brown
an onion, to make the whole house smell of good things cooking, to
add tomatoes from a can and fresh tomatoes as well, to play with the
seasoning. He stood over the simmering pot, our newly tall son, adding
oregano and basil, but also a pinch of sugar, a shake of cinnamon.
Tasting, absorbing, and tasting again. And we attempted to draw wise
parental lessons: If you can do that, you can certainly doctor tomato
sauce out of a jar.

And as we cooked, no question, he became a little less worried and
a little more confident about living in the woods for a couple of weeks.
But me, I became downright messianic; it had occurred to me, as we

messed around in the kitchen together, that I had discovered the secret of life—or at least the secret of parenthood. Teaching him to cook had revealed to me the one essential message that I felt I had to transmit—the key to the universe.

You are going to become an adult, I wanted to say. *Not in any two-week bonding experience, though that may have some value, but over the next years, you are going to become a grown-up. And what does it mean to be a grown-up? It means being able to take care of yourself. You have to be able to support yourself, in whatever style to which you wish to become accustomed, and you have to be able to provide the basic necessities of life for yourself, like food and shelter. In other words, you have to be able to scramble your own eggs in the morning, sew on the button that's just come off, create for yourself the kind of home in which you want to live, and then keep it going. That's it; that's all. If you can't do those things, you aren't a grown-up, and if you can, you're there.*

I had never known that that was my message. In fact, I had never known that I had a message at all. Orlando is my oldest child, and it is over his poor defenseless head that I generally lob my maternal trial balloons. At Orlando's every age and stage, the surprises of parenthood have emerged from the great multicolored cloud of human experience to bite me on the leg. And it turns out that I do have a message, to a child on the brink of adulthood, and the message is about taking care of yourself and browning onions and the meaning of life.

You want your child to know who he is. You want it to turn out that who he is is someone nice, someone worth knowing. You want him to have tastes and opinions, and know what they are—and of course, down deep, you want him to have tastes and opinions you understand. But then you want to feel that you're sending him out into the world with the wherewithal to accommodate and enjoy those tastes and opinions. You want him to be, as my grandmother would say, a person. And your job is to help him along toward that independence, that awareness, that competence. And that's the meaning of life.

And cooking consolidated it all. Or crystallized it, or made it gel, or kept it from curdling, if a food metaphor is indicated. Cooking is about taste—understanding what you want, what you like, what you crave, what moves you deeply—and then about having the skill and knowledge to call that something forth from the raw ingredients. Cooking is knowing who you are, and then doing something practical and delicious with that knowledge.

So off he went to the woods. Looking back, he says dismissively that the food was pretty simple. With the other boys in his squad, he cooked macaroni and cheese, burgers, chicken stir-fry. He made many grilled tomato-and-cheese sandwiches over the fire, and some toasted peanut butter–and-jelly sandwiches into the bargain. But he also got a little bit fancy now and then—he made garlic bread to go with that doctored tomato sauce, and he cooked the spaghetti properly. His squad ate well, and he didn't have to dig latrines and chop wood—or at least no more than his minimum share. And of course he did lots of other things. He bathed in the icy lake and climbed the high ropes. He volunteered to "solo"—to spend a night alone in a sleeping bag in the woods—during which he happily read a 700-page fantasy novel by the light of his flashlight, feeling that he had finally achieved a certain nirvana, able to read blearily into the dawn, no parent to come checking for light under the door and give lectures about school tomorrow and needing to be well rested.

And then he came home, and yes, he seemed more adult, more independent. And yes, the ninth grade did seem to be forged into a stronger group. So we could all, as parents, breathe first a sigh of relief that the school to which we had consigned our precious children seemed to know what it was doing, and then a sigh of gratitude that we ourselves would never have to go live in squads for two weeks in the woods of New Hampshire.

But now I had a son who could cook. He had learned the lesson: You can make things you like. You can look at ingredients and figure them out and create the thing you crave. His cooking ever since then has followed certain idiosyncratic paths. He got very good at making an Armenian pomegranate dip, muhamarra, that we often buy from the nearby Armenian grocery—but that is much much better if you buy the pomegranete syrup and make it fresh, not to mention the pleasures of working with that sweet exotic potion. He took over a certain dish we usually make at Thanksgiving, mashed potatoes with onion and basil and Parmesan, and started supervising it to see it was done right—the potatoes mashed enough, the cheese spread evenly. He acquired a George Foreman grill and became a specialist in grilled panini. He could be asked, in a pinch, to assemble the pasta for dinner—to make, for example, an old family favorite of dubious ethnic integrity that we call spaghetti pastramara, essentially spaghetti carbonara made with pastrami—or is it pastrami and eggs made with spaghetti? One way or another, it's a dish Orlando likes—and now a dish he understands.

It started as a kind of trick: We'll teach you to cook, and you'll use it to get out of splitting kindling—you'll use it to make friends up in the woods. But it's not a trick; it's a real and true and timeless message about what it means to grow up and go out on your own. Know how to make the things you like and need. Understand where food comes from, and how it is transformed from raw ingredients to finished project. Take care of yourself properly, and you will also be able to take care of other people. And that's the meaning of life. Or at least, the meaning of parenthood, because, after all, the subtext is always about getting a child ready to go away and grow away, equipping him for a journey on which you will stay behind. But it is somehow a great comfort to know that as your child takes that journey, when the moment comes—as it so often does—for spaghetti, he will know how to make the sauce. It was a revelation, he says now, how easy it was to make something good.

Mashed Potatoes with Onion, Basil, and Parmesan Cheese

Please note: This recipe is originally from *The Splendid Table*, by Lynne Rossetto Kasper (William Morrow, 1992)—"Basil and Onion Mashed Potatoes," pages 345–346. I have included various small changes (which mostly reflect our laziness and willingness to cut corners) in how we prepare it.

5 lbs. potatoes (*she calls for "small red-skinned"; we usually buy Yukon gold*)
4 tbs. olive oil, *plus extra*
2–3 large onions (*she says 2 large onions, minced; we like lots of onion, so we usually use 3, and we don't mince them— we chop them pretty coarsely*)
1 bunch Italian parsley (*she calls for ½ cup, minced; we use a bunch and chop it—again, coarsely*)
4–6 large cloves garlic, minced (*original recipe calls for 2*)
½–¾ cup fresh basil leaves (*she uses ½ cup minced; we use a little more and, again, chop it coarsely . . . there seems to be a theme here . . .*)
½ cup water
Salt and freshly ground black pepper
1½ cups milk
2 tbs. butter
6 oz. Parmigiano-Reggiano, coarsely grated

(continued on page 140)

Scrub the potatoes, cut away any obvious bad spots, cut them into quarters, and put them in a pot with cold, salted water to cover. Cover pot, turn heat to high, bring to a boil, lower the heat, and partly uncover; cook until potatoes are easily pierced by a fork.

Heat 3 tablespoons olive oil in a large skillet. Add onions and parsley. Turn heat to low and cover, and cook 20 minutes or until onions are soft and transparent, stirring occasionally and adding more oil if needed. Uncover, turn heat a little higher, and continue to cook, stirring, till onions are golden-brown. Stir in garlic after a few minutes, and then, when onions are brown, stir in basil; cook 1 more minute, then add the water and scrape up any brown bits in the skillet. (This is a Lynne Kasper trademark, and we try to always do it.) Add lots of salt and pepper.

When the potatoes are ready, drain them in a colander (she peels them; we don't), then dump them back into the pot and mash them enthusiastically. When they are getting to be pretty well mashed, add the the onions and herbs, the milk, the butter, and another tablespoon of olive oil. (She wants a texture like very thick whipped cream, we tend to go for a little lumpier.) Lightly oil a 9- by 13-inch baking dish, spread with half the potato mixture, then with half the cheese, spreading it evenly, and then with the other half of the potatoes and the rest of the cheese.

Bake at 350°F, lightly covered with aluminum foil; after 35 minutes, remove foil and bake another 5–10 minutes.

Spaghetti Pastramara

This can be more or less rich, depending on mood and ingredients. Go with 3 eggs, less cheese and pastrami, and the eggs dominate—great comfort food. Increase the cheese and the pastrami, and it gets richer and more decadent. . . .

1 lb. spaghetti	4–6 oz. pastrami,
2–3 eggs	cut into small squares
6–8 oz. Parmigiano-	Salt and pepper, to taste
Reggiano, grated	

Cook spaghetti in boiling water until al dente. While spaghetti cooks, beat eggs well in a bowl. Drain spaghetti, and toss hot spaghetti immediately with beaten eggs, mixing well. Add grated cheese, continuing to toss, and then the pastrami. Mix thoroughly. Season with salt and pepper to taste. Serve immediately.

CHAPTER FIFTEEN

Milking Reindeer

Sheila: Perri put it to me recently on a perfect, crisp, cool, fall morning, just as we were setting off on a drive to admire the New England fall foliage.

"I would contend, Mama, that for all your own pioneering working-mother status, and the pride I am sure you legitimately take in your daughters' accomplishments, that a certain slightly insidious double standard is still at work when you look at your children. Basically, I am accusing you of what may be a classic Jewish mother syndrome, or may stretch wider than that: I think you look at me and think that Larry is a hero to put up with me and with my nonexistent homemaking inclinations—that whatever contributions he makes around home and children are truly princely—and I think you look at my brother and feel that he needs to be taken care of, and again, that his own behavior in taking care of his own children is, well, princely. In other words, I am accusing you of contributing, in your own highly liberated way, to the Jewish prince syndrome."

"Who, me?" I was astonished, as I always am when I'm confronted.

She continued on her tangent. "Or maybe it's not fair to call it Jewish—maybe it's part of the wider multicultural phenomenon in which you feel grateful to anyone who takes a daughter off your hands

(even to the point of paying a dowry)! But then you worry that anyone who marries a son isn't really good enough to deserve him!"

I shook my head. I like to see myself as a just creature.

For the next few hours as we drove, while I tried to note the foliage,
I brooded about her words, answering the charges in my head. First,
we stopped to pick apples in a Massachusetts orchard, then we continued on to Fruitlands Museum, the site of Bronson Alcott's utopian
farm experiment, for lunch.

In 1843, when Louisa May Alcott was ten years old, her father and
Charles Lane, an English philosopher, along with a half dozen high-
minded Transcendentalist friends, set up a communal farm in Harvard, Massachusetts; they hoped it would be paradise on Earth. They
would live as one family sharing work, food, and ideas. They spurned
money. They wanted to be the very best that humans could be.

Others joined them; some departed; sometimes there were as many
as fifteen living on the farm together.

Perri: I would just like to state, for the record, that my mother has
every single little piece of this story slightly wrong. For example, we
picked apples *after* we went to Fruitlands. And while I may have
broached this subject with her as we were setting out—okay, I did
broach the subject—the rather fluent cadences above are actually
quoted from an e-mail I sent her, attempting to provoke her to write
on this subject. I mean, I don't actually speak in sentences that include
parentheses, thank you very much.

On the other hand, I did want to provoke her. I thought it was a
topic we should take on—my mother's apparently invincible double
standard. I knew I was right and she was wrong, in all sorts of interesting ways—and it was a chance for me to torture her with various triv-
ial and small-minded resentments I've cherished for years. What could
be better?

I can't remember what actually set me thinking about all this.
Maybe it was an argument that Mama and I got into back when we
started talking about this book. She had complained that she hadn't

gotten a thank-you note after she sent a baby present. The young man who had had the baby—the new father—was the son of my mother's good friends, but she wasn't complaining about *him*. Instead, she expressed this as a grievance against his wife, whom she didn't know at all—why hadn't *she* sent a note?

"Why didn't your friend teach her son to write his own thank-you notes?" I asked, irritably.

"That's not the point," my mother said.

"Yes, it is too," I said, brilliantly. "You're being a sexist, and that's all there is to it. I've never written a thank-you note in my life to one of Larry's relatives—when they sent us baby presents, Larry thanked them, or they didn't get thanked, I guess. I never asked. I thanked my own friends and family." And then, to my increasingly intense irritation, I could see that in my mother's mind, this was all adding up to a little more luster for Larry's golden crown—he writes thank-you notes! What a saint!

And yes, the truth is, it's an old grievance. When our kids were little, I noted my mother marveling over Larry's ability to handle a young baby but never over mine. When she was watching, our daily life somehow became a little bit of a performance, with my mother applauding. Of course, as you may have noticed, I squirm a little when she makes a big deal out of my own domestic abilities—when she comes out with these kind of slightly disingenuous accounts of my cooking, or my family life, in which it turns out, inevitably, that *hey, Perri is a great cook,* or *hey, Perri's child-rearing techniques looked a little funny to me, but they turned out to be sheer genius!* So if I object when she does that, how come I object again when she fusses over Larry but not over me? Mothers and daughters—there's no logic to it, is there?

But even if I'm not logical, I'm right about this. She has a double standard, in which she's perhaps absorbed some of her own mother's views about the general helplessness and incompetence of men, but she's a kinder, gentler person than her mother was, so this translates not into contempt but into a desire to see these helpless ones cared for properly, and to celebrate past all reason any small domestic accomplishments they may possess. And her code word for the dissatisfactions she feels when women my age don't leap to do their duty is *feminism*. She explains all sorts of behavior that she considers inadequately feminine—failing to write a thank-you note to your husband's parents' old friend, for example, by saying, "She's a feminist, I guess." And what she means by it, I think, is *Thank God my daughter found someone to put up with her,* and *No one will ever be good enough to marry my son.*

Sheila: Ah, Perri, good enough to marry our son is not the issue anymore. Life was easier when the stupid traditional suspicions about suitors' wealth, family, beauty, and intelligence still prevailed. It's far more complicated than that these days. The young women I see around me or I hear about now are lovelier, glossier, better dressed, nipped and tucked into shape, Botoxed, massaged, manicured, pedicured, exfoliated, and gloriously miniskirted and well educated. Their radical sisters with their hair braided into dreadlocks arrive with rings in their noses or tongues. Many in both groups have had advantages undreamed of by me, by my generation, by all previous generations. They have absolutely no time at all to think or reflect because when they are not advancing their careers, they spend every possible minute of their busy lives, public and private, talking on cell phones. They're—how can I put this delicately? They're privatists.

They are noteworthy for their declarations of independence, long lists of things they don't do. In their struggle to gain equality in an unfair world, it seems to me, women have become wary and unwilling about their social roles; there's a great lack of trust, and little desire to invest in their men. That appears to be what happened to your generation, which is also your brother's, and to the next one, your sister's, as well.

They're an alien breed, hard for me to recognize.

Mrs. Alcott, highly educated and a social worker before she married, was the only woman to stay the course, to stick it out with the commune. She did all the "woman's work" at Fruitlands. She was not a Transcendentalist philosophically, but she loved her husband and followed him loyally. He said of her fondly that she liked the domestic chores. But then, Mr. Alcott has always been characterized as a dreamer.

Perri: I don't know what world my mother is living in. As she has mentioned several times, she doesn't see very well. Who are these Botoxed, miniskirted, dreadlocked young women she imagines? I think she reads things—through her magnifying glass—and she glues them together, in a somewhat fevered way, and conjures a strange society, an "alien breed." This is not me—or my sister—or the young women she teaches at her community college. I mean, some of them may sometimes wear short skirts or pierce their noses, and certainly people talk on their cell phones, but I'm just a little dubious of the overall picture she's put together here, and of her firm conviction that she understands what motivates them. Or maybe I'm just worried that even though I am neither manicured nor exfoliated, she includes me in their number (as I call her each morning on my cell phone, on my way to advance my career), and she judges me, in some irredeemable sense, a selfish privatist, whatever that is.

Sheila: Perri, remember who you are talking to? A woman who is more than three score and ten, who absorbed the singular noble obligations of wifehood and motherhood with her mother's milk, a woman who ingested and assimilated certain eternal verities as she chewed her zwieback. Don't judge me too harshly if I sometimes have trouble figuring out exactly where I stand—think about the commandments that have echoed loudly in my head all through my life:

A husband must be well dressed, for he goes out into the world. (Do his laundry. Iron his shirts carefully.)

You owe him a hot breakfast every morning and a substantial hot dinner every night. (Home-cooked meals, of course. Restaurant food is poison.)

The children are your job; he knows nothing about their care and is not interested, nor should he be. It's not manly.

You are important; no one will ever love a child as much as his mother.

A mother has keen instincts about her child, which make her intuitively knowledgeable about everything.

It goes without saying that she knows more than the doctor, with all his highfalutin education.

A good mother, night and day, must remain constantly at the bedside of a sick child.

The greater the mother's sacrifice and suffering, the more rapid the child's recovery.

Loud keening is a true maternal skill. (Tearing the hair out seems to have vanished, perhaps because of the enormous cost of hair transplants.)

The secret family recipe for chicken soup must quickly be conjured up to work medicinal miracles.

Never forget that all this is done in a flat with floors clean enough to eat off. (Even when I was a child, I thought this last one strange.)

I never gave much thought to where my father was when I was sick during my own childhood. Men were background material, somehow never to be counted on to do anything substantive in health crises or emotional crises. My father's bailiwick was an unknown mysterious place called *going off to work,* which he frequently could not reach. His vital role was to somehow provide money for us.

So is it any surprise that when a child is not well today I have an absolute conviction that the mother must be there as caregiver? Do I believe the father cares as deeply for the child and is as capable? Of course . . . but that doesn't curb my judgmental eye from its automatic roving as it seeks the mother.

Perri: Actually, it's interesting that my mother should choose that particular example. The question of who should stay home with a sick child is one of those recurrent sore points in my own life—I've probably had this fight with Larry a hundred times or so. Each time it starts out as an ostensibly civilized logistic negotiation: "You teach tomorrow; I see patients. Can you skip your afternoon lecture and get home in time for me to go to this one meeting I absolutely can't cancel?" . . . And each time, or almost each time, it degenerates into a mean-spirited and resentful psychic shoving match, with a predictable and pointless list of subtexts: *You're selfish; I'm a martyr. You don't take my work seriously; I don't take your work seriously. You always do this. I always have to do that. I do more than my share, and you don't appreciate it.* And as in most long-term relationships, either party is equally capable of reciting any of the lines, with profound conviction.

These fights, I understand, were the consequence of a child-rearing decision we made more than two decades ago and have essentially never regretted—we sent our children to day care. And day care means plenty of minor—and some not-so-minor—infectious illnesses. In the pediatric infectious diseases trade, where I have spent a certain amount of my professional time, we cite numbers ranging from six to twelve infections in the first year that a child spends in close contact with other children—at whatever age this first exposure takes place. Whether it's your six-month-old or your six-year-old, that first year of hanging around with a group of peers, getting to know the microbes that live in their noses and mouths and gastrointestinal tracts, is full of interesting fevers and stomach flu and little upper respiratory bugs.

We lived through this times three children—an older son who specialized in ear infections, a daughter who got an occasional ear infection but distinguished herself in particular by an absolute refusal to swallow any medication ever under any circumstances whatsoever, and finally a younger son who never bothered with a single ear infection but ran a temperature of 105 for days every time he got the most minor virus.

So Larry and I had this fight over and over. Late at night, when it became clear that a runny nose was turning into a fever and a cough.

First thing in the morning, when a child woke up hot to the touch. Middle of the night, when a child threw up all over everything, and in the middle of the process of cleaning up, we would look at each other, bleary-eyed and worried, and ask the question "What about tomorrow? Who stays home?" And, maybe worst of all, long-distance, when one of us—usually me, I have to admit—was out of town, and the other one—usually Larry—realized that instead of coping alone with day care dropoff and pickup, it was now an issue of coping with a radically disrupted schedule, a child needing care and attention. No wonder it turned quickly into not-so-veiled accusations about who had seriously problematic priorities, who really did or didn't care about the children, who really didn't take whose work seriously.

The funny thing is, I often interpreted these fights, with resentment and hostility, as fights about professional credentials rather than about gender. That is, I thought Larry had written a highly suspicious and self-serving code in which he had decided that only someone with a medical degree could properly care for a young child with the sniffles. He used to imply, it seemed to me, that there was something highly cavalier in the way that I, a qualified pediatrician (or even, way back when, a qualified medical student, a qualified pediatric resident), was willing to leave my sick child in the care of a mere civilian. Surely, if I really cared about this sweet and feverish little sufferer, I would stay home and offer the benefit of my special expertise! How could I even contemplate going off to work, offering other children my attention, when my own was ailing at home? How could I even suggest that the attentions of a nonphysician, like their father, could compensate for the very special highly trained diagnostic and therapeutic skills that only I could bring to the sickbed?

And I was always left furiously repeating the same arguments: "And just where did *your* mother go to medical school? What about my mother—where did she get her medical training? How come millions of parents without M.D.'s take perfectly competent care of children with minor illnesses, but just because I'm a doctor, you abdicate all responsibility—you act like putting on a Band-Aid is a major surgical procedure—'Oh, let me step aside so the doctor here can take care of this!' Get over yourself—anyone can put on a Band-Aid, anyone can give Tylenol to a kid with a fever, anyone can brew up a pot of chicken soup. Your mother brought up three children—and she took care of them whenever they were sick. Call her up and get her soup recipe!" And on and on and on.

And then, to my intense annoyance, my own mother caught the bug from Larry. She was visiting us once, and Josephine got sick with some little fever or other, and my mother, who had seen her own children through mumps and chicken pox and dozens of cases of tonsillitis and upset stomachs, started acting as if I were the only authority in town. Should she put a cold cloth on Josephine's forehead? she asked me anxiously. Should she give her something else to drink? Did I want to examine her? She was anxious and deferential, and it made me a little bit frantic. When *I* get sick myself, I still wish for my mother to take care of me and make things okay—I mean, what did I do when I went into labor? Called my mother, right? My medical degree, it seemed to me, had completely subverted the natural order of the universe.

Sheila: Actually, when you children were small, if you got sick, Papa was the organized, sensible adult during the crisis. But I was always there, imagining the worst, terrified, bargaining silently with God (who I wasn't sure I believed in). By the time you were seven, Papa and I both had full-time jobs, and his entailed fewer hours than mine, but I was the one who stayed home with a sick child, and I would not have had it any other way. I absolutely believed my presence was essential to my child's recovery.

Perri, do you remember the old story about the Copenhagen housewife who put an ad for a household helper in the paper? A vigorous-looking, attractive young woman, a Laplander, her hair in two thick braids, applied.

The housewife began to identify the chores that the job involved. "The windows must be washed."

"I don't do windows," the applicant said, forthrightly.

"The floors must be swept."

"I don't do floors."

"The dishes must be washed promptly after meals."

"I don't do dishes."

It went on this way until the housewife protested in despair. "If you don't do windows or floors or dust or cook or wash dishes or care for children, then what do you do?"

"Oh!" said the young woman brightly, with a huge, endearing grin, "I milk reindeer!"

Today I am surrounded on the streets of Manhattan by high-powered, suited, stiletto-heeled beauties, most of them reindeer-milkers. They don't cook, clean, or sew. Their laundry is washed by machine, dried by machine, and often folded for a fee. In their expensive little apartments, they are totally geographically challenged, unable to find their way to the coat closet, the shoe rack, the laundry hamper to put things away. The floor, particularly the central area of the living room, often is where they dump everything. Coats, packages, shoes, laptops, mail lie there abandoned, much of it never to be recovered again as new layers accrue.

I long ago embraced the idea that my ancestors were monkeys and that we, their descendants, are imitative and learn from others and pass the learning along. It was a pleasing idea to me that my daughters would be newer, smarter women with many more advantages. And our granddaughters? What wouldn't they be able to do?

The answer is housework.

Perri: Reindeer? Monkeys? Maybe the "answer" is zookeeping. Here we are again in the complex bestiary of my mother's mind. Who are all these stiletto-heeled beauties, whose domestic arrangements she seems to know so well? I don't get it—I don't really see why the Lapland joke is relevant, but then, I guess I am one of the reindeer-milkers (stiletto-heeled reindeer milkers?). To me, it seems that my mother is stuck in some dissatisfied endless loop, resenting young—or younger—women who are able to escape some of the very things that she claims she herself always resented and wanted to escape. My mother claims to have hated housework—to have distinguished herself in the suburbs by *not* being house-proud, while all around her other mothers were hiring decorators and redoing their homes. She manages perfect doublethink: contempt for those who put time and energy and money into their homes (you should hear the tone of disbelieving amusement when she says the word *decorator*), contempt for those who, at least in her imagination, dump their laptops in the middle of the living room floor (hey, Mama, maybe their feet hurt too much from their shoes to walk as far as the table).

And what does she mean, *their laundry is washed by machine, dried by machine?* How does she wash and dry her own laundry, by pounding it with stones as she stands knee-deep in a river? My mother lives in Manhattan, and when she wants to do laundry, she takes the dirty clothing down to her basement and puts it in a—guess what?—washing machine, where hot water and detergent do the work. And then she moves it to a—wait for it—dryer. And then, yes, she takes it back up to her apartment, and she folds it neatly, and she puts it away—and she seems to feel she deserves some kind of a special citation for this. If you ask me, my mother can't decide whether she is a free-spirited bohemian or a compulsive neatnik, and she is happy to assume either mantle as it suits her, and either way, there is always a certain moral superiority.

Sheila: Who would have believed that I, who have been occasionally accused of leaping up to wash dishes before I'm through chewing my food, would have daughters who believe stacked dirty dishes and pots in a sink are an architectural triumph?

I'm no zealot. I recognize that sloppiness is only a venial sin. . . .

But what the sloppy person doesn't realize is that the neat person can't just forget it and relax. My head spins and my hands ache with the need to put things in place, and since I can't really do that in someone else's home, I am upset. *I need to put my children's houses in order.*

Take heart, Perri, time and evolution are slowly solving the problem and we are making progress. I suffer much less from the neatness-and-order syndrome than my mother did. She raced to empty and wash the ashtray each time a smoker flicked an ash or a match in it. I never do that! Of course, no one smokes in my house. But if someone did . . .

At Fruitlands, the only time Mrs. Alcott rebelled was during the crisis of the oil lamps. She did all the mending for the commune, at night, after the rest of the farming and household chores. She had weak eyesight. When the Serious Thinkers decided that they could not ethically rob the whales of their oil, so they would have to give up lamps and burn pine knots instead, Mrs. Alcott announced that each man would have to do his own mending.

The lamps were immediately restored.

Perr—we have a long-standing joke, you and I: If I behave myself on a visit and sit still through a meal without straightening things, you'll let me do the dishes. That is what I strive for; nothing makes me happier than emptying your sink. And if you unearth a dish towel— any rectangle of absorbent cloth—and let me dry them instead of letting them drain, the visit is unalloyed gold.

I have a truly wonderful daughter-in-law who holds a difficult and challenging administrative job. She does not like housework. So she doesn't do it. She doesn't like to cook, so she doesn't. The same is true of sewing. There's an impressively long list of tasks she doesn't do. There's a part of me that says, *More power to her.* But there's another part of me, the mother-in-law part! After all, I had some of those same inclinations and subdued them and forced myself to do the nasty stuff for almost fifty years.

Perhaps when my daughter-in-law refuses to do all that household/ kitchen labor, she is negating all my years of washing and waxing when I could have been typing. Or perhaps it is just meanness in me. You know, like the old doctors who objected to humanizing the hours for interns: "We put in all those hours. Why should they get off so easily?"

Charles Lane, father of one son, felt strongly that the Alcotts had too many children (four daughters), and he argued that leaving the family with its ties and going off to live with the celibate Shakers would improve Bronson Alcott's character. Mrs. Alcott vigorously opposed him, and she carried her point; the family stayed together.

Years ago, I'd have argued that doing chores one hated built character, that it was admirable to take on unpleasant responsibilities and handle them, but I don't believe that now. My eyesight is so poor, I can't see dust or small litter on the floor these days, and I'm glad, *glad* of it, so my character hasn't been improved by decades of obligatory domesticity.

To whom does the future belong? Not to women like me. We generalists who pick up after people, who are impelled to sweep and dust, to mop and scrub, will disappear. Our sons, those eligible young men, those princes, will all somehow have to become reindeer-milk drinkers. They and our daughters will have to develop new skills for their new social roles, just as we did.

I had completed this avalanche of deep thought and was ready by the time we'd arrived at Fruitlands to bombard Perri with my conclusions. But first I had to eat the delicious Fruitlands mushroom quiche and savor the excellent coffee.

At midday, the Alcotts and their companions ate mostly apples and fresh bread baked by Mrs. Alcott, washed down by cold water. They were vegetarians and drank neither coffee nor tea, spurning imports. They wore no cotton, for they were abolitionists; nor wool, because it robbed the sheep; nor leather, because it meant death to animals. They wore only linen. The Fruitlands experiment lasted six months and ended in disappointment and disaster. The farm failed, and the communal group broke up. Bronson Alcott was ill and depressed for a long time afterward. Charles Lane returned to England with his son; there he remarried and had five more children.

All of this thinking made me realize how much I dislike people like Charles Lane who tell others how to live.

When lunch was over, I excused myself to go to the ladies' room. I wandered aimlessly in the corridor a bit. My vision is poor. I came upon a door. I looked around and saw no other doors. Since this one had the *diaper changing* symbol on it, I did not hesitate. I assumed it was a unisex bathroom and used it. My emergence seemed to startle the elderly man waiting outside. I smiled at him in a friendly and en-

couraging fashion—a unisex bathroom . . . oh, brave new world!—
and went back to our table.

My family was vastly entertained when I reported my adventures.

"That was the men's room you used, Mama," Perri said softly. "The
ladies' room is down the corridor to the left."

"But the door has the diaper table, the diaper-changing symbol," I
protested. "That's always on the ladies' room door."

"And are the fathers supposed to change diapers in the ladies'
room?" Perri teased.

She was right. When I saw that door, it had not occurred to me that
a diaper-changing table could ever belong in the men's room.

Perri was too polite to rub it in, but I saw the accusation in her eyes.

Yeah, you, Mama, her eyes said. *Yeah, you.*

The handwriting on the wall is clear. And it will remain there permanently, for there will be no eager practitioners of housewifery with
sponge and Lysol to wash it away.

PART FIVE

Bodily Harm

CHAPTER SIXTEEN

Truth and Beauty

Perri: It was Saturday morning and my mother was visiting me; we were going to spend the day writing together and talking about this book. Larry was away at a conference in Berlin. I got up relatively early—but of course, my mother was up earlier. I thought with automatic regret about how I hadn't provisioned the house for her visit—why hadn't I bought a pack of English muffins so she could have the breakfast she prefers every morning? Instead, in my non-breakfast-eating house, she had toasted a slice of sandwich bread—I hoped it was this week's sandwich bread. And because Larry, the resident coffee fanatic, was away, she had been able to make herself the mug of instant coffee she prefers, instead of having him grind beans and brew her a cup of something she admits is more delicious but dislikes because it's also more "trouble." Anyway, she had already had her toast and coffee by the time I came downstairs at eight forty-five.

"I'm going out," I said. "I'm going out to get my hair cut. Back in an hour. And if Anatol isn't awake by nine forty-five, would you wake him up and tell him to get dressed and try on these ice skates to see if they fit—he's invited to go skating with his friends later this morning and I don't know if this is where Larry left the skates he's wearing this winter." And I put on my coat and ran out the door before she could try to make me a cup of tea.

Actually, I wasn't going to get my hair cut at all. I was going out to get my hair colored brown. And by the time I got to the hair salon, I was all roiled up about the complications of my life and my schedule and my family and my vanity. I said hello to Linda, also known as "Tattooed Linda," since there are two different Lindas who work at the salon, and sat down resentfully in her chair, thinking something like this: *Why can't anything ever be simple for me? Why is everything always such a mess?*

So okay, here it is: About a year earlier, I had come, somewhat belatedly, to the realization that most women my age (midforties) had started coloring their hair. That is, in any gathering, most women still had black hair or brown hair or red hair or blond hair, while I was beginning to look in the mirror and see a generous sprinkling of white and gray. A couple of friends had confirmed it—like it was no big deal at all. It seemed to me that I had a choice: I could cut my hair short and let it change color as it wanted, or I could leave it long and start coloring it too. But there was something about the idea of my frizzy, long, leftover-hippie hair now streaked with white that was just too— just too something. Too Cambridge, too aging modern dancer, too witchy, I don't know.

So I wandered into the hair salon around the corner and I met Tattooed Linda, whose arms were indeed lavishly ornamented, and who mixed up a particular pot of brown stuff and colored my hair back to something close to my original hair color. And then, of course, I had to keep going back to see her. But I couldn't quite manage to do it regularly enough; I kept finding myself back at square one, looking in the mirror and seeing the speckles of gray and white, and realizing that I had let the whole process drag again. And somehow, it was always hard to fit in one of these appointments. Tattooed Linda, I'm sure, thinks of me as someone who is always impatient to leave, always running out of the place with wet, wild hair.

Also, as I've said, I don't really like having people touch me and work on me. Yes, I kind of like the feeling of having someone else wash my hair, but even that bothers me a little. I have had a professional manicure once in my life—doing research for a novel I was writing, in which the main character was going to have a manicure—and the whole experience made me horribly twitchy; also, my cuticles stung for days and I didn't really feel comfortable with my hands again until the polish wore off. I do get my toenails done once in a while in the summer, and that doesn't bother me as much, though again, I don't get them done regularly enough so that they always look good, I wait till the polish is chipped and almost gone. I have a gift certificate for a massage languishing on my desk—I've never had, or wanted to have, a professional massage. No, it goes further than that—I dread the idea. I read travel articles about women at spas getting wrapped or steamed or massaged, and I shudder.

Sheila: I was The Smart One and my sister, Marilyn, was The Pretty One.

So how come I was never singled out for the $500,000 MacArthur Fellowship for geniuses? How come my sister was never chosen Miss America? Each of us spent more than seven decades thinking of herself in that limited way, for those were the labels our mother affixed to us early. Tied to us twenty-four hours of every day all during our early childhood, with no help or babysitters, that was the way our mother came to see us: The Smart One and The Pretty One.

She must have felt imprisoned during all those years of work and worry. She loved us, but we were needy, constant companions, as all small children are. Did she know she was creating a rivalry? How could she *not* have known? Did she care? Did she do it purposely? Why? To spur us on? To foster competition? Because, in her unhappy way, she was jealous of our youth?

Probably a little of all of those.

As a result, I grew up longing desperately to be pretty, and my sister always yearned to be smarter. To the end of her life, Marilyn underestimated her intelligence and her abilities. Though she raised four fine children, managing for many years as a widow with minimal income, most of her sentences began, "I don't know anything about this, but . . ." She apologized continually. It was as if being The Pretty One canceled her right to have any opinions and preferences, canceled her right to have a mind. When she was a dinner guest and had a choice of food—white or dark meat from the turkey, for example— she could not venture a preference. She would only take what no one else wanted.

I, all my life, have taken shamefully little interest in my personal appearance. It's easy to blame everything on one's mother, I know, and I'm much too old to refuse responsibility for my actions, but I've wondered how glamorous I'd be if "That one's The Smart One" and "This one's The Pretty One" had not eclipsed the possibility that someday, I too might be pretty. These labels provoked rivalry as well as guilt. I never won a school prize without putting my sister in the shadow, and she, receiving compliments on her appearance, must have known how jealous I was.

We were neither of us extraordinary except by this parental attribution. And we were not alone; among my friends, I could count The Dumb Ox, The Skinny Melink, The Clown, The Princess, The Wild Animal, and The Schlemiel. Recently I had lunch with an acquaintance who is still actively fighting her childhood sobriquet, The Little Chaza (pig). Though she is lean, and has been since adolescence, she is "Atkins-ing," and consulted endlessly with the patient Thai waiter, who had limited English, about low carbs. How could he know she was haunted by the ghost of childhood greediness?

Perri: All around me in the hair salon, I thought resentfully, were women who thought of this whole process as a treat. An hour or so out of your week devoted to your appearance, devoted to taking care of yourself, to making yourself look good and feel good. I tried to imagine their feelings—the harmless self-absorption of wrapping yourself in a smock, of letting someone wash and trim and color your hair. There were people around me getting complex treatments— tinfoil in their hair, multiple different colors, complicated cuts. There were people chatting avidly with the men and women cutting their hair—I never know what to say to Tattooed Linda, and I'm sure she thinks I'm profoundly unfriendly, unconversational, always pressed for time, and eager to get out of there. Mostly, I wish I could read right through the process, but of course I have to take my glasses off, and without my glasses, I can't read.

So she slathered my head with the brown stuff from the pot, and I sat there trying to calculate whether I would be done in time to get home and take Anatol to his ice-skating date. Anxious again, hurried again, counting the minutes. So much for making an early Saturday appointment. And then I started wondering whether my mother—or more likely my daughter—would notice the difference in hair color when I got home. I had left the coloring way too long this time; my hair was full of white strands. And why hadn't I just said to my mother, I'm going out to get my hair colored? Why was I ashamed at the idea that my daughter might notice? Or why, to ask it differently, if I didn't want people noticing, couldn't I schedule myself regularly enough so that my hair color would be consistently brown, rather than periodically piebald?

Mostly what I felt, I think, was a kind of general frustration: Why are the things that seem to be so easy—and natural—and even plea-surable to so many other women, so hard and fraught and compli-cated for me? Here I am, after all, a professional woman in my forties, the mother of three, earning a reasonable salary—why does coloring my graying hair back to its original brown loom as such a project, so fraught and complex and loaded with various kinds of embarrass-ment? And for that matter, I suppose I was thinking, why don't I get it about all the other little steps of female vanity that seem to come easily enough to everyone else? Is there anyone else out there my age who has never owned—or successfully used—a hair dryer? Anyone else who just washes her long (frizzy leftover-hippie) hair every night and braids it back, too clueless to use what Tattooed Linda calls "prod-uct," too out of it to understand about cuts and styles? Why don't I understand—why have I never understood—about moisturizers and makeup? Why can't I tolerate makeup on my face—or, for that matter, I thought, extending the list of my feminine inadequacies, why can't I tolerate pantyhose on my body? Why am I fat when everyone else in my peer group is thin?

Of course, I had mothers and daughters on my mind; my mother was visiting, we were planning to spend the day writing about mothers and daughters. It was my mother I had left in charge in my house, it was my mother I hadn't told about getting my hair dyed—it was somehow also my mother I was blaming for all this. I grew up with a mother who didn't understand about vanity. She didn't believe in taking trouble over her body and her appearance, any more than she believed in taking trouble over her coffee. Something had been left out of my makeup, and it wasn't just makeup. And here I was, now, leaving it out of my daughter's makeup. How was she supposed to know about hair dryers and "product"?

Sheila: Poor Perri. Her problem goes well beyond vanity—my peculiarities are not limited to my feelings about my appearance. There are so many things that I don't get—that I've never gotten—or that I just get wrong. I may have had a categorizing mother, and I may have refused to classify my children, but my daughter's problem is that she has a peculiar mother. I've always been this way. Mort used to muse wildly and most entertainingly about my singularity. He'd begin with the oddly epicanthic folds of my eyes. Probably, way back, I'd had a distant ancestor, he hypothesized, who was carried off by one of the Mongol hordes.

More recently my forebears lived in the shtetls of Hungary, and Mort tried to make a legend out of that, a suggestion that I came from a weird folkloric place of outliers. He quoted my father, who said his village was so poor, the only man who had a jacket was the mayor. That's why he was mayor. I could go on, but it's all speculation. Maybe I have something unexpected in my genetic makeup, or maybe I really do come from the country of the strange. What I do know is that all my life, well-meaning conventional folks tried to socialize me, but I was me from early on. Sometimes I subdued the me in me for a brief time, trying to be one of them, but it never really worked.

Take whistling: I've been a serious whistler since adolescence. In the 1930s, girls didn't whistle. "A whistling woman and a crowing hen never come to any good end," my grandmother and my aunts—and, of course, my mother—warned me constantly. To this day, when I'm alone, I often whistle. Loud.

Recently, in the laundry room of my apartment building, an elderly lady introduced herself to me, saying, "I hope you don't mind my intruding. I have been listening to your 'Ode to Joy.' I've heard you whistling many times before. You and I are the only two who do it. Ach, how my mother hated that!"

Mind? I embraced her. I didn't know there was another one.

A better example: You know how Yo-Yo Ma has his instrument? His cello? Of course. Well, I have my instrument too. My bugle. The World War I silver bugle my bandmaster presented me with in 1942. Most of my life, I've been a crackerjack bugler.

To answer the constant badgering I endured as a young woman about my unladylike choices, I developed perfectly good rationales. For the whistling: In the 1940s I was lucky enough to find a steady job on Saturday nights as a babysitter (fifty cents an evening). The catch was that my employer was a widow, which meant that when she came home late at night, she had no husband to walk me home. I had to walk home after midnight through the slums of Brooklyn alone. I devised a means of accompaniment, a loud whistle, which kept up my courage—and probably woke up the neighborhood. The "Marseillaise," with its rousing *"Aux armes, citoyens, Formez vos bataillons . . . ,"* was particularly bracing.

The bugling, which mortified my respectable older female relatives (during parades, they stayed indoors), was a source of income; I spent summers as camp bugler in the Catskills. I held on to my bugle, and during our family's long exile in suburbia, I frequently bugled "Mess Call" at dinnertime to summon everyone expeditiously. "Mess Call" was not common practice in Leonia, New Jersey, but the neighbors tolerated it. I have the bugle in my coat closet now, but alas, there's no one to call to dinner.

Perri: That's all very well, but there is no reason why the lady playing the bugle on her suburban porch couldn't have spent ten minutes with a hair dryer before she came out to make an exhibition of herself. But we didn't own a hair dryer. And my mother hates getting her own hair cut so much that she cuts it at home with a little curved pair of manicure scissors—and then, if it doesn't come out well, she goes to a discount hair-cutting place where they charge twelve dollars or so, and grits her teeth until it's over. My mother has never been tempted—has never even thought of being tempted—by massages and spa treatments and any of that stuff. As she says, she just doesn't get it—and neither do I.

Sheila: That's just the beginning of it. There's shopping. I hate shopping! And I hate looking for clothes for myself the most. When I go into a store, I head right for the sale rack, though I have enough money to buy whatever I like. I never do that. Sometimes Perri comes along and bullies me into buying something lovely, but it's a scene. Yet I truly love and admire beautiful garments—on other people. I can't buy them for myself, and I'm reluctant to accept them as gifts.

Along with frugality in purchases goes an impossible frugality in use. I carefully save my best clothes till, though they're unworn, they're old and outdated, while I go around in *schmattes* (rags). I'm probably the worst-dressed woman who ever taught in a college—and there's heavy competition. Do I want to look weird? I've asked myself many times, *What am I saving my good garments for?* Who knows?

Why did I smoke a pipe at college? Why did I wear jeans long before girls were wearing them? Why don't I tweeze my thick eyebrows? *Because it hurts* doesn't seem to be reason enough for other women. Why is the main floor of Macy's, with all its cosmetic counters, alien territory to me? Why don't I use face creams and lotions and mud packs to avoid wrinkles and telltale age marks? Why have I never dyed my hair, which whitened prematurely and is now snow white? Mornings going to work, for years and years now, I have been most often the only white-haired woman on the A train.

Why do I hate to have anyone work on me or even touch me to beautify me? Last Mother's Day, my son, David, gave me a SoHo luxury spa gift certificate for a massage. It took six months to get me there. The masseuse could not believe I had never had a massage. I was a novelty. I left her to her wonderment and promptly fell asleep. So why did I need a massage? I promptly fall asleep at home without hundred-dollar massages! Why am I the way I am?

Perri: And yet, of course, I also knew—and acknowledged, as I sat there letting the various chemicals soak into my head—that growing up with my mother, I had somehow escaped the crippling feelings about beauty that nag at many women. I haven't spent a lot of time in my life worrying that I couldn't have anything I wanted because I'm not pretty enough. I don't believe that my life would be different—or much better—if I were beautiful. I don't generally feel particularly self-conscious leaving the house, even on my worst hair days—once when I was standing at the cash register at the hair salon, paying my bill, a woman about my age came in off the street and started begging them to squeeze her in—she was on her way to a party, she said, and she had realized she couldn't possibly go unless something was done about her hair, and it was an important party, it really mattered, and could they please help her out. And they did. And I felt as if I was listening to alien beings speak a gibberish-based dialect (I mean, her hair just looked like hair, that's what it looked like).

Linda shampooed out the dye, combed out my wet hair, and I thanked her and tipped her and ran out the door, wet strands of newly brown hair blowing around my face in the February wind. Ran home, found Anatol dressed and ready, thanks to my mother, and yes, the skates fit. Drove him to his friend's house, dropped him off, complete with skates, wondering what his friend's mother (thin, carefully cut blond hair, short and athletically bouncy bob) made of my newly dyed wet look. Sat down to work with my mother on our writing, got up, went to the bathroom, and braided back my damp brown hair. Later on that day, my mother remembered my haircut—remember, she doesn't see so well—and asked me whether I was satisfied with it. Sure, I told her, it was just a trim anyway.

Sheila: It's surely not that I do not want to be pretty. Attractive. Favorably noticed. A part of me has probably always wanted that. But the rest of me gave up long ago, I think, in childhood, perhaps because of the way my mother always said (and I mean *always*) that Marilyn was The Pretty One and I was The Smart One.

Anyway, the adults said brains were more important than looks in life. They didn't say when. Somehow that didn't seem to be true during my adolescence and college years, when dating and courtship were paramount concerns. My mother felt my eyeglasses were a tremendous handicap and urged me not to wear them.

"Which is more important—to be able to see or to look pretty?" I demanded.

To which she said, "You don't have to see everything."

"I do," I said, and of course, I wore them. I needed them badly to see, and besides, wearing them had become a point of honor. I would not wander around half blind just so I'd be prettier. Anyway, smarter was supposed to be more important.

I was smart enough to figure out that if you're poor and badly dressed, the choice is either to continue to compete against the odds or to go your own way. My way for the rest of my life was to pay no attention to current styles and rules—indeed, to blank them out—and to develop a sense of what my own integrity was. Besides affecting my outer appearance, this integrity manifested itself in strange ways, physically as well as psychologically. Some drugs and medications violated my sense of self. When it was commonly thought that estrogen treatment was beneficial to middle-aged women, my gynecologist prescribed it, but I immediately hated it and the way it made me feel—not like myself—and I stopped taking it.

I am not the Puritan that Perri is. I use powder and lipstick because I like their effects, but I've forsworn all other cosmetics. I don't wear perfume, though I once did; I get no pleasure from it since my husband is gone. I don't wear clothing that isn't comfortable, and I gave up high heels many years ago.

When I look in the mirror, I see a familiar beetle-browed old face capped by white curly hair. She's not The Pretty One. And it may be a misnomer to call her The Smart One. But one thing's certain. She's the one she started out to be. She's taken her mother's advice at last and given up wearing glasses. They no longer help.

CHAPTER SEVENTEEN

Who Needs a Doctor?

Perri: Several years ago, I had a bad cold that wouldn't go away. My voice sounded terrible, and my mother was worried. Now, it is my general policy never to tell my mother very much about my health. I can't stand solicitous inquiries, and I find that the loving concern of others often gets in the way of my own precious denial. But in this case, my mother could hear, day after day, when we talked on the phone, that I sounded lousy. And she wanted me to go see a doctor.

I pointed out that I *am,* in fact, a doctor, and therefore would know if something major was wrong with me. I pointed out that there's nothing doctors can do about a bad cold. I pointed out that I hate going to doctors, and that I get that directly from her.

She still wanted me to go. So I offered her a deal—if she would go get the mammogram that was a couple of years overdue, I would go see my primary care doctor and get my cold checked out. And we kept the bargain—both of us. Though it is only fair to point out that we were both confirmed in our prejudices: My doctor looked me over and told me I had a lingering bad cold, which I already knew, and my mother's mammogram was negative, so they told her she was healthy—which she already knew.

My mother believes, I think, that when a doctor finds something wrong with you, it is partly that doctor's fault and partly your own fault for going to see the doctor in the first place. My father, on the other hand, believed devoutly in preventive medical care; no one has ever more faithfully kept his primary care appointments and followed every recommendation for blood tests or referrals. And every time the doctor found an abnormality—his blood sugar was out of control, his prostate-specific antigen level was high—my mother was torn between a sense of gratitude that they had caught the problem early enough to do something about it and an accusatory impulse. *Well, what do you expect if you keep letting them draw your blood?* I imagined her saying—or thinking. And then when my father died suddenly and unexpectedly, I know that part of her grief was a kind of frustrated anger that all his careful conscientiousness around his own health should have led to this.

And even though I'm a doctor—and a primary care physician at that—I cleave much closer to my mother's attitude than I do to my father's. I don't like going to the doctor, I don't like having tests done, and I always have this sneaking feeling that if I don't have the test, they can't find the problem, and if they don't find the problem . . . well, then, the problem isn't there. As I said, I cherish my denial.

Sheila: Doctors? Who needs them? I grew up in a home where there was a strong antagonism to doctors. They cost money, and we were poor. They wanted to examine our bodies, and we were modest. We never mentioned our unmentionable body parts—not even to one another, and certainly not to strange men. We pretended the dirty parts of our bodies weren't there.

There was the abiding belief when someone was not well that if the illness wasn't named, it might go away. It may have become a joke now, but in an orthodox Jewish home in Williamsburg, Brooklyn, during the 1930s, chicken soup was an effective all-purpose medication. In addition, we had hot baths and cold compresses and castor oil, and we could wish and pray to help drive the sickness away. But over and above all these remedies, it was not naming the problem which protected us, which kept the illness from turning into something real.

In those days, there was no money for bread—so going to the doctor was a luxury—or maybe, better, a disaster. You went only if you absolutely had to; the sick person was blamed for draining the family coffers. I was a tomboy and often hurt myself playing rowdy games. When I was eight, in a street game of Kick-the-Can, the can was kicked into my knee, tearing the skin badly. My mother, weeping with fear, ran downstairs and immediately carried me to the doctor. Tenderly, she held me in her arms while he stitched up the wound. Then she really let me have it, yelling at me, spanking me, raging to other family members about what I had done. "Who ever heard of a girl behaving this way?" she demanded, and she talked about that knee for years. I didn't understand how she could love me and pick on me simultaneously. But I understand now when I think about my mother, bringing up three children in desperate poverty, with no health insurance of any kind—and it is one of my reasons for supporting socialized medicine.

The older women in the family whispered about "women's troubles," and various of our female relatives suffered from those vague illnesses. At my grandmother's house, when someone was seriously ill, a mysterious woman would arrive to do "cupping," a terrifying process in which little heated glass cups were applied to the patient to draw the poisons out. My grandmother also had various herbal medicinal teas. So private were illnesses kept that I have no idea what my older female relatives died of. Women's bodies were our secrets, and they were not nice secrets.

When my older sister first menstruated, my mother slapped her. "To keep the color in your face," Mama explained. That scared me, rather than reassuring me, so I never mentioned my own menstruation to her. Oddly, my mother never asked.

I grew up distrusting doctors. I had a healthy body and I managed to wish away—or overcome—whatever minor ailments I had. I was lucky, I suppose. And I am inordinately fond of chicken soup.

Perri: I did not grow up poor—or religious—in Williamsburg in the 1930s; I grew up middle class and secular in Manhattan and the New Jersey suburbs in the 1960s and 1970s. And my mother, by then, had learned to name the various parts of the body—of her children's bodies, if not her own—without embarrassment. I did not get slapped when I reached puberty; I got the first edition of *Our Bodies, Ourselves,* with an inscription from my parents, as a birthday present. And my memory is that my mother treated our childhood illnesses with perfectly appropriate medical attention. No cupping, no castor oil, no desire to keep anything secret. Of course, we had good health insurance. So we had checkups and vaccinations and antibiotics, the odd tonsillectomy when appropriate, dermatologists for our acne. There were real medicines in the medicine chest—the kind that cost money. My mother's one big medical secret during this time, I suspect, was that she was not taking care of herself.

Sheila: It's true—once I had children, I became a frantic doctor-caller. The children were so small and helpless, and they got so very sick. As soon as a child's illness seemed threatening, I needed to consult authority. My husband had been a Merchant Marine ship's purser, and therefore the medic on board his ship at the end of World War II; he was calmer, and sometimes he restrained me. He didn't think that every little fever needed an emergency medical visit—but he did believe in regular checkups. He could talk me out of calling the doctor unnecessarily for our children, but he couldn't talk me into medical care for myself. If anything did seem to be going wrong with me, I reached immediately for a simple benign explanation. For example, one day right after I had my third child, I noticed that my shoes were too tight, and I told my husband that my feet must have gotten fatter during the pregnancy. It turned out that instead, I was having a life-threatening allergic reaction to penicillin, and my whole body was starting to swell up.

So yes, I saw the doctor when I was pregnant, and I hated it for all the reasons I had learned growing up—the embarrassment, the concentration on the parts of my body I preferred to ignore, the risk that a problem would be identified, named, and made real. After each child was born, I stopped going to the doctor—or even, really, having a doctor of my own. It drove my husband crazy.

However, we agreed about our grown-up daughter, Perri. She did not take good care of herself. She never got enough sleep, she undertook too much, her diet was haphazard, etc., etc. She was incredibly eagle-eyed and outspoken about our illnesses or minor physical disabilities, but she neglected herself. And this from a doctor! She was supposed to be a model, an example! Wasn't that in the Hippocratic oath?

Perri: For crying out loud, I was a medical student—then an intern, then a resident—and throughout, a mother of young children. Of course I didn't get enough sleep; of course I was stressed out. But growing up, I had somehow acquired an invincible conviction of my own basic good health, and to this I now added a very special kind of doctor's denial: *illnesses happen to patients; they don't happen to me.* It's kind of the opposite of the famous syndrome in which some medical students diagnose themselves with whichever obscure disease they happen to be studying; some of us just decide we're immune to everything. And, like my mother, I got most of my medical care during my pregnancies. I was a cranky, if reasonably compliant, obstetrical patient—but as soon as each baby was born, I wanted nothing more than to be out of there—out of the bed, out of the hospital, out of the doctor's supervision, out of the role of patient and back in the role of doctor, where I belonged. So sure, I could worry about my parents' health—but where the hell did they get off, worrying about mine?

Sheila: Then in middle age, my eyesight grew worse and worse, and once again I came up with an explanation that had nothing to do with any illness of mine: I started to complain that the lightbulbs were defective, and the house was darker. My husband forced me to be examined. The diagnosis was glaucoma. A part of me hated that doctor for naming it and making it real. Though he treated me and arrested the disease, I never quite forgave him.

But these days I am humbled, reduced to dependence on doctors, who have taught me to name my body's malefactors: cholesterol and high blood pressure and macular degeneration. I am what my daughter the doctor calls a compliant patient; I take my medications every day, antioxidants and Lipitor and hydrochlorothiazide and Toprol XL. I resent them, but I take them. So my pharmaceutical list, which for so long included only chicken soup, has broadened, and I see my doctors regularly. But deep in my heart, I hold fast to the belief that the doctors are partly to blame for finding all these ailments—and that the rest of the blame is mine, for letting them look in the first place.

CHAPTER EIGHTEEN

Insecurity

❧

Perri: My mother and I were in a hotel room in Atlantic City. It's funny—the way hotel rooms keep coming up, you would think we were always checking in somewhere or other, but it's actually pretty unusual for the two of us to share a hotel room. It's true that we've made a couple of trips together, and it's also true that every now and then, when I have a business trip in the New York area, she joins me.

It's also true that hotel rooms seem to crystallize certain things. They take us out of our several domesticities, out of our routines. Nobody has to be caretaker or homemaker or hostess. My mother, of course, tends to make her hotel bed as soon as she gets up, but she doesn't try to make mine. (When I stay at her house, I try to remember to make the bed as soon as I get up out of it; otherwise, she sneaks in while I'm in the bathroom and does it.) Even so, hotel rooms somehow shift the foundations—or the focus—a little bit, and we see each other in a slightly different perspective.

So we were in this hotel room in Atlantic City. I was attending a knitting conference, promoting a book of knitting essays I'd written. My mother does not knit or crochet—or do anything else that could remotely be considered crafty. Just as she lived untouched through the suburban craze for self-actualization in the 1970s, she was also completely immune to macramé and all other handicrafts; the suburbs were full of women with looms and potter's wheels, and the suburban night was full of classes, and it all went right by my mother. So the presence of several thousand crazed knitters in Atlantic City bemuses her, but she wanders the convention market with no desire at all to snatch up a skein of multicolored mohair or pick up some novelty yarn and start a simple garter-stitch scarf. I, on the other hand, was well past my first hundred dollars' worth of yarn and trying to figure out how I could possibly get all this wonderful new stuff onto the plane with me.

I had flown from Boston to Philadelphia and then come by shuttle van to Atlantic City. My mother had arrived the next day by bus (naturally) from New York City. The plan was this: In the morning, we would take a shuttle van to the Philadelphia airport and together take a flight back to Boston, so my mother could spend a couple of days visiting my family. I hooked up my computer to the hotel room phone and went online and bought her a ticket; my mother was deeply impressed, as always, by my remarkable computer skills.

And then, with everything all set, she thought of something: She had come away without her passport, so she had no federally issued picture ID. She has no driver's license, of course, and she's never bothered to get the alternate alcoholic beverages commission ID. When she flies, she carries her passport, but she had set out for the Greyhound bus to Atlantic City without it.

Together, we looked through her wallet. She had a variety of cards—a voter registration card, a credit card, an ID with her picture on it from the college where she teaches. Would they let her on the airplane? My mother was terribly anxious, repeating over and over that she couldn't believe she could have been so stupid, that she had spoiled everything, that it would be better for me to go back to Boston without her. So I called the airline to ask, and an agent took me through a list of alternative forms of identification—and remarkably, one option was a picture ID—any picture ID—together with a voter registration card. I hung up the phone and announced, triumphantly, to my mother, that everything was okay, that she happened to have the perfect combination of identification cards. Everything was fine; we would fly out of Philadelphia as planned.

But my mother was not reassured. She was certain that they would refuse to let her on the plane. She would consent to go to Philadelphia with me the next day only if I promised, absolutely, that under those circumstances, I would immediately abandon her; I would get on the airplane, smugly holding my driver's license, and she would make her way to the bus station and find a bus back to New York. Because I believed the airline agent, I agreed to this condition, rebelliously thinking to myself that no way would I ever abandon my mother at airport security. Of course, if by some chance she wasn't allowed onto the plane, I would go with her to find a bus—or a train—and I would take care of her. But I didn't say any of this; I just told her, honestly, that it wouldn't turn out to be a problem, and we went to sleep.

At least *I* went to sleep. The next morning, as we got ready to go, my mother told me that she had lain awake all night in the dark, worrying over the possibility that she might not make it through Philadelphia airport security and feeling stupid about having left her passport at home. She looked drawn and tired—and therefore older than she had looked the night before.

As we rode the shuttle van to Philadelphia, I kept thinking about September 11, 2001. It was because of September 11 that my mother faced airport security so intense that it was even imaginable that a seventy-seven-year-old woman might be turned away as a security risk. It was because of September 11 that my mother now needed a passport to travel within her own country.

But what I was remembering was the morning of Tuesday, September 11, 2001, when I arrived at work and heard about the destruction of the World Trade Center and, of course, I called my mother, who was at home in New York, to see if she was all right. I knew that she taught her class on Tuesdays, and I knew that her college was right down by the World Trade Center, that she in fact got off the subway at the World Trade Center stop, and I was completely panicked. It's probably what almost everyone did that morning—call people they cared about in New York City. And some of them, of course, were not all right.

But my mother was fine—safe in her apartment more than two hundred city blocks north of the Twin Towers. She hadn't left yet to teach her class, which met in the middle of the day. She had been watching the news, of course, and she was deeply distressed—but she wasn't at all afraid in any way. Well, no, to be fair, she was worried about one specific thing: She told me that she thought she should probably leave a little bit earlier than usual, since the subways might be running slowly.

"Mama," I said, "there won't be any subways running to the World Trade Center. There won't be any school today."

"You think they'll really cancel school?" she asked, shocked.

"Mama," I said, staring at unbelievable images on my computer screen, "promise me you won't go down there."

So that's what I was thinking about as we rolled toward Philadelphia—what scares my mother and what doesn't scare my mother. And when we got there, the security guards were happy to accept my mother's voter registration card, together with her school ID—except that this unusual form of identification automatically doomed her to a special thorough search, which flustered her badly. I could see her thinking resentfully that this never happens on the Greyhound bus. When we finally found ourselves on the plane, bound for Boston, my mother immediately fell asleep, worn out by fear and worry and travel. I took out my laptop to work on an overdue article, and instead, I found myself writing a letter to the woman asleep in the next seat:

Dear Mama,

    Last night you said you couldn't sleep for worrying about our return to Boston—not a fear of flying, not a fear of traveling, but a worry that you would get in trouble or be turned away because you didn't have your passport. You often describe yourself as very frightened, very easily afraid . . . and yet you live alone in Manhattan (in an apartment that my sister can't sleep in without checking all the windows . . . do you ever check the windows?), travel back and forth on the subway without a second thought, walk home from the subway at night. . . . Do any of these things ever scare you? They scare other people, you know—I work with healthy young people who wouldn't think of walking New York streets at night or riding the subway late in the evening. Don't make a face—they aren't too middle class; they're just scared, like some people are scared of flying. Think about how you felt after September 11—were you physically scared? Were you worried for your own safety? Were you worried about public transportation? (Remember the anthrax moment, when many people stopped taking the subways?) Did you think, even for a minute, about leaving Manhattan and moving somewhere safer? (My brother did . . . he talked about moving to the suburbs because Manhattan was such a target. . . . My sister did . . . she talked about applying for a job in Australia.) Did you think about packing an emergency escape bag or buying a gas mask? If not, why not?

Mama, what if you made a list of the things that scare you and the things that don't—I mean, really scare you—I'm trying to think of physical fears . . .

Childbirth—were you really scared? You couldn't have been, or you wouldn't have been able to do it in Trinidad.

I know you don't like ferris wheels or roller-coaster rides—but you aren't scared of downhill skiing, are you? I am—I've gone cross-country skiing but never wanted to try downhill—but you used to do it, didn't you?

And I know you don't like boats. Do you mind big ones or only small ones? How much is fear; how much is seasickness? And you don't mind flying at all, do you?

What about illness, Mama—I don't get the feeling that you read news reports and start to worry that something you've been eating or doing (sunburns) is going to hurt you. I think of this because every time an article comes out in the news to say that something causes cancer, parents turn up in my office to tell me they're worried, or my sister calls to ask if I think she might have been exposed—but not you, Mama; never you. . . .

I guess this builds up to the question: Are you scared that you're going to get sick with this or that—or are you just scared of losing independence? I'm thinking about the way Papa worried about illness and death. Can you place yourself somewhere on this spectrum?

And finally, world events—I remember calling you the morning of September 11. What you weren't was scared—and after as well. Can you think back to other scary world events—WW II, the Cuban missile crisis? Were you scared? Did you think of changing your life, of buying protective gear, or moving somewhere safe? You didn't, did you, not for a minute. So, Mama, are you just plain brave, or do you think there is something generational here— something about growing up during a war and taking part in air raid drills and wondering whether the bombers would come?

I finished writing my letter. My mother was still asleep in the next seat. The frightening thing had not happened; she had not been challenged at security or denied permission to board the plane or sent out on her own to find her way home from Philadelphia. She was safe and at peace, airborne and asleep.

CHAPTER NINETEEN

The Urban Widow's Tale

Sheila: I don't want to die with my boots on. I want to be wearing my firmly laced, English-teacher walking shoes when I go—my oxfords, of course. What could be more appropriate?

I wander lonelier than any cloud, day or night, in Manhattan at all hours. My restlessness shouldn't be hard to understand. I'm a widow as well as a liberated suburbanite returned after a twenty-year exile. During my explorations, I often take a subway train or a bus, or I walk—if possible—before I consider taking a taxi. My children don't understand. They think I'm cheap and foolhardy, that I worry them needlessly. Like a child, I'm reduced to phoning them late at night once I'm safely home. I hate that part worst of all.

When they're feeling mellow and affectionate, they think their difficult old mother is brave.

Piffle. I'm not brave at all. In fact, I am about as craven a coward as is possible; however, I take my cue from Henley: "I am the master of my fate; I am the captain of my soul."

So for me, the gravest dangers lurk in what I have responsibility for, in what I can control, in what is ultimately up to me. My antennae pick up different signals than other people's, and once I'm alerted, the situation is desperate and I have to take radical steps. It's been that way all my life.

I know when I need to save myself!

The first time was in the summer of 1944, after my junior year in high school, when I had a terrible fight with my mother. I ran away from home, moving to a small Manhattan hotel. I got two jobs: I pasted labels on paint cans, days, and I sold hot roast beef sandwiches at McGinnis on 50th Street and Broadway from six to twelve, nights. For two months, I literally tiptoed in and out of that dumpy hotel, terrified. I had never been on my own; I was a minor. I feared arrest, disgrace. I was alone. I feared the city. My impossible hope was to save enough money in those two months to be able to finish high school.

How did I manage to survive during that frightening summer? I had *no choice*—that's how. I'd realized that if I continued to live in my parents' home, my life would be smashed into shards.

Yet I had to finish school. It took even more resolution after the summer to return home in September. I knew I would flee again, permanently, and that knowledge sustained me. I fled once high school was done, and I didn't return.

I was seventeen then. I was terrified, so I acted when I saw there was no alternative. That was not bravery. That was a desire to live asserting itself. *Run, Sheila, run, or you will die!*

Now I'm seventy-seven and again I live alone in Manhattan. I have limited vision. In fact, I'm legally blind and have been so for some years. My vision is worse in dark places. When a taxi takes me home at night, I cannot see much around me. Nor can I read the meter. Sometimes taxi drivers get lost; I'm no help to them. And often they are immigrants, Punjabis or Moroccans with rich accents. My hearing is rotten, so I can't decipher what they say.

I know the subway system. I navigate it with relative ease. I don't feel threatened while riding it. I stay out of completely empty cars, and I move away from visibly psychotic fellow passengers. Somehow, without effort, I always look shabby enough so no one wants my wealth.

When I walk about at night, I try to behave intelligently, to stay in lighted, populated areas. I could not live in this city if I were afraid of it. I would be a prisoner, as much of one as I, a nondriver, was in the smothering, safe suburbs.

Each of us has her own cache of personal fears. I live in a second-floor apartment. When my younger daughter stays overnight, she always checks the windows. It never occurs to me to do that. I keep the windows open when the weather is good. I do not feel threatened: I enjoy life in Manhattan, and I am not afraid. I feel safe in the city—in my city and in most cities, in fact: Calcutta, Tokyo, London, Paris, Port of Spain, Beijing. They have opened their doors and their alleyways and parks and spectacular markets and vistas to me . . .

There have been times when I've unexpectedly been courageous. Or at least not scared. When I got pregnant with Perri, I was so happy to be having a baby, at last. After all, I was thirty! Living in a wooden shack in the tropics with no refrigerator, no running water, no windows or screens, I forgot to worry and loved the experience. I knew, I just knew it would be all right. And it was. When Perri's siblings were born, here in the United States, I was already proficient at the process.

On September 11 when the World Trade Center was destroyed, I don't think I comprehended—I was simply unable to believe what I heard and saw on television. Somehow my mind would not allow it. I was convinced that there would be school, nevertheless, that day, in my college, which is close by the WTC. I never miss a class if I can help it, so I resolved to go. Fortunately, Perri phoned, and she had to really work at talking me out of taking the subway downtown.

Maybe not fearing great public disasters is the result of being a child during World War II, when the destruction was far away. I remember being afraid for the Austrians and the Czechs and the Jews but not for myself. It wasn't real. And so events like September 11 and the Cuban missile crisis have seemed slightly unreal, slightly distant, as if by definition world events must take place at some distance and threaten the safety of others.

But plenty of things scare me.

Water does. I cannot swim—though I passed the Brooklyn College swimming test, twice across the pool—I've never liked water. Rowboats and the like give me no pleasure. Canoes or kayaks seem like diabolical inventions to be avoided. I have more courage about large ships. I mean *large*! A long time ago, I went to Europe and back on the "queens" via Cunard. I think the vastness of the ships, along with a husband, an ex–Merchant Marine who could swim, was reassuring.

I stay clear of amusement parks. Ferris wheels and roller coasters and the like absolutely pulverize me and always have. Even the merry-go-round and swings make me violently dizzy. Bumper cars are my idea of a thrillingly dangerous ride. When I was young, I ventured to learn to ski. It was exhilarating, and somehow not frightening, perhaps because I never moved up past the baby slope. There, I was content. I don't like heights anyway.

I find big dogs threatening. I was bitten on the knee by one, in childhood, and I suffered the sequence of rabies shots. I'm uncomfortable near dogs and resent them as fellow passengers in apartment-house elevators. I think rude thoughts about their owners as we ride together, and the dogs sense my enmity, for they glare at me malevolently.

Taking off and landing in airplanes, I clutch the armrest and shut my eyes, but otherwise I'm perfectly calm even during long, difficult flights to places like Japan or Indonesia. I'm not sure why. Perhaps, again, because what happens is not up to me. I readily surrender responsibility to whoever is in charge and let them—the pilots, bus drivers, train engineers—do the worrying.

I do worry about my children and grandchildren. Curiously, I am much more anxious when they are here in the city near me than when they are far away. This oddball reaction is in accord with the principle that if they're here near me, I should somehow be able to help.

I am petrified by all business negotiations, no matter how minor. Though I've been a writer for fifty years, I suffer whenever I need to call my editor or even my agent, *who works for me.* Job interviews, conversations regarding academic promotion, meetings with my accountant or lawyer—any business-related activities—really send me spinning. It's as if I were entering a dangerous whirlpool and I can't swim. I've wondered if this is a vestige of my Depression childhood; any encounter my parents ever had with "officials" (Home Relief in-

vestigators, school principals, teachers, landlords) was always trau-
matic.

What frightens me most now is the vision of my elderly self as helpless, dependent on others. I long to be a functioning adult till my very
end. I know my children love me and will care for me, but *I do not
want them to have to.* I fear pain and deformity and dementia and
dread them for the alterations they make in the self. I do not want to
lose control. When I was depressed after my husband died, I tried
Zoloft, but I couldn't bear the meretricious self I became. I want to die
me, just as I tried to live.

I don't fear death in the same way I fear debilitating illness. Death
seems a natural evolution of this body that has served me so well for
so long. It makes sense that the body should wear out. I can imagine a
time of great weariness when eternal rest becomes a comfort. Nor do
I brood about death or worry about it. It has already claimed so many
dear to me; it is simply the great inevitable chasm that looms ahead.

Memory bridges it. Memory comforts and soothes. And allows one
to go on living in the richness of the past. I hope that among the
thoughts of those who are fond of me and survive me will be how
much I loved the city and the independence it offers. I have requested
cremation so I won't have a tombstone with a legend on it. Let the legend be recorded here. It is simply: "Of her own free will, she never
took a cab."

PART SIX

A Woman's Work

CHAPTER TWENTY

Our Brilliant Careers

Sheila: Until I was twenty-three, I had a single standard when looking for work: If it paid any wage at all, I would do it. I was a babysitter during the 1940s, fifty cents a night, and a dollar on New Year's Eve. I washed the dishes for some and tidied the living room, as well, for that half-dollar. Those were the years when I perfected my whistle, as I walked home from my babysitting job through the Williamsburg streets. I whistled louder and louder to keep my courage up. I bused tables at Bickford's Cafeteria and sold cream cheese–and-nut sandwiches at Chock full o' Nuts, part-time. I bugled in cemeteries on patriotic holidays; summers during my adolescence, I waited tables in resorts in the Catskills, or I served as bugler-counselor in girls' camps.

After I ran away from home in 1944 and spent the summer doing two jobs, my father sought me out. "An unmarried Jewish girl does not live alone," he argued. I had one more year of high school, so I went back.

Perri: I can't imagine not working. I can't imagine not having a job of some kind to go to. I can't imagine not having professional colleagues, and a working world—and I can't imagine not earning a salary. My own job history, however, will look much more like the story of the privileged child I was—most of my jobs, at least from high school onward, will be the jobs that my parents let me do because they sounded interesting—or the jobs I had to do to advance along the career path I had chosen—graduate school, then medical school, then medical training. Still, here's my list:

BABYSITTING: When we lived in suburban New Jersey, I was a big-time babysitter, especially around the age of eleven or twelve. Standard practice back then was to pay a dollar an hour and leave a twelve-year-old girl to ransack your house. We were looking for copies of *Everything You Always Wanted to Know About Sex* but Were Afraid to Ask*™ by Dr. David Reubin, and I must say, we usually found them—at least until the best-seller list evolved, and they were replaced by copies of *The Joy of Sex*. By the time that became standard household equipment, I had outgrown the babysitting. So the rates had gone up and the service had declined since my mother's days in Williamsburg—although nowadays, of course, we hardly leave twelve-year-olds alone in the house themselves, let alone put them in charge of two or three young children. . . .

THE FLOATING HOSPITAL: The summer I was fifteen, I volunteered on this hospital ship that took poor families out onto New York Harbor every day and provided amusements as well as various kinds of health care and health information. The following summer, when I was sixteen, they hired me to work on the play deck, where it turned out that my main value as an entertainer of New York children was that my hair, which at that time was short and curly, would hold cornrows. Almost every day, four or five small girls would work me over, braiding elaborate patterns into my hair, all the while falling over with laughter at the sheer ridiculousness of a white girl with cornrows in her hair. This was my transition to college: My parents and my siblings set off on a cross-country drive, and I lived in a Barnard dorm and kept my job, thrilled to be on my own in New York, and also, I'm afraid, very much aware that I was not cut out to be a professional player-with-young-children.

Sheila: For me, babysitting was my salvation. It got me out of my parents' house; it got me through college. In 1945, I took a job as live-in babysitter, room and two meals a day but no wage. I moved out of my parents' home for good, attending Brooklyn College (which was free) and working weekends roasting nuts in hot oil in the window of the giant Planters peanuts store near Times Square. This arrangement lasted all through my undergraduate years. Those years as a live-in babysitter were as much revelation as my college courses. I was hired because the family's live-in maid wanted a chance to live out and have more freedom. She was so valued, the family took me in and she continued to work for them. So I went from the cold-water flat of my parents to a lush private home in Flatbush—wood fires, paintings, books, music, civil conversation—near the college, served by a full-time maid. Two little boys, three and five, were my charges; their parents went out often at night, and I stayed in. The ambiance of pleasant, middle-class family life was a shock. The first time a glass of milk was spilled at table, I froze, waiting for the consequences. No one got upset. The father simply reminded his son to be more careful. The maid wiped up the milk, and the meal continued. I was dumbstruck. Did people really live like this?

Summers, I waited tables in the Poconos. The summer of my senior year, I worked in a clothing factory operating a "joker" machine, which identified cut parts of a garment so that all the proper parts of the same fabric would be matched. I was so terrible at it that the manager, who had a kind heart, was constantly shouting at me, "For this you have to go to college?" But he kept me on all summer.

Perri: Well, I had various part-time jobs in college—I signed up with the student employment service and was sent to clean houses, including one apartment in which everything, including the carpeting, was pure white, and the nervous woman who lived there watched me carefully to see that I didn't leave any splotches in her already immaculate igloo. I babysat for the alumni children during reunion week and was tipped handsomely by somewhat tipsy, unimaginably middle-aged twenty-fifth reunioners, as they staggered back to their rooms in the dormitories and found that I had kept their children safe. The only hard part was insisting to the extremely savvy and entitled thirteen-year-old girls that no, they could not go join the teenage group's party, because there was a fourteen-year-old cutoff. A couple of years ago, as I attended my own twenty-fifth reunion and left my own children in the charge of the obliging undergraduate babysitters, I thought back to those middle-aged drunken parents. . . .

Sheila: After college, I took the white-collar job of my parents' dreams: receptionist and secretary in the New York School of Mechanical Dentistry, and hated it. I lasted about a year.

Desperate, I fled to Iowa City, where I'd been accepted at Paul Engle's Writers' Workshop. I got a full-time job, eleven P.M. to seven A.M., five nights a week, at the Iowa State Psychopathic Hospital, which was actually on campus. I worked nights as an aide, sitting on the darkened ward, doing my homework and writing, interrupted only by disturbed patients and trips to lock and unlock toilets. This job enabled me to complete two master's degrees.

Perri: The next few jobs I had were connected to school. I was a teaching fellow at Berkeley, when I was in graduate school, thinking I would be a biologist, before I changed my mind and applied to medical school. I was a teaching assistant in the big premed introductory biology course, in the invertebrate biology course, the ecology course. Then, during the first two years of medical school, desperate to earn some money toward my expenses, I taught Harvard's required freshman writing course. I found myself, of course, grading papers during my medical student lectures, letting my teaching slide when I had medical school exams—and then, intermittently, turning all my attention to the teaching, hurling myself at it in a frenzy of creative energy as a way to avoid studying for my medical school classes.

And then, right after medical school, came internship and residency in pediatrics—this is technically something between a job and an educational experience—you do get paid, however minimally, to be a resident, but you also have to do this particular job in order to qualify as a doctor. My residency was back before the current rules limiting hours and night call, and it featured those proverbial thirty-six-hour days, and yes, I hated it and I loved it and my family suffered and I learned a lot. I prolonged the residency-like experience with a couple of years of pediatric infectious diseases subspecialty training.

At one point, like my mother, I ended up on a psychiatric ward. What is the significance of that particular convergence, we ask ourselves? I worked for a year as the medical consultant on a pediatric psychiatric ward—I had just had my second child and I wanted to work part-time. I think, in retrospect, that I probably didn't have the experience or the background that I really needed to do that job with confidence. I was helping to take care of kids—mostly teenagers, some younger children—who often had both major psychiatric problems and also major medical issues. For example, there were lots of girls with big-time eating disorders. My job was to worry about their electrolyte disturbances (which can provoke heart arrythmias and kill them). And the problem was, of course, that we had to sort out whether peculiar behaviors—refusing to get out of bed in the morning, sitting sullenly and staring off into space instead of participating in group therapy—reflected physical problems or behavioral acting out. It was a fascinating job, and I was terrified every minute.

Sheila: After graduate school, I found a teaching job. From 1951 to 1957, I taught English and history at Julia Ward Howe Junior High School in Harlem, a rough but interesting girls' school. My first published novel, *Come Back on Monday*, comes out of those years. It was fueled by my rage at the callous opportunists who administered the school. I bought a pair of orthopedic shoes in 1951, my first year at Julia Ward Howe, because the stupid principal ruled that no teacher should sit down during the school day. She insisted that the shop teacher wear a jacket and tie all day too. There were many such in-house edicts, but after a while my friends and I—most of the teachers on the staff were young and idealistic and working at their first jobs—grew smart and sneaky and developed ways to get around the rules, ways to engage our students and open up their worlds. Dance classes in the halls. Trips. Guest speakers. Writing contests with prizes. A school magazine.

Our students were rebellious but energetic, and many of them were very ready to be interested. There were plenty of problems, but we were determined to teach them, to change things in Harlem, to give them a chance. And we did see change; some girls made it into the specialized high schools like Music and Art; some began to think of college. On the other hand, it was a hard, poor neighborhood, and many of our students were hurt or destroyed. Vicious street fights were regular after school, and often, girls yanked earrings though their opponents' earlobes. We persisted in our belief that we could teach and our students could learn—and when we had small victories, we celebrated. One year we prevailed on the principal to let us do a faculty show for the kids. When she heard we proposed to do *A Christmas Carol*—Dickens—a classic!—she agreed. She was big on classics. We did the play humorously, casting the tallest male teacher as Tiny Tim. He was a hilarious sight carried onstage by our Bob Cratchit, the short, dumpy shop teacher. We performed for all the assemblies, and the kids loved it. The principal's comment afterward was "It is inappropriate to handle a literary classic this way."

I reluctantly left Julia Ward Howe to go to Trinidad with Mort on our first field trip. The one great joy I had in leaving was that I would no longer be under the reign of this martinet. She was too stupid and bureaucracy-minded to see the incredible resources she had available to her in her troop of lively, dedicated, idealistic young teachers, just as she was too stupid and prejudiced to see the potential in her students. But I loved the students, and I loved the women I taught with. Many of my old colleagues are still my friends today; some of the dearest of them have died.

The happy ending: In 1965 my husband, on an errand on 50th Street in Manhattan, saw a posting that the Borough of Manhattan Community College, a new branch of the City University of New York, located there, needed lecturers in English. I applied and was hired, and after forty years, I still work at BMCC. I love to teach. There are those who say it is the stand-up comic in me that is thus gratified, for a class is a captive audience. Perhaps. Or more likely, I think, teaching, like writing, is a way of dispensing the treasures of my life. Fiction and good writing delight me. My attention and imagination are wholly engaged.

So if there's some one thing that gives me vast pleasure, I believe it's my obligation to spread it around. Teaching in the City University of New York, for me, is a great privilege, for it was the real birthplace of my mind. At BMCC, I introduce the motley student body—as motley as we were in the 1940s, though the ethnic mix was a different one—to so much variety and opportunity. They read and they write, and they are often astounded at the richness and kookiness of their own imaginations. And as their teacher, I make the trip with them, and it takes me far. These days in the classroom, I journey away from the sadness of loss and age and wander with my students' writing to endless possibilities. That's the privilege of a teacher.

I have been blessed.

Perri: I don't know if this is my happy ending yet, but it's certainly a reasonably happy place for me to be—I'm a community health center pediatrician. I took a part-time job at Dorchester House, a neighborhood health center in Boston, and I still work there, seeing patients in primary care. And I do love walking into those exam rooms and getting my chance with child after child, family after family, to solve a problem, answer a question—or just help a little bit along the way. Like my mother, I find myself drawn to a poor urban population; I'm fascinated by the journeys (in every sense) of new immigrants and the complexities of poverty and social mobility. Some of this is the do-gooder in me, of course, but some of it is that certain stories, certain populations, certain problems interest you and draw you, and you can't exactly explain why.

And a little over a decade ago, I got involved with this sweet little book program called Reach Out and Read. I had written an article about the department of pediatrics at Boston City Hospital, where I did my pediatric infectious diseases training, and about the challenges of taking care of poor inner-city children, and one of the programs I had featured had been the literacy program in the clinic. They had volunteers reading aloud to kids in the waiting room, they had doctors talking to parents about how important it was to read to young children, and those same doctors gave each child a new book at every checkup from six months to five years of age. I had interviewed one of the doctors who founded the program, and he had talked eloquently about what a book could mean in a young child's life—but also about what a book couldn't mean, about how important it was to give books but how it still didn't solve the problems of unstable families, unsafe neigborhoods, overwhelmed and overcrowded schools. And then when he was leaving the hospital to take another job, he asked me to pick up the book program, and then the chairman of the department suggested we write a grant to help other hospitals replicate it . . . and then it took over my life. Reach Out and Read is now a national nonprofit, with thousands of sites in clinics and hospitals and health centers and private practices, training tens of thousands of doctors and nurses to advise parents about reading aloud and giving out millions of books every year. I am now a fanatic.

And okay, that's my life—running back and forth between Dorchester House and Reach Out and Read, seeing patients and trying to make sure I follow up on their problems, training doctors about literacy, begging for book money, running the Reach Out and Read National Center. As my mother says, I have been blessed.

Sheila: For me, having a job shores up my sense of worth. The years that I was a stay-at-home housewife and mother, I felt the diminution of that pride in work. Irrational? Nonetheless . . . I work now because I love what I do—I inhabit a world I know—but also because going to work bespeaks a kind of independence largely absent among women in my childhood.

Teaching is a noble calling. People—children particularly—are eager to learn. All a teacher needs to do is make the learning tempting. Stand-up comedy and eccentricity are my favorite resources. These days I tell my college classes, before they notice for themselves, that

I'm nearly deaf and nearly blind, so they need to speak up and listen, and they should regard me merely as a harmless, aged relative. They do, and really, I am.

You should be absolutely honest with yourself about what you like to do. The longest days of my work life were at my worst-of-all job: secretary-receptionist. It was my worst-of-all job because paramount among my responsibilities was keeping records. The records were important; the students were on the GI Bill, tuition paid by the U.S. government. They were there to learn, but I didn't help them learn— I only did the paperwork. From this job I learned what I already knew: I was an execrable typist, bookkeeper, stenographer—and I should not have been in that office. My parents' white-collar dream was my nightmare.

For me, interacting and working with people is vital, perhaps because I spend so much time alone, writing. Waiting tables or busing them or sitting up all night with mental patients was continually interesting and challenging. I welcomed the unexpected.

Carrying one's lunch guarantees a good lunch no matter the job. These days, I eat with colleagues and sometimes with students. They *never* bring sandwiches but instead frequent the fast-food stands that have moved into college cafeterias. Together, we talk and joke. I carry my lunch so I can literally have a movable feast.

Perri: I, on the other hand, never carry my lunch. (Yes, Mama, I know, it's because I'm bourgeois—hopelessly, irredeemably bourgeois. Years of making school lunches have soured me on the ritual of packing food—I have bad associations with little Tupperware containers and insulated boxes. They call up images of the late-night realization that there's nothing in the house, or the smell of the lunch box that someone forgot and left overnight at school.) Sometimes I order out, if that's what's happening in the office. At Dorchester House, there's a Vietnamese restaurant right across the street. I know the menu so well I can order by number.

But I agree about the pleasures of office contacts, the joy of patients. I have not wanted to live what I imagine as the quintessential writer's life, alone in a room with my mind and the blank piece of paper. Or rather, I have sometimes yearned after that life—but yearned only after little bits of it, an hour or two in the morning, a whole day here or there, a wonderful couple of weeks. That's not how I want to live from month to month and year to year. I like to leave home in the morning and go out into the world and be part of its workings. I know what makes the world interesting to me, and, as a writer, I know where my stories come from.

CHAPTER TWENTY-ONE

Watching You Work

Sheila: Perr, when your phone rings and it's a patient in trouble, I listen to your end shamelessly as you elicit information and give instructions and prescribe and then, later, follow up. Even after all these years, I am amazed at your gentle, cool, authoritative voice: the voice of a doctor. What the shaman was to the tribesman, the doctor is still to me. I believe that to cure or to palliate and comfort is to bless. Of course, whenever I ask you for medical advice, you get grumpy, and you always preface your answer with "Mom, I'm not an old people's doctor . . ." But then you either help me or send me to someone who can. I don't think doctors like to recognize that their parents are old and vulnerable.

Perri: Actually, what I say is, "Mom, I'm a pediatrician." By which I mean that I don't know anything about high blood pressure or high cholesterol or estrogen replacement or any of the other things that afflict adults. I'm not telling you that I'm not interested, I'm telling you that we're outside my area of expertise. But I do recognize that you think all doctors know everything—it's not your fault; it's somehow a part of how you were raised, and I have to admit that I enjoy the reverence. Go ahead, tell me more about my gentle, cool, authoritative voice.

Sheila: I'm no doctor, heaven knows, but I do have one skill that you don't yet have, a parental skill. I am an unmitigated first-rate *kveller,* a deriver of vicarious pleasure and pride from my children's accomplishments. And that is why I am inordinately, idiotically, suffused with pleasure when I watch you work. When I listen to you lecture. When I read your articles and short stories and novels. Whenever I sit in your living room or beside you in the car, and you're on call and the phone keeps ringing. Whenever people say nice things about you.

You're my oldest child, so you came first, but I'm equally aggressive and obnoxious about all three of my children. Their defeats are my defeats and their victories are also mine. Your father and I never managed that separation that some families accomplish: adult children having separate and discrete lives. Of course, I must bear silent witness (though I often have strong opinions and even diagnoses!), but I know better than to voice them.

Years of analysis and thousands of dollars would, no doubt, prove that my behavior is payback for my own mother, who never noticed accomplishment: The little girl with the eyeglasses saying, "Look, Ma, I'm a college teacher, I'm a writer, I'm a mother, a wife. . . ." Perhaps.

So I watch Reach Out and Read grow and flourish, and I listen to your lectures on literacy and how vital books are for children, and I take great delight in the independence and freedom of your professional life. You've often said to me that I found my own way, while you were the "good girl," the suburban middle-class daughter, who did the expected, who went to college then to medical school. But you are more than that, because you understood there was freedom to do what was meaningful and right for yourself, and when the time came, you seized it. Surely that is what carpe diem truly means.

Perri: I have seen my mother teach now and then over the years. In fact, she taught a writing course in my alternative high school, and I took the course. But I wasn't really watching her very closely. I appreciated her excellent comments and her careful handling of the class— and her professional writing teacher's unshockability, as I and my high school classmates wrote our adolescent sagas of sex, drugs, and rock and roll. But really, when I was fifteen years old, I think my mind was just too fixed on me to appreciate my mother as a teacher. I know that when I was younger, I sometimes went to her college with her—I have distinct memories of the old-fashioned purple mimeograph sheets she used to hand out in her classes, which I read with interest. I met a wide variety of authors on those pages—Dorothy Parker, D. H. Lawrence, Ernest Hemingway—and probably, I watched my mother teach, but I guess I just took it for granted.

Anyway, I recently went to class with my mother, under strange and even tragic circumstances. Her older sister, Marilyn, "The Pretty One," was dying in a hospital in Brooklyn. She was my mother's oldest and closest friend, and the only other one left from that original family of five back in Williamsburg. Marilyn lived alone in an old-age residence in Brooklyn, and she had not been well for a long time. She couldn't see, couldn't walk without a walker, and she had a variety of serious medical problems. But she and my mother talked on the phone every day, and sometimes, when the weather was okay, my mother made the long subway trip out to see her, and they went to a restaurant together.

Something happened to these two sisters, and I assume it happened back in their childhood, to make them both apologetic about taking up space in the world. My mother apologizes all the time—if I sat in her living room and I asked her to get me a glass of water, and she got up to get it while I sat there and read the newspaper, and then, as she brought me the glass of water, if I shifted my legs slightly so as not to trip her—my mother would say, "I'm sorry!" Meaning, *I'm sorry I disturbed you and crowded you and made you move your legs while I was bringing you the drink of water you asked for.* Well, her sister was even more extreme. She apologized to everyone for everything. When she had her massive stroke, my cousin told me, and the aide came in the next morning and found her in bed, my aunt tried hard to tell her, "Don't call my children; they have to go to work!"

My aunt Marilyn was the gentlest, sweetest, kindest person in the world—that was what we always said about her, and it was true. She had a hard time—she was widowed very young with four children and no money—but she held the family together, and she brought everybody through, and she lived to enjoy years of matriarchal grandmotherhood, which she thoroughly enjoyed.

But she had had a massive stroke, and she was in the intensive care unit of a Brooklyn hospital, and she was dying. I had flown in from Boston, and my cousin, the oldest of Marilyn's children, had picked me up at LaGuardia Airport. My mother came out to the airport as well, carrying her briefcase. Her idea was to come out to the hospital with us, be there for the family meeting, and then hurry back to Manhattan to teach her class at one PM.

In the end, she didn't come to the family meeting. She said she didn't want to see the pictures of her sister's brain. She said that Marilyn's children knew what Marilyn wanted—and indeed they did. So she went into the ICU and sat beside her sister and held her hand and talked to her. My cousins all knew what their mother had wanted. She had told them she was tired; she had told them she did not want a ventilator or a feeding tube. She had told them she wanted them to let her go, when the time came. And it had become clear to all of them—and to my mother, and to me—that the time had come.

The family meeting ended. The doctors left. There would be papers to sign and legal procedures. My mother came back into the room, and my cousins asked her, tearfully, if they were doing the right thing, and she tearfully told them that they were, that they were doing what Marilyn had wanted, and what she herself would want. "Marilyn is already gone," she said.

And then my mother said that she needed to get back to Manhattan to teach her class. I tried to persuade her to skip the class—to call the school and say there was a family emergency—but my mother refused. She had a briefcase full of papers she had marked, and the students would all be arriving, and they would be expecting their papers. And they would be bringing the papers that were due today—how could she stand them up? No, she had to go, she said, and she had to get there on time. I was torn between staying with my cousins, to provide what doctorly support I could, and going with my mother. The cousin who had driven to the airport made the decision for me: "I

don't want your mom traveling alone. I don't want her on the subway," she said. "Go take care of her."

So we took a taxi into Manhattan (you know how she would have
traveled if I hadn't been there), and I watched her teach her class. And
I watched her become—not a different person, not at all. I watched
her, well, become herself. It was a terrible, tragic, disconcerting day—
but for two hours of it, she was fully engaged, outside herself, using
everything she had. She gave them back their papers, carefully scruti-
nized through her special magnifying glass, marked in red, line by
line. She gave them an in-class writing assignment. One page: "You
are anyone you choose to be, in New York City: a homeless person, a
student, a rich man, an immigrant, a nun. You board a bus and sit,
and your foot kicks a blank envelope under your seat, which turns out
to be filled with hundred-dollar bills. What do you think as you sit
there? How do you behave? Finally, what do you do?"

They read their pages aloud. She leaned forward and listened, following what the students said, reading their lips, telling them to speak
up if she couldn't hear them clearly. She laughed at their jokes and
pointed out their successful images, commented on their abilities to
build suspense or delineate character. I sat at one of the student desks,
leaning on the desk arm of the chair, and I could tell the students were
listening. They listened to one another, and they listened to my
mother. They could tell that she cared, that she thought their para-
graphs were important, and that she was willing to bring everything
she had—her hearing, her vision, her brain, and her memory—to bear
on their writing and their stories.

I watched her up in front of that class—and of course, I was in a
strange and emotional state myself—but it seemed to me that I was
seeing my mother for the first time. *This is who she is,* I kept thinking. *This is who she is.* She needed to come and do this for
two hours so that she can remember who she is. I thought—again with
much confused emotion—about the various things that people have
suggested to my mother as possible occupations since my father's
death: volunteer work, grief groups, adult education, hobbies. None
of that was right. Even the people she loves best—family, children,

grandchildren—were only one part of the picture. What she needed, really, was this. She needed work, she needed to be using herself—all of herself—in this particular way.

The class ended. The students were interested and engaged up to the end. She collected the papers they had written, and they wrote down the details of the next assignment. They said good-bye, and several of them lingered to ask questions or go over comments on the papers she had handed back. My mother answered every question, concentrating her hearing, reading their lips. She packed the new set of papers into a folder and packed the folder into her briefcase. She took my arm. She was ready to go back to Brooklyn and say good-bye.

CHAPTER TWENTY-TWO

There Are No Old Babies

Perri: I wasn't absolutely sure what my parents would say when I told them I was pregnant. On the one hand, I assumed they were interested in being grandparents—someday. On the other hand, I was a first-year medical student, and they were helping out with my massive tuition, while I taught freshman English and went into debt, big time, with student loans, to cover the rest. Larry was a graduate student, finishing his dissertation, with no way to know where the jobs in his field might be. My parents had never pushed the idea of grandchildren, and I knew they were heavily invested—both emotionally and financially—in my medical education, and I wondered whether they would consider this a dubious time to have a baby. I was, of course, not reckoning with the deep, primal desire to become grandparents. Just because they hadn't pushed it, I had naively assumed that grandchildren were not on their minds. It turned out, of course, that they had been heroically restraining themselves from bringing up the subject; they were ready and waiting for a grandchild, and they seemed rather disconcertingly confident that the child care arrangements and the finances and the will-Larry-find-a-job-and-if-so-will-it-be-in-the-same-state stuff would all work out.

So during my first trimester, I signed up for a spot at a day care center. Clearly, this child was going to need someplace to go every day.

We never thought seriously, as far as I can remember, about having a babysitter come to our house, both because Larry was home writing his dissertation when he wasn't teaching and because it somehow seemed self-evident to us both that we didn't want to rely on any one person. The university had several affiliated day care centers, and spots were hard to come by, so we got ourselves on the list. It never occurred to me that my parents, who had been so enthusiastically confident about the advent of grandparenthood, would have any doubts about these arrangements.

Sheila: All three of Perri and Larry's children spent their infancy and early childhood in day care. Magic words—now. But I remember twenty-one years ago when Perri first spoke them, broaching the concept: All-day, from eight to five o'clock, infant and toddler care. It was revolutionary to me. But she and Larry had already made their careful plans. They weren't consulting me; they were telling me. The baby would go to day care five days a week.

An infant to be sent out into the world on its own to be cared for by strangers? That was how my mind heard it. Every morning. Like the postal service. Neither snow nor sleet . . . How could they even think of such a thing? It was bewildering. It was actually frightening. Since I couldn't admit to being old-fashioned, I raised practical objections. "But you're going to be nursing!"

"I have a breast pump, and I'll leave milk for the baby in the day care refrigerator."

Whoever heard of such a thing? Not me.

Thus I was introduced to the breast pump, an ingenious device. *A mechanical wet nurse,* I silently derided it. I felt that I had wandered into Huxley's *Brave New World.*

It was hard for me to be comfortable with these plans. "The baby will be exposed to a million germs by the other children. Who knows what they have?"

"Ma," Perri lectured me in her "doctor" voice. "Typhoid Mary will not be in the day care center. Most infections in kids are passed hand-to-hand, and the children won't be handling the baby. Besides, exposure to germs triggers the immune system to make antibodies that fight off infections. Some scientists think social contact reinforces the immune system. It's a good thing for the baby."

"Perri, we're talking about a new baby."

"Mama, there are no old babies." She was laughing at me.

"A very little baby."

"Oh, I don't know," she said, patting her sizable stomach. "Seems good-sized—even large—to me."

I knew enough to keep quiet. Who cared, really, what I thought?

Perri: Honestly, I don't remember this conversation. I suppose we must have talked, my mother and I, about what I was planning to do with the baby, but I have actually been repeatedly surprised, as the years have gone by, to hear my mother refer to her initial deep doubts about day care, and to her memories of how we argued. I remember her being very well behaved—keeping her opinions to herself, cheering me on. I wonder whether I was actually so worried myself about how things would work out—about whether we would be able to do this at all—that I simply shut out questions and doubts.

On the other hand, you do realize here that we are asking my mother to write about her grandchildren, and that she thinks they are perfect, and that therefore all decisions I made about them have to have been the best possible decisions, since they yielded the best possible grandchildren. Get ready to hear how all my apparent eccentricities were actually strokes of genius—no matter what she really thought or felt—and no matter whether some of my decisions were a little bit dubious. It's all going to turn out perfectly, and for two cents, she'll show you some photos she just happens to carry in her purse.

Sheila: Perri's smart-ass line "There are no old babies" was a quote. She was quoting me in an argument with my own mother. It set me to brooding about my own long and checkered history.

In 1958, I interrupted my teaching career to have Perri, at thirty, and I didn't go back to work. I became a stay-at-home mother. David was born two years later, and for the next five years, I stayed home. My advantage over other women in similar situations was that I was a writer, and I could still steal a little time to do my thing. So mornings, I got up at five, or else I went to bed very late, and I wrote.

After seven years of pushing the swings, refereeing the playdates, and baking lumpy cupcakes, I'd had enough. My husband sensed this, and, on an errand to pay car insurance, passed a new college just opening in the Times Square area, and he picked up a job application for me.

I began teaching evenings at Manhattan Community College, which offered education to students working in Midtown. Teaching part-time after seven years of domesticity was bliss, and I stayed at it. In 1967, when I was forty, Mort and I decided that if we wanted one more child, it had better be soon. Forty was pushing the bounds of motherhood in those days. I continued to teach part-time till, when I was in the ninth month of pregnancy, a full-time tenure-line position opened at the college. I was eligible, I wanted that job, and I got it.

But when I told my mother and mother-in-law, they both were appalled. "But what will you do with the baby?" they chorused. "A new baby!"

"There are no old babies," I reasoned. I wouldn't let the guilt strategies enmesh me. "We'll hire someone."

"A stranger? Who leaves a new baby with a stranger to go to work? You're not starving."

There was much more of the same, but we hired a young woman from the Dominican Republic, who grew to love the baby, and as the baby flourished and grew plump—the grandmas' major criterion for health—they were placated, more or less, and life moved on.

Perri: I know we had babysitters—actually, we called them housekeepers. To be honest, I don't remember them clearly. Maria, the young Dominican woman, mostly took care of my younger sister, the one born in 1967. Soon after my sister was born, we moved to the New Jersey suburbs, and Maria kept working for us, commuting from New York every morning. But in the suburbs, in 1968, ten-year-olds like me didn't need babysitters. My brother and I walked to school each morning—no adult needed—and walked home in the afternoon. And then we were more or less free to run around the neighborhood and play with various neighbor children in various neighbor backyards. Nobody tracked children's specific whereabouts—certainly, it was nothing like the scheduled extracurricular activities and carefully arranged playdates that we all suffer through nowadays. But what that meant, I think, was that Maria mostly took care of my baby sister. I know that her life took a wrong turn—that she got married, and the marriage didn't work out well, and that my mother was worried about her, and that she refused all help, and that she finally killed herself. I know my mother was deeply upset—but I remember her grief better than I remember any emotions of my own.

There was a second woman who came and worked for us after that. Again, I remember her as someone who took care of my sister, not someone who was particularly relevant to my own life. She was older, and passionately fond of knickknacks—for years, whenever I saw some particularly ornate candle or china figurine, I would think to myself automatically that Mrs. C would have liked that.

I think both of these women did their jobs perfectly well. In my memories, they were very peripheral to my own absorbing child-centered universe. I do think that I somehow took away from these experiences a strong sense that I did not ever want—well, to have someone else in my house. Did I sense the complexity and the pressure of this relationship—the way my mother worried about whether Maria was being abused by her husband, or the way she worried that Mrs. C occasionally seemed a little tipsy? Or are those just stories she told me afterward, which resonate more for me now that I have children of my own? I don't really know, but I do know that by the time I had my first child, I knew what I wanted: the model in which everyone leaves in the morning—off to job, off to school, off to day care. And who knows, maybe I did argue my case fluently when my mother objected—fluently and ignorantly, since she was absolutely correct that day care would mean one infection after another, and instead of worrying about whether the housekeeper would get sick, we worried about whether the baby was getting another fever.

Sheila: In 1972, we visited an aunt and uncle on the Bet Zera kibbutz in Israel. There, I first learned about the children's house, where all the young ones on the kibbutz lived and slept and ate their breakfasts and lunches, under the supervision of several adults who preferred being with children. Meanwhile, the other adults worked in the fields and orchards. The workday started in the cool dawn and ended at three in the afternoon. Then the children spent the long afternoon and evening with their parents. They played and swam and ate and studied together and talked. Then the kids trooped off to bed in the children's house.

This concept was new and strange to me, and I expect I was hostile to it. After all, wasn't I doing all the domestic stuff *and* working *and* writing? Surely the absence of the kibbutz mothers must be damaging their offspring. I could not imagine my children sleeping nightly under another roof. Wasn't I the one to be at hand if they woke ill or distressed? No matter that I hated getting up at night, wasn't I the only one?

I put it to my aunt, who had three young sons: Didn't she feel strange allowing others to raise her children? Didn't she mind?

First she laughed, entertained by the question, which she thought particularly American. (And particularly naive or even stupid?) "Why should I mind? And how is it strange? My sons see me after I've finished the work of the day. I can give them all my attention. I don't have anything pulling at me that I must do. It's not necessary for me to say, 'Go away. I haven't time for you.' I never once put them to watch TV because I was busy. Look at my sons. Do you see anything wrong?"

Of course, nothing was wrong. I was as limited as my mother and mother-in-law had been. It is as if each of us found it necessary to justify the way we did things as the right and only way.

When my friends and contemporaries, both the neurotic ones and the happier ones—all raised by full-time, stay-at-home mothers—reminisce, there is often great bitterness over the injustices of their childhoods. They don't set out to malign their parents, but too many unhappy memories crowd out the happy ones. If the traditional methods were so great, why haven't we turned out better—and happier?

Perri: You never know where you'll end up with my mother—now, all of a sudden, we're on the kibbutz. I suspect this is once again ingenuous—my memory is that my mother often referred to the children's house system when I was growing up, and that she yearned for it in a vague old-socialist kind of way, as she yearned for a classless society and social justice. Never mind that she would have hated working in the fields or in the orchards. She would have liked—or she thought she would have liked—life with a communal dining hall, and no meals to cook and no dishes to wash. And she would have liked—or she thought she would have liked—the children's house system. I suspect her of having invented this historical conversation with my aunt, just as I suspect her of having invented the arguments she thinks she had with me about infant day care. In both cases, my mother was actually holding dialogues with herself, putting forth the questions, the doubts, the worries, and then answering them.

Me, I am no old socialist. I never thought for a minute that I wanted to live in an egalitarian worker's paradise where I would pick oranges by day and eat in a communal dining hall. And I like retreating with my family into my own house at night. In fact, I'm so territorial about my own house that I could never hire a regular babysitter.

For whatever reason, in my ignorance, I always knew what I wanted. And now, in retrospect, I can identify many things about day care that work for me. I loved sending my babies into the baby room in the morning, a room of soft floors and padded corners and bright-colored chewable objects and busy boxes. In fact I loved watching my children adjust to each age-cued room—this is a two-year-old's place, this is a three-year-old's place. I loved the professionalism of the teachers—the energy with which they seized opportunities, never mind the trouble and mess. I remember dropping off a three-year-old (I no longer remember which three-year-old—among my children, we accumulated some fifteen years of day care, and the memories blur a little) one grim rainy morning, only to have the teacher tell me—cheerfully!—that she thought it might be fun to make the sand table into a mud table just for today. I nodded my enthusiastic approval, trying not to grimace, and got the hell out of there before the mud arrived. I loved the order and routine of day care, especially since we lived in such chaos at home—and most especially during the stressed years of my training. At day care, snacks arrived on time—and no one tried to palm off two-day-old Chinese takeout on you instead of graham crackers. And after snack, everyone sang the cleanup song, and no one fell asleep on the couch the way Mom did last night, instead of doing the dishes (well, throwing away the used takeout containers).

I know we were lucky. It's a university community, and we had great day care. And I give the great day care great credit—those teachers do a job that I could not do. They made a friendly, welcoming place, and my children lived in it, all day, every day, for years. And the truth is, it didn't take my mother long to realize that her grandchildren were perfect, and that therefore, they must be attending the perfect day care programs.

Sheila: Every conversation I report, needless to say, took place exactly as stated. My historical accuracy is impeccable. And the fact that Perri has blocked out memories of my articulate concern just shows you how carefully she was really listening. But yes, she's right, the day care turned out well. I need to celebrate the pleasure my grandchildren got, as they grew older, from spending their days with others their age and with gifted teachers. They loved going to day care. They made friends early, and they kept many of those friends. They were socialized and not afraid of people or new foods or new experiences. A parent from every family contributed a half-day's work each week to the center, furnishing extra help and also allowing the parent to watch and assist the child at play.

Ben, a gentle boy, enjoyed it all immensely. (This was before he became Orlando.) He learned all the songs and happily absorbed the friendly, peaceful, ecologically minded ideals of the liberal, academic institution. No television. No weapons or war toys. No bullying. It was a blessing to have a child in a benign, caring environment, where he was being imbued with the values I cherished.

So here is my favorite story about his values: One morning in the three-year-old room, my grandson was playing with a Tinkertoy set, while his fond father was assisting in the day care center. The child was engrossed in a complicated construction.

A teacher came by, noted him hard at work, and stopped to say, admiringly, "Ben, what you've built with those Tinkertoy pieces is really wonderful. What is it?"

Earnestly, without looking up, Ben replied, "It's a bird feeder. I built a bird feeder."

The teacher was delighted. "What a good idea! A bird feeder, so all the little birds will get a chance to have something to eat. How kind of you to think about the little birds."

Ben smiled, and his listening father felt proud.

Then the teacher turned to talk to another child, whereupon Ben lifted the elaborate construction and aimed it at the teacher's back, calling out with gusto, "Bang, bang! I shot you with my bird feeder!"

Alas, he shot down some of my birdbrained ideas about the perfect child-rearing environment.

CHAPTER TWENTY-THREE

Knitting Patterns

Perri: And now, finally, we come to a chapter that truly belongs to me. My mother has much to say on almost every subject, but when it comes to knitting, she needs to stand still and let herself be measured. She does not knit, and I am sure she does not understand the appeal. This is, after all, my mother, who cannot understand why anyone would knock herself out trying to bake a cake when the bakery does such an excellent job. Imagine how she feels about spending hours on a handmade scarf.

I, on the other hand, knit passionately, if not always expertly. And I knit across the generations, perfectly mindful of all the symbolism involved: knitting for my children, knitting for my parents, trying to tie the family together, shaping warm garments to hug people closely. But nothing is ever simple across generations. How can I knit for my adolescent daughter without burdening her with an object she'll feel self-conscious wearing and feel guilty leaving home? Her friends can walk into a store and pick out gifts she'll use and appreciate; I strike out regularly even with earrings and carefully selected clothing, chosen to resemble her other clothing, bought at the same chain stores. . . . And how can I knit for my mother, who wants no gifts, who wants no trouble taken on her behalf? Once I gave her a little scarf I had knit, and she seemed pleased. She looped it decoratively around her neck and wore it to a party. I told her it looked wonderful, and I said I wanted to make her another, in a different color, a different yarn. "But Perri," she said, "I only have one neck."

Nothing is ever simple. When you knit for the people you love, you are acting out of generosity, of course, but you are also intruding, just a little, into their lives. *Take me with you out into the world,* the scarf says to your teenage daughter. *Wrap me around your neck and let me protect you and keep you warm.* No wonder it makes her squirm just a little; no wonder you rarely hear a teenager boasting: "Hey, guys, my mother knit this for me!"

Still, I love to knit, and I visit my productions on those I love. Here is the story of two projects—mother to daughter and daughter to mother, in which we pursue the tangled, colorful, sometimes scratchy ball-of-yarn metaphors: watch me try to tie it all together, work toward beautiful patterns, and avoid obvious lumpy knots.

PART I.

Fearful Symmetry: The Story of Josephine's Shawl

It started, as so many things do, innocently enough. It started, as so many things do, with a single ball of yarn. It was really, really soft—it was Plush by Berroco—and it was purple. A friend had made a decorative little scarf out of the same stuff in green, and I had fingered it with pleasure—really soft, really fun. So she bought me a ball, in a nice lavender, and I needed a small suitable project.

I would make a scarf for my daughter—she was fifteen, she likes purple, she likes soft and strokable fabrics. But she doesn't really like scarves—the most successful scarflike item I ever got her (note that I do not say *that I ever made her*) was a big red pashmina rectangle that she likes to wrap around her neck or her shoulders in winter. It's soft and strokable (though I would not by any means care to go bail for the origins of the so-called pashmina, since I bought it from a New York City sidewalk vendor for ten dollars) and warm and bright, and though she uses it as a scarf, it's really more of a shawl. Very well, then,

I would make this fluffy purple thing more of a shawl—and I cast on for a much wider object.

And by then it was already no longer completely innocent. Here I was, willfully choosing to cast on for a project much much bigger than my single ball of yarn could ever accommodate. And here I was, already, treacherously allowing myself to fantasize that with the right color, the right texture, I could knit something that would resolve all the mother–daughter tangles. I was imagining a shawl that would also be a kind of security blanket—so soft and appealing that Josephine would have to wrap it around herself whenever she studied, in the winter, in Massachusetts, in our drafty old house. She would wear it up in her room, stroking it over and over, as she worked on her homework. She would wrap it around her sedate blue peacoat when she went out, for warmth and color and that secret, hard-to-quantify comfort. In other words, I cast on confidently for something that I allowed myself to imagine as a tangible harbinger of maternal love, acceptable to an adolescent, capable of delivering comfort, scholarly inspiration, warmth, and—why not?—protection. I had one completely inadequate ball of fluffy lavender yarn, and I proposed to knit something magical.

Not to pursue the metaphor too closely or anything, but of course I soon saw that I was running out of yarn. *No problem,* I thought, *too much solid lavender would be boring anyway.* My friend had mentioned that she was going back to that same yarn store, and I asked her to pick me up a few more balls of Plush—any colors, as long as they went well with purple. And when the white and the cotton-candy pink yarn arrived, I happily began striping, here a wide purple band, here a quick alternation of thin pink and white and pink and white. The thing, whatever it was, was growing.

The thing, whatever it was, was no longer in any notable way reflective of my daughter's taste. I mean, Josephine likes purple and she likes pink, but there's a reason why that successful pashmina purchase was a simple solid color. Her tastes are conservative—navy peacoat, red scarf, button-down shirts from the Gap. I may like the idea of adding colors and striping randomly, but she tends to go for pinstripes. She looked at the growing object, and she tried to be polite. Yes, it was soft. Yes, it was nice to touch. But there didn't seem to be any pattern to it. Could I assure her that it would be—she paused—*symmetrical*?

So I did—I assured her that it would be. Never mind that symmetry had not, until right then, crossed my mind. Left to myself, I would have been happy to meander along, adding different colors, ending when the thing seemed long enough—I had, in fact, saved some of my original purple ball, planning specifically to have the last color match the first color, but I didn't think it was necessarily enough for perfect symmetry, for the exact same number of lavender rows on the other end of the shawl. But Josephine loves order and method and pattern, and I could see that a symmetrical shawl would be much more comforting and much more welcome than anything more random. So I promised symmetry. And in a certain sense, that freed me up—I could do anything I wanted, I reasoned, with mixing yarns and striping colors, as long as I saved enough of each color and texture to work my way out from the midpoint in perfect matching mirror image.

I was running out of yarn again—this thing was big. Soft, yes, colorful, yes, but also just plain big. It covered my lap in its colorful softness whenever I spread it out to knit. I went to my local yarn store and looked for the next stripes, the next colors. They didn't have Plush on hand, but they had some other soft, fuzzy white yarns—slightly different textures, slightly different white stripes. I found myself wanting to add something to the white to make it more interesting, and I came home with a skein of Squiggle, pink and magenta dangling tails. One skein of it turned out to contain a great many—well, squiggles—and that rather took over the middle part of the shawl, white plush yarn knitted together with all these little dangles. When I wanted to take a break from knitting, I spent some time pulling all the little tails through to the right side of the garment.

Josephine acknowledged that the squiggles were kind of cool. "Will it really come out symmetrical?" she asked. "Yes," I said, "I promise," as I added on more white with dangles. She sat down beside me and began pulling the tails through to the right side, and I showed her a ball of dark purple fuzzy stuff that I had brought home. "Will it be okay to use this for the center panel?" I asked. "Then I'll start knitting my way back out again, matching everything, stripe for stripe." "Sure," Josephine said. She hesitated. "Can you put this pink stuff with the dangly things on the purple too?" she asked, and I was delighted. Here was my magic shawl encouraging my daughter to cut loose a little bit, to choose frivolity and extra colors and—quite literally—novelty yarn.

So I did. The center of the shawl would be a wide white stripe, then a wide dark purple stripe, then a matching wide white stripe, to signal the beginning of the perfect symmetry—but they would be united by silly pink squiggles. I marked the central row of the central purple stripe carefully: Here was the mirror-line, the symmetrical point of origin, the mother row. Well, actually, every row was the mother row; this was the mother shawl, or the mother of all shawls, or the mother of all shawls made by a mother.

If I say to you, "I am not a particularly symmetrical person," you will probably imagine for a moment that one eye is blue and the other is green, or that my shoulders are slightly out of true. And in fact, as a pediatrician, this is a conversation I have regularly with the observant parents of young infants, who have detected subtle mismatches between the two sides of a baby's face. In fact, it's a conversation that I had, as an observant parent of a young infant, with my own pediatrician, when I noticed that my youngest child had one eye that was slightly larger than the other, and my pediatrician assured me—as I often assure parents—that these common small facial asymmetries do not mean anything pathological, that they in fact add character and personality.

But when I say that I am not myself symmetrical, what I mean, of course, is something more metaphorical, or spiritual, or characterological. I mean that since I live with a rather high level of disorder in all aspects of my life, I swear no particular allegiance to symmetry, or to any other kind of all-determining pattern. I admire order, but I am also firmly pledged to the aesthetics of randomness and happenstance. Josephine, on the other hand, is the one long-suffering orderly person in a chaotic household. Her books are perfectly arranged on the shelves of her room—and she has taken a certain amount of family grief because her fondness for consistency is so strong that she will banish a book from those orderly shelves if it does not match its companions in shape and size. That is to say, she owns four Harry Potter novels in hardcover, and one in paperback, and the paperback is consigned to the communal chaos of the playroom. Josephine preferred the incomplete but perfectly matched set. Better to be without volume two than to compromise.

As I worked my way away from the mother row, and outward from the purple stripe at the center, I was nervous. Did I have enough lavender for the necessary four stripes, three narrow, one broad? Had I saved enough cotton-candy pink? I felt strongly the obligation—Josephine had shown herself willing to tolerate mixed colors, stripes of different widths, and even dangling ornamentation—but I knew that one stripe too few would always bother her.

And as it turned out, I was running out of cotton-candy pink. Very late one night, I found myself on the Internet, desperately trying to order more Plush yarn. And oh, woe, there were two different pinks—and even when I put my bleary eyes right up to the screen, I couldn't tell from the picture which was which. I ordered a skein of each. And there I was, stalled in the home stretch, in the middle of my wide pink stripe, which would have to be followed by those three little tiny pink stripes, alternating with white stripes.

My mail-order yarn arrived. And God be praised, one of the pinks was the right pink. A different dye lot, of course, but you would hardly notice that among the varied colors and the novelty squiggle. Out of the wide pink stripe, into the white stripe and then the lavender stripe, and then that rapid alternation of narrow pink and narrow white. We were truly galloping toward the end here, pausing every row or two to count the rows on the starting side again, absolutely determined to match those stripes precisely.

Well, I finished the shawl. And I could fold it exactly in half along my marked mother mirror row, and match the two sides stripe for stripe. I thought back to invertebrate biology, which I loved back in college and in graduate school, and about how much attention we had paid to the different kinds of symmetry—most symmetrical organisms are like my shawl, bilaterally symmetrical around a central mirror plane, but there are also echinoderms, like the starfish, which have a more complex radial symmetry. It all goes back to the development of the embryo—cells can line up and cleave and divide around a plane of symmetry, shaping the developing organism. These ideas seemed somehow very profound to me, late at night, as I triumphantly concluded my shawl with a seed stitch lavender border, matching it row for row to the four rows of seed stitch with which I had begun, back with my original single ball of yarn.

Embryology, the development of the organism, mothers, daughters, pattern, randomness—it all somehow worked into the desire to create something soft and warm and comforting. But it is always more complicated than it starts out to be—I knitted in my own randomness, and my own poor planning, didn't I, and I attempted to teach my daughter some lessons about experimenting and playing games with color. But I also listened to her, and I hoped that she would every now and then wrap herself in this thing, this shawl, this mother garment, in the privacy of her own room—I knew better than to think she would wear it out of the house. I pictured her deciding one chilly night to wrap herself up in the shawl, I pictured her unfolding it—naturally, she keeps her clothing neatly folded and put away; naturally, I keep my own garments randomly piled on chairs. And perhaps she would pause with the shawl still folded precisely in half to acknowledge the complex intentions that went into it—and most of all, to admire the precise symmetrical matchup of stripe for stripe, color for color of the two symmetrical halves on either side of that mother mirror row.

Shawl

Only a maniac would follow these instructions precisely; these are my best guesses, working backward, at the colors I used and the number of rows per stripe, but for heaven's sake, mix it up a little bit!

This shawl is worked in stockinette stitch with a seed stitch border of 4 rows on each end, and 5 stitches on each side to keep it from curling.

MATERIALS

YARN: A combination of yarns in complementary colors—I used pinks, purples, white, all in soft, fuzzy textures—I used mostly Berroco Plush and Chinchilla—and a complimentary shade of novelty yarn for accent—I used Squiggle in pink.

NEEDLES: Whatever size allows you to work comfortably and somewhat loosely with those main fuzzy yarns—I used 10½ circular needles, which were convenient as the shawl got bigger.

DIRECTIONS

KNITTING: Cast on (I think I used plain old e-loop cast-on) an uneven number of stitches—I used 61.

5 rows border, * K1, P1 * repeat to end of row, K1.

Knit body of shawl in stockinette stitch with seed stitch border (can place marker 5 stitches from each side if desired):

- Row 1 and all odd rows: K1, P1, K1, P1, knit to 4 stitches from end P1, K1, P1, K1.

(continued on page 222)

- Row 2 and all even rows: K1, P1, K1, P1, K1, purl to 5 stitches from end, K1, P1, K1, P1, K1.

STRIPE PATTERN I USED (APPROXIMATE)

- With Plush yarn: Lavender border and 17 rows; 2 rows pink; 2 rows white; 3 rows pink; 2 rows white; 2 rows pink; 5 rows lavender; 4 rows white, 9 rows pink

- White Chinchilla and Squiggle together: 2 rows, then with lavender Plush alone, 5 rows; white Chinchilla and Squiggle together 8 rows; lavender alone, 6 rows

- White Plush and Squiggle together: 13 rows

- Dark purple Chinchilla and Squiggle: 13 rows

- For perfect symmetry, now repeat backward, starting with 13 rows of white Plush and Squiggle together, 6 rows lavender alone, 8 rows white Chinchilla and Squiggle held together—continue working backward with symmetrical stripes, ending with 17 rows of lavender—and then 5 rows border

- 5 rows border: * K1 P1 * repeat to end of row, K1

Bind off.

Sheila: Just because a person doesn't happen to knit doesn't mean she has to be left out of the conversation. I think it's amazing that Perri can knit. I think it's more amazing that her brother David, the child of parents who struggled to pass the required gym course in college, is an athlete. I think it's amazing that their sister Judy—born and bred among monotones—has a sweet voice and sings professionally.

Look, I can't explain where they come from, these gifts and talents, even these inclinations and ambitions.

Perri is the daughter and, on my side, the granddaughter, of women who could do no skilled handiwork at all, even back in the days when such skills were expected. Perri knits and writes about knitting and wants to knit things for me. Isn't this backward, knitting for grandma instead of grandma knitting? How did this happen?

I always greatly admired beautiful handiwork and coveted the various skills, but I grew up to be what you might call a Shakespearian knitter, which doesn't count. I refer, of course, to the line, "Sleep that knits up the ravell'd sleave of care . . ." That is, I'm a terrific sleeper but a terrible knitter. And yes, I've tried. In early adolescence, when all the girls in Williamsburg went from what we called "horse reins," long woolen chains hooked on spools, to knitting and crocheting, I gamely attempted it, but it quickly became apparent that any wool I touched turned to knots. I lost my neighborhood boyfriend after I knitted him a scarf.

My mother could not knit or crochet; she said she had never been "handy." Actually, we had several pretty cross-stitched holiday table-cloths from her trousseau—I remember an especially lovely pale green linen one—so once upon a time, Mama had known how to do em-broidery, but that was gone, left behind in her frivolous novel-reading days. She could sew—that is, she could mend torn garments—and I can do that as well, but neither she nor I could ever do much creatively with our hands. My sister, more mindful than I of her maternal obligations, did manage to produce a few nice small baby sweaters, when her children were young. After that first scarf, I never completed anything. In fact, I gave up; I recognized ineptitude.

Perri's other grandmother, my mother-in-law, taught Perri to knit. Perri was Grandma Mimi's first grandchild, and Grandma Mimi was a patient, humorous teacher, proud of her pupil's progress and gener-ous with her praise. When Perri was young, she would sit on the couch and knit while Mort read aloud. Now she knits on trips—riding in the car, riding on the train, riding in the taxi. She says she en-joys it, and I suppose she does. But she didn't get it from me or my side of the family. I wonder if one day I will have a female descendant who bugles. It's a rare skill for females, so I certainly hope so. A perfect reveille is a wonderful thing.

Perri: I wanted to knit something for my mother. I wanted to make her something a little bit complicated and a little bit fancy. I know she has only one neck for scarves, and only one torso for vests and sweaters, but I felt her wardrobe could be expanded. I wanted to knit her a tangible work of devotion and an insidious piece of luxury goods.

PART II.
How to Knit Your Mother a Vest and Win a World Championship: A Twelve-Step Program

STEP ONE: *Take your mother to a high-end yarn store.* (Well, actually, it was that knitting conference in Atlantic City, and there was a huge yarn market set up in the exhibition hall. I wandered from stall to stall, buying yarn for one future project after another, shawls I'm going to knit someday, kimono jackets—the colors called to me from either side of the aisle; the textures were there to be fingered and rubbed and sniffed. I was giddy with colors and drunk on yarn; I could have knit a blanket to wrap around the world, it seemed to me. And my mother kept me company, wandering bemused past mohairs and Icelandic wools and acrylics and silk blends and cottons and cashmeres, past mass-produced balls and hand-painted skeins and ceramic buttons and quilted knitting bags. And it all tempted her not at all. She admired the colors, but somewhat abstractly, from a distance, like a confirmed skyscraper dweller at a garden show: Very pretty things you have here, to be sure, but why on Earth would I ever want to buy any? What would I do with them if I had them?) Feel a desperate desire to buy expensive, beautiful yarn, in large quantities, and tell your mother that your fondest wish is to knit something—anything—for *her.* And of course she'll say, "Don't go to any trouble." And of course she'll say, "But I already have so many clothes." And of course she'll say, "But where would I wear it?" But press her and press her, and finally she might allow, rather hesitantly, that she would like a warm vest since she is often cold.

STEP TWO: *Make her select the style and pattern she prefers.* A vest! Jump on top of it right away. Absolutely, a vest it is, and a vest it shall be. The perfect vest. Point out vests left and right, display samples, homemade models proudly worn around the exhibit hall by accomplished knitters of every shape and size. Stockinette, garter stitch, cabled, basketweave, seed stitch, Fair Isle, lacework—what does she prefer? Button-down or pullover? Round-necked, V-necked, crew-necked, shawl-collared? (My mother tried to retreat—she didn't really need a vest, she said. She couldn't possibly choose. She couldn't see well enough to choose. Whatever I wanted, whatever I thought would be best, that would be fine with her. Something simple. Something cheap. Something warm. I acted just a little bit hurt; here I was, eager to devote hours and hours to her vest, and she couldn't even take the time to decide whether it should button down the front or pull over the head! She apologized profusely and reminded me that she didn't really *need* a vest in the first place. She peered at the various vests I indicated. Okay, she said, something button-down, something with a little texture to it, nothing too hard to knit. We saw a vest hanging on the wall of one of the exhibit booths—a simple button-down pattern, no fancy collar, no fancy two-color knitting. My mother pointed at it: something just like that, she said.)

STEP THREE: *Make her choose the yarn.* Ask her whether she wants the vest to be a solid color or to be variegated. Explain to her what *variegated* means—yarn that has been dyed so that one skein contains many different colors. Ask her how warm she would like the vest to be—does she want it thick or thin? Ask her if she has preferences about the material itself—let the words *lambswool, chenille, cashmere, mohair, alpaca, microfiber, one-ply, two-ply* come cascading off your tongue. Get a little more technical: *sport weight, worsted weight, bulky weight.* Your mother will look longingly at the one particular vest that originally attracted her attention. "Just like that," she'll say. "Whatever yarn that is, that's what I want." (In fact, my mother had chosen a vest made out of a particularly beautiful hand-dyed variegated wool, made by a company called Wool in the Woods. The woman in charge of the booth was one of the women who runs the company, Anita Tosten, and she took charge of us efficiently. The wool we wanted was called Bobcat, she said, and I would need two slightly different colors to work with. Or rather, since each "color" was actually multicolored, I would need two slightly different color combinations. She picked out a whole set of them, and together we backed my mother against the wall and made her choose.)

Buy the yarn and the pattern book, *Knitting with Hand-Dyed Yarns* by Missy Burns, Stephanie Blaydes Kaisler, and Anita Tosten. As the chosen hand-dyed yarn is being rung up, your mother will suggest that maybe, in the end, it would be better to find a cheaper, mass-produced wool. She will point out that she really doesn't need anything fancy. Remind her that you will be spending hours and hours of your valuable time with this wool running through your fingers, and that you would be grateful if she would allow you the small luxury of beautiful hand-dyed wool to work with. She will agree, but still look troubled: It's okay for you to want to work with fancy yarn, but not for her to wear it. Realize that your mother is still mentally stuck back in the time of World War II, when knitting your soldier a sweater was the patriotic and economical thing to do; she thinks knitting a sweater should be cheaper than buying a sweater, and when you consider what she is willing to spend on a sweater for herself, that gives you a total budget for yarn of maybe eight dollars. Finish buying the yarn and get the hell out of there before she realizes how much it actually cost. Hum patriotic songs under your breath as you clutch the bag of yarn and hustle her away.

STEP FOUR: *Worry about the gauge.* The book says that to get the vest to come out the right size, you should be knitting with whatever size needle makes the stitches come out so that 14 stitches equals 4 inches.

Knit a little square of fabric with size 10½ needles and worry that the stitches are just slightly too small. Knit another little swatch with size 11 needles, and decide that these stitches are just slightly too big. Feel a little like Goldilocks. Agonize over this for a while. Argue with yourself that it's always better to err on the side of slightly bigger, slightly looser. Acknowledge that you prefer the tighter look of the fabric knit with the smaller needles. Talk yourself into working with the smaller needles, knowing that you will worry the whole time that the vest will come out too small.

STEP FIVE: *Knit the back.* Wait for a special occasion. Carry the balls of yarn and the needles and the pattern book around with you. Sit down with an old friend to watch game seven of the 2004 American League Championship Series between the Red Sox and the Yankees and realize you are too nervous to watch the game without knitting. Pull out your two different balls of Bobcat and cast on. This vest is worked in a 3-by-3 pattern—knit 3, purl 3. Realize, in the true superstitious spirit of baseball, that those knit 3 purl 3 repeats are essential in helping the Red Sox pitchers strike out the Yankee batters. Knit right through the bottoms of the innings when the Yankees are up, muttering to yourself, "One-two-three out, one-two-three out." Put the knitting down and watch when the Red Sox come up to bat.

(And after the Red Sox won the ALCS and went on to play St. Louis in the World Series, it was perfectly clear to me that I had to keep knitting my mother's vest while watching the games, and that if I didn't, and the Red Sox pitchers had trouble getting batters out, Boston would lose the World Series, and it would be all my fault. I knew my mother wouldn't want to see that happen; she may live in New York, but she comes of Brooklyn Dodgers stock, so she hates the Yankees and loathes George Steinbrenner. Furthermore, as the mother and grandmother of fanatic Red Sox fans, she was with us all the way. My feelings of profound responsibility about working on the vest fit perfectly with the heavy superstitious mood hanging over Boston, as we waited and watched, dreaming of our first World Series championship since 1918. People followed their good-luck rituals religiously, wearing their lucky caps—or shirts—or underwear—for game after game, sitting in their good-luck spots, repeating their good-luck mantras. A little ritualized knitting didn't seem particularly out of line. And what can I say? Once I started knitting my mother's 3-by-3 vest during the other team's half of the inning, the Red Sox won every game: They beat the Yankees in game seven and went on to win the World Series in four games. I don't want to take all the credit, but I certainly did my bit.)

STEP SIX: *Knit the two front panels.* Follow the pattern's advice to knit these simultaneously, right front and left front growing together on your needles. Since you are also following the pattern's advice to alternate your two colorways every two rows, this will leave you with four different balls of yarn, two for each front panel, hanging off your work. This will provide all kinds of tangle possibilities. Make the front panels a little too narrow. Worry while you're knitting the panels that the vest is going to be too small and too tight.

STEP SEVEN: *Knit two extra side panels.* Measure your mother. Try to convince yourself that the nice broad back plus the two puny front panels will go around her perfectly. Give it up and decide to improvise two little strips to go at the sides under her arms and enlarge the circumference. Give up as well (maybe you're getting tired) on alternating the two different yarns. As a result, let the two side strips be a little different in tone and shading from the back and front panels. Convince yourself that this will only make the vest more interesting, more beautiful, more distinctive. Remind yourself that anyway, your mother doesn't see very well.

STEP EIGHT: *Sew everything together.* By now, baseball season will be long gone. Knit the shoulder seams together. Sew the two side panel strips to the back. Sew the two front panels to the side panels.

STEP NINE: *Pick up stitches and make the borders at the front, neck, and armholes.* Try to keep the two sides even—same number of stitches at each armhole. Fail to get this precisely right, but decide it looks even enough. Make nice wide border strips in the front, to give your mother a couple of extra inches even beyond the side strips. It's getting on toward spring now; begin to feel a little anxious that by the time this vest is finished, the weather will be too hot for your mother to wear it at all. Feel very guilty about this.

STEP TEN: *Sew on the buttons.* Use a set of fused-glass buttons that you bought a couple of months ago and have been carrying around ever since, tucked into the plastic bag with the balls of Bobcat yarn and the increasingly crumpled photocopy of the pattern. Actually, it's a Boston Red Sox plastic bag that you happened to have had way back at the beginning, because you had loyally bought a couple of Red Sox T-shirts; you stored the sweater in it on that first memorable game seven night, and of course, you couldn't ever change the bag after that. A lucky plastic bag is a lucky plastic bag.

Resolve not to tell your mother, ever, that the buttons for her sweater cost thirty-something dollars. Take a personal satisfaction in their deep color and their rich beauty—as if you are tricking your mother into wearing jewelry.

STEP ELEVEN: *Work in the ends.* Do this with a crochet hook on a long drive to Brattleboro, Vermont, with a good friend. Let your friend do all the driving, hunker down in the passenger seat, and painstakingly work in one end after another, reminding yourself that the vest needs to be finished soon because the warm weather is coming. Get the vest finished as you're pulling into Brattleboro and the sun is setting; roll it up and stuff it back into its lucky plastic bag with a sense of triumph, and try to work the stiffness out of your shoulders.

STEP TWELVE: *Give it to her.* Invite your mother to come meet you at a medical conference in Washington, D.C. Tell her you'll have a fancy hotel room she can stay in. Point out to her that you can get some work done on your book together. Tell her she needs to see the National World War II Memorial, and the Franklin Delano Roosevelt Memorial. Pack up the vest and put it in your suitcase. Fly to Washington, D.C. Take a taxi to the hotel. Check in. Tell the woman at the desk that your mother will be joining you later and should get a key to the room but that you're not exactly sure when she's coming, because she's taking the Greyhound bus from New York City, but she doesn't know which bus. Go off to the first day of your conference.

Call the hotel reception desk once or twice during the afternoon to ask if your mother has checked in. Late in the afternoon, return to your hotel room to change into more comfortable clothes. Turn the air-conditioning up. Get a call from the desk, which is now completely on alert for your mother: She's here! They're sending her right up! Wait for her knock, greet her, hug her. Agree that it's pretty chilly in the hotel room—and in Washington in general. Offer her the vest to help her keep warm. Help her put it on. Admire it. Admire the knitting. Admire the colors in the yarn. Admire the buttons. Find yourself unable to resist telling her, "Those are some fancy buttons, Mom. They cost more than thirty dollars!"

Walk proudly beside your mother as she wears the vest to visit the World War II Memorial on the Mall in the afternoon. In the evening, take her to see the FDR Memorial, which reflects the years of her childhood and the four terms of the man she still thinks of as *her* president. Note the other tourists who are also from her generation—they stand out among the school groups and young families who crowd the memorial, even after dark. The older people are stepping carefully and leaning in close to read the many inscriptions by the light provided. Take your mother's arm. Read the inscriptions aloud to her when the light is too dim for her. Let her tell you that the vest is just exactly what she needed to keep her warm.

Vest

The most important instructions I can give you here are to go on out and buy the book *Knitting with Hand-Dyed Yarns*. I will try to give you honest instructions for what I did, but if you want different sizes or really expert directions, go with the original! The vest I made was designed to fit a bust size of 40 inches and a length of 21½ inches.

MATERIALS

YARN: 2 skeins of Wool in the Woods Bobcat (100% wool; 200 yards/183 meters per skein) in 1 variegated colorway; 2 skeins in a contrasting complementary colorway.

NEEDLE: 10½ needles or size required to obtain gauge of 14 stitches to 4 inches in pattern stitch—or maybe just a tiny bit less (I think mine was really 15 stitches to 4 inches, if I'm being honest).

NOTIONS: Nice-looking buttons—the original pattern calls for 7, but I used 6

MISCELLANEOUS: Stitch holders, markers

DIRECTIONS

Pattern stitch—3-by-3 over multiple of 6 + 3 stitches. All rows: * K3, P3; repeat from * to last 3 stitches, K3. Alternate the two different yarns, working 2 rows with one, then 2 rows with the other throughout.

(continued on page 232)

BACK: Cast on 69 stitches, work pattern stitch, changing yarns every two rows, until back measures 12 inches (though I always go a tiny bit longer than the pattern says to, so I probably went to about 12½ inches).

ARMHOLE SHAPING: Keep the pattern going—bind off 3 stitches at each side once—63 stitches. Bind off 2 stitches at each side once—59 stitches. Decrease 1 stitch at each side every other row 4 times, for a total of 8 decreases—51 stitches. Keep working straight until the back measures 20½ inches.

NOTE: The first bind-off of 3 stitches on each side will mean starting each row P3, K3, but otherwise, leave the pattern intact; after that you will have to be aware of the pattern because rows will not necessarily begin with a multiple of 3. Keep the pattern intact!

ONE OTHER NOTE: Just for fun, I actually varied the pattern and put a 5-by-5 basketweave inset in the middle of the back; very easy to do in that I just took the 5 central 3-by-3 repetitions and made them into 3-stitch blocks for a basketweave, purling on top of knitting and knitting on top of purling over that section for 4 rows, then reversing the stitch so that each stockinette block is topped by a reverse stockinette block for the next 4 rows—and I repeated this till I had a little inset square 5 blocks wide by 5 blocks high. It doesn't stand out in high contrast, but it gives the back some extra textural interest. . . .

NECK SHAPING: Continuing to keep the pattern continuous, work 16 stitches; place the next 19 on a holder. Tie on a second ball of yarn and work the last 16 stitches, then work both sides at once, and bind off 2 stitches at each neck edge once.

You now have 14 stitches on each side. Keep knitting both sides in pattern stitch until the back measures 21½ inches. Then put the two sets of shoulder stitches on holders.

FRONTS: WORK BOTH PIECES AT ONCE: The directions say to cast on 35 stitches for each side and work in the pattern sequence, switching colors every 2 rows as you did in the back, *but* since this is not a multiple of 6 + 3, you will have to make an adjustment to the pattern at the beginning and end of each row. If you want to do this, consult the book and do it properly; I made the executive decision to decrease the two fronts to 33 stitches each, which allowed me to go on knitting mindlessly in pattern stitch—but led directly to the skimpyness of the front panels and my subsequent decision to add in side patterns.

In either case, work the front panels till they reach the same measurement of the back when you started armhole shaping—12 or 12½ inches. Then, keeping continuity of the pattern stitch (and watching out, as above, for rows where you will no longer start with 3 stitches, repeat the armhole shaping as for the back, so you have 24 stitches on a side. Keep working until the sides measure 18½ inches. Then, keeping the pattern going, bind off 4 stitches at each neck edge once, then bind off 3 stitches at each neck edge once, then bind off 2 stitches at each neck edge once. Each side is now 15 stitches. Decrease 1 stitch every other row 3 times—each side is now 12 stitches. Work until the fronts measure 21½ inches (or are exactly equal to the back). Place shoulder stitches on holder.

OPTIONAL SIDE PANELS: If the total circumference of the vest now seems a little too snug (because of dumb executive decisions you made about gauge or about making the fronts with

(continued on page 234)

fewer stitches than the original directions said or just because the intended wearer has gained a little weight), consider making side panels: Make 2 at once, and use only 1 of the 2 complimentary yarns. Cast on 9 stitches for each panel and work in pattern (K3, P3, K3 all rows; repeat to end) until strips measure same as distance to armholes. Place stitches on holders.

FINISHING: Knit shoulder seams together, using 3-needle bind-off.

ARMHOLE BANDS: With the same yarn used to make the side panels, pick up and knit 1 stitch in each garter-stitch ridge, knit the 9 stitches off the holder into the band, knitting 2 together at each end of the strip (K2TOG, K 5, K2TOG), join into a circle, and knit for at least 3 rows. The original pattern calls for 3 rows, all knitting, but I made the bands wider, and since I was doing this on a circular needle and I liked the garter-stitch look, I actually knit 1 round, purled the next, knit the next, purled the next, and then did the bind-off in knit. Bind off loosely in knit.

NECK BAND: With the same color used for the armhole band, begin at R neck edge. Pick up 18 stitches to shoulder seam, pick up 5 to back holder, pick up the 19 stitches on the holder, pick up 5 to the shoulder seam, and pick up 18 stitches to the left front edge. Knit at least 3 rows. Again, I wanted a slightly wider band, so I did 4 or 5. Bind off loosely in knit.

RIGHT FRONT BAND: Mark for buttonholes, starting 1 inch from neck edge, with bottom button 15 inches from neck edge and other markers evenly spaced, depending on how many buttons you're using. With your band yarn, pick up

1 stitch in each garter-stitch row, knit 2 rows, then make but-tonholes: Knit the row; bind off 2 stitches at each buttonhole marker. Next row, knit, cast on 2 stitches over the bound-off stitches. Next row, knit. Bind off loosely in knit.

LEFT FRONT BAND: Pick up same number of stitches, 1 in each garter-stitch row. Knit at least 5 rows. If you're still anxious about the circumference of the vest, add another couple of knit rows. Bind off loosely in knit. Sew the buttons to the left front band. Work in the ends.

Give it to your mother.

PART SEVEN

*Take Your Old
Ma to India*

CHAPTER TWENTY-FOUR

Air India's Poster Girl

Sheila: In December 2004, I was visiting Perri, and I noticed a pile of colorful guidebooks to India—*Lonely Planet, Frommer's, Fodor's*—had appeared on the Cambridge living-room floor that is Perri's vast bookshelf. On this same visit, I began to hear certain mutterings about Perri's need to travel during winter break in January—one short month away.

Constantly restless, my elder daughter is always ready to take off somewhere—Parma, Tokyo, Athens, Venice, Dubrovnik—so it wasn't hard for me to deduce that something big was afoot. I never suspected that the big thing afoot might be me. Or that the foot (both feet, in fact) would have to be bare most of the time. I understand that according to certain religions, shoes profane holy sites, where the soul is nurtured, but I am a woman with a rubbery old soul and extremely tender soles.

Ah, what one is asked to do for one's children.

So anyway, when she actually put it to me: "Mama, let's go back to India," I was not surprised by the destination. But I was absolutely staggered by the projected dramatis personae. I'd never dreamed that she would think of taking me along.

I was, after all, past my seventy-seventh birthday. For decades I have been legally blind, able to see only small objects up close (under my nose) and large things limned in the distance. Glaucoma and macular degeneration, in lethal combination, have viciously burrowed away at my vision. Who in her right mind invites such a person to go sightseeing?

Each morning, as I don my earrings, I also pop in my hearing aids. My breakfasts are all prefaced by handfuls of pills, and my waking hours end with similar doses. I hate them all, except for my twilight medication, which, my favorite doctor assured me, was essential for my heart, blood vessels, and memory: a glass of red wine or a gin and tonic.

All in all, I was hardly the poster girl for an Air India ad.

"Think about it, Mom: India!" Perri's enthusiasm makes her an excellent pediatrician. But it also makes her dangerous. She offers the unlikely because she actually believes it is possible. "If you're up to it," she urged, "I'd love to go with you."

Thinking about it actually made me weep. We were not strangers to India, having lived for a year in West Bengal, in 1963–1964, while Mort studied a small rural village as it became industrialized. That year in India was a major event in our lives. In preparation, Mort and I had studied Bengali till we could speak fluently as well as read and write. The two of us had learned to love the language. We'd been so childishly proud that we could read the work of the great Bengali poet Rabindranath Tagore in its original language.

So we lived in a small town a couple of hours outside Calcutta. Perri, then five, pigtailed and clad in a white uniform, attended the Loreto Convent, while David, three, in navy blue short pants and checked shirt, went to the Assemblies of God Mission School. I remembered my New York Jewish son coming home to announce proudly he'd learned a hymn, and then singing the words he thought he had heard:

Jesus loves me, this I know
Because the Bible tells me so.
He will wash away my skin,
Let his little brother come in . . .

The Indian year had been a tumultuous, wonderful time. Like the year in Trinidad, it was a landmark in our domestic history, a touchstone for memories and family legends. In 1978, Mort's book *From Field to Factory: Community Structure and Industrialization in West Bengal* appeared. I also gathered material during that year, and I published two novels set in India, *Bahadur Means Hero* (1969) and *A Perpetual Surprise* (1981).

My husband's interest in India and Indian religions was permanent. We'd returned to travel through India as tourists in 1983. Later, Mort became interested in Sai Baba, a Hindu guru who claims to be God and works miracles for his followers, materializing gold objects before their eyes or creating ash, which drips from his fingertips. We had attended the meetings of his followers in New York and Trinidad, and Mort's book about him, *Singing with Sai Baba: The Politics of Revitalization in Trinidad,* appeared in 1991.

But all of that had happened long ago, and it had happened because I married an anthropologist. Mort had been the traveler, the scholar whose questing mind and endless curiosity had moved us about wonderfully. An anthropologist gets paid for wandering the earth and studying its cultures. I was never an initiator of journeys, but I was always willing to go anywhere—to Trinidad and the various Caribbean islands, to Japan, to China, to Israel, to Egypt, to Indonesia, to much of Europe, and to Morocco.

Mort brought India into our lives. Fascinated by Indian culture and religions, he'd immersed himself in Indic studies. When he died suddenly in 2001, his death deprived me of not only a beloved husband but also of a best friend, an invaluable literary editor and critic and the pilgrim who had blithely and intrepidly led me afar to *seken straunge strondes.* I felt lucky to have had such a rich and fulfilled life. Left alone, I had no desire to travel anywhere.

"What do you say, Mama? Are you up to it? After all, you prowl all over Manhattan at any hour. Why not India? In January, it's warm and lovely."

"Perr, Papa's gone. It's a different India without him. Besides, I'm too old. I can't see. I can't hear. Why would anyone want to travel with me?"

"I know it's an irrational impulse," she said, with her usual sympathy, "but I do. I want to travel with you. It won't be the same without Papa," she agreed, "but it will be India. All that you remember is there; all that you loved is still there." She went on to talk about Delhi, old and New. She said she wanted very much to see Calcutta, where she had last been as a child of five, and she opened the guidebooks to read to me about the glorious green Maidān and the bustling thoroughfare of Chowringhee for shopping. And then there was so much more we had neither of us ever seen. She'd already assembled a list of great eating places in India from various gourmet-travelers' accounts. She was amazingly well informed. India had totally invaded her imagination.

Perri: I want to make it clear that I was by no means sure we were really going to do this. It was my idea to go to India, but it was kind of an idle idea. I had traveled with my mother to Trinidad, and it had worked out—but Trinidad is a Caribbean vacation, a single flight south from John F. Kennedy International Airport. I suggested India mostly because these days, it's hard to get my mother to express much interest in travel, in seeing new places, or even in returning to places she's touristed. Suggest a museum and she's likely to remind me that she doesn't see very well. Suggest Paris or London or Rome and she'll shrug and say, "But I've been there." Suggest someplace she's never been, and she'll shrug again, as if to say, "If I was never interested enough to go before, why should I bother going now?" In some ways, I think it's part of a larger lethargy that she's struggled with ever since my father died, part of a larger, harder, what's-the-use-of-anything question.

And yet, and yet . . . she zips back and forth between New York and Boston on the Greyhound bus. If you give her a good maternal pretext (the premiere of my brother's movie in LA—or a conference I was hosting in San Francisco), she'll happily hop on a transcontinental flight. She bopped around Trinidad and Tobago with me quite contentedly (except for getting seasick on the glass-bottomed boat). So I suggested India, kind of the next step after Trinidad. It was the other exotic field trip that my parents took; they carted my brother and me off to a small town in West Bengal in 1963, and the four of us lived there for a year. I was five and David was three, and I think I remember India pretty well—but my memories and perceptions are those of a five-year-old. India was where I learned to read. India was where I was when JFK got shot—a subject I recycled over and over in those essays we had to write every year in elementary school. I was in school at the Loreto Convent in Asansol, India, where the missionary Irish nuns mourned his death as a Catholic—and Irish—tragedy, and I enjoyed a brief period of celebrity as the first—and only—American mourner. India was a whole variety of sights and sounds and smells and tastes; India was rules of behavior at mealtimes (eat with your right hand only) and religious festivals. After we came back, I read lots of stories about India, and sometimes I felt a special connection—I read "Rikki-Tikki-Tavi," for example—and became so retrospectively terrified about the possibilities of vengeful poisonous snakes that I had nightmares for weeks about cobras and kraits . . . from my bed in a New York City apartment.

I knew India had a special place in my mother's mental geography—as it does in mine. I knew she was still committed to the idea that India was interesting—or, perhaps, that she was still interested in the places she had lived long ago. I also knew, of course, that India is a challenging place to travel—definitely in the advanced traveler's category. I had been back once myself, in 1986, to spend a month of my medical school clinical rotations in a Delhi hospital, a chance to pursue my interest in infectious diseases and get a good look at everything from leprosy to tuberculous meningitis.

So I suggested it to my mother. How about a couple of weeks in India in January? And I saw the idea take hold. She came up with places in India she wanted to go. She blocked out the time. She sounded excited.

Sheila: That conversation was only the first of many as Perri spun her wondrous web. I was soon caught up in those gossamer strands of possibility. I began to venture a suggestion or two—just as if I really thought we might be going. "Could we go to Puttaparthi and see the God Incarnate?" I wondered. Mort was fascinated by Sai Baba and his followers and had attended many worship ceremonies, but he had never actually seen the great man himself.

"Why not?" Perri embraced the idea. "Then, Mama—you're up to it? Wonderful! Leave everything to me. I'm going to book it all on the Internet!" And just like that, she did.

The only thing she forgot was that we would need visas. And when she remembered, a week before departure, she panicked and I despaired. She was flagellating herself for her poor planning, and I was remembering our tangles with Indian bureaucracy in the past. In 1963, Mort's research had been delayed three months by a customs officer's refusal to release our tape recorder because he suspected we were importing it to sell illegally. A hundred-dollar machine! And then at the end of that year, just before our departure, we were threatened with detention because we hadn't filed Indian income tax papers— even though we'd had absolutely no income in India. For weeks, the tax official kept inviting us back to tea to discuss our "tax problem." Only a last-minute letter from a "big man" at the Ford Foundation secured our departure. Time—and clerical complexity—had impressed me as part of India's infinite mystery.

Things weren't the same anymore, apparently. The Indian consulate, in this Internet age, had downloadable visa applications posted on their Web site. Perri downloaded them and faxed me one. Oh, glorious machines! We immediately filled out the forms and hastened to take photos, execrable pictures in which we looked like ax murderers. Who cared?

Luckily, I lived in exactly the right city for the next step. In the early morning, first thing, the heavy snowstorm notwithstanding, I set forth to deliver our vital documents to the consulate office on East 64th Street.

It was, even at that early hour, exceedingly crowded. The guard at the door somehow found me a vacant chair, one of only three in the entire room. "Sit here till your turn, Ma," he advised. "I will call you."

Sweet. The title was an affectionate one in deference to my white hair.

After he signaled and I delivered the applications, he cautioned me. "Come back promptly at three forty-five, this afternoon. Passports are given out between three forty-five and five o'clock. Not later, Ma."

I was so impressed by his specificity, I returned in very good time— along with the hundreds of other morning applicants. We then all stood shivering together on line on East 64th Street until we were herded into the small anteroom that could not possibly contain us all. I was part of a largely Indian crowd, babies, old women, restless young people, all bundled up in damp winter coats and now packed into this overheated New York office. There were no chairs in sight. There were no explanations. The guard was terribly busy doing nothing. *I'll just catch his eye and ask him what's happening*, I resolved. *He'll remember me—Ma.* But since the morning, he had mastered the art of looking nowhere, and his eye was not to be caught. Perhaps he was embarrassed by the situation.

It was evident that the passports were not ready. So we stood waiting—squeezed together like livestock in a pen—for almost two hours. In time, some derisive grumbling began, then increased among the waiting men. The women remained silent, but the men were guessing what might have happened: the clerks had fallen asleep in there; they were having their tea; they'd lost the only pen, and so on. Slowly the tone turned sullen, then angry. People jostled for more space, and now and then someone would give up loudly and push his way out.

I began to fear the situation might turn ugly. It was very crowded, and it would be impossible to get out if there were trouble. The genius of the Internet and the fax machine had been vanquished by Indian bureaucracy. All we needed was a clue as to what was happening, but there was none.

Disheartened and weary, I considered giving up and leaving—if, indeed, I could edge my way out. I thought about Indian bureaucracy— and then, with real doubts, about how hard the trip to India might be. What was I doing, going to a country that couldn't even keep its promises about giving out visas? The whole trip seemed like a burden and a challenge, and all I could imagine were dangers and bureaucratic screwups and angry crowds. But Perri was counting on me. I had talked her out of travel insurance. We didn't need it. We were healthy; we'd go and come back on time. We'd never missed a plane. But without visas, we were going nowhere. Inhaling so I was skinnier and required less room, I stayed put.

At ten past five, the windows opened and the passports materialized. Immediately, people relaxed and began to joke. "You thought you wouldn't get one, eh, Ma?" the guard chided me, as I moved past him. "You looked so angry, I said to myself, 'Ma is vexed too much.' " He laughed heartily. What a good joke!

I held my tongue. I knew what was important: I was clutching the passports, the visas were there, and we were on our way to India!

CHAPTER TWENTY-FIVE

Oy, Calcutta!

Perri: I don't think I remember Calcutta from 1963. I have strong memories of that year in India, but those memories date from our stay in a house in a town a few hours outside Calcutta, from my time at the Loreto Convent, from the year of daily life in India that took me from five years old to six years old. They are the memories that, while I was growing up, were reinforced over and over by various kinds of story-telling. There was that patented response I developed to where I was when JFK was shot. There were the family legends, like the time David was bitten by a stray dog, and had to get the whole series of rabies shots. There were the memories that attached to various souvenir items on my bedroom shelves—the plaster bust of Rabindranath Tagore, the Nobel Prize–winning Bengali poet, that I had been given on my sixth birthday; the graceful purple sari–clad dancing lady doll on her round wooden base. And then there was my hair, of course; Indian girls measured their beauty by their long, dark hair, parted in the middle and worn in two braids for little girls, one braid for older girls. In India, we had lived near a family with five young daughters, and in the mornings, they would line up, smallest to biggest, and each would braid the hair of the sister standing in front of her. I had absorbed this aesthetic and wanted only to have two long braids to my waist, though I knew my hair would never be anything more distinct than an unremarkable brown. Still, I refused to cut it, wore it parted in the middle and braided every day until seventh grade, when we moved to a suburb in New Jersey and I came up smack against a different and rigorous (and infinitely uglier) code of aesthetics. My school in New York City had been tolerant of all sorts of styles of hair and dress, partly because it was full of Columbia University families from all over the world. In New Jersey, girls made fun of my braids, and no one aspired to waist-length black hair. Eventually, in a foolish and futile attempt to meet New Jersey standards, I chopped off most of my hair. It didn't work, of course; I still didn't look right. And I regretted that lost long hair for years, which may help explain why I am now, all these decades later, still wearing my hair long, pinning it up every morning and braiding it back every night.

India definitely had marked me. It was so different from any memories that might have persisted from back-before-India. I remembered the India of 1963 in bright colors and dramatic stories—religious festivals with enormous painted statues of gods and goddesses worshipped and celebrated and then paraded through the streets to be dumped in the river . . . the trip to see the cave paintings at Ellora and Ajanta . . . blistering daily heat and torrential monsoons. Everyday life in India was full of excitement—the monkeys that would jump into the courtyard of our house to steal loaves of bread . . . the adventure of bouncing along dirt roads in the back of my father's Land Rover . . . even the ritual every evening of going to sleep under a tent of mosquito netting, with my mother ducking inside the tent with me, armed with a flashlight, to hunt down any mosquitos that might have breached the defenses.

But I had no strong memories of Calcutta. We had lived there for a month at the beginning of the trip, so I had been at my youngest. Whatever my impressions of Calcutta might have been, they had been covered over and buried deep by all the months in Asansol. I was curious to see Calcutta, but that had more to do with the city's reputation than with chasing down any particular memories or personal history. I knew I had attended something called the Free Jewish Girls School of Calcutta—but I had no memory of the place.

Even so, after my journey to Trinidad with my mother, I was not at all surprised that our time in Calcutta evolved into a search for the lost town of the early 1960s. I had booked us into the Fairlawn Hotel, a Calcutta guesthouse at which the sun has not yet quite set on the British Raj. You turn off a congested Calcutta street, with pavement-dwellers spread out on either side, with rickshaw wallahs resting and waiting between the shafts of their rickshaws—you turn into the driveway of the Fairlawn Hotel and find yourself in a green oasis of artificial vines, plastic fruits and flowers, and colored fairy lights. The hotel soldiers on with its traditions—the gong at mealtimes, the resolutely British colonial food, the white gloves and turbans on the servers, the upstairs lounge filled with British royal family bric-a-brac and clippings. Mama and I were installed in an upstairs room with two single beds and a bathroom with a hot-water geyser. When we came back down, we made the acquaintance of the proprietress, who was sitting—not to say holding court—out on the verandah. Sumptuously coiffed and carefully made up, Mrs. Violet Smith greeted us and efficiently turned us inside out to determine our business in Calcutta.

Sheila: I was anxious about Calcutta, a city I had both loved and feared. The Calcutta I remembered—the historic home of glorious Bengali art and music, of Bengali culture, the birthplace of Tagore—in 1963 had been crowded with homeless families living in Howrah Station and the surrounding streets, each cluster of kin living on a cloth spread on a small rectangle of pavement with its own invisible boundaries. You couldn't walk on those sidewalks of destitution.

Whenever traffic was halted for a red light, car windows were immediately curtained with hungry faces, mostly the wan faces of children or mothers holding up tiny babies, pleading. My own small children were frightened and curious. It was impossible to explain such poverty.

In that Calcutta, when I walked along a street, and particularly when I was in the markets, hordes of ragged children grasped my clothing and my legs and hung on begging, as they raised their clenched hands to their mouths to signify hunger.

"Chase the beggars," an Indian friend advised me sternly. "You must be firm. Chase them away."

"I can't," I pleaded.

"You can't live here otherwise," she warned me.

We had only stayed a month, and I'd left for rural Bengal with relief. Now, *Calcutta,* the colonial name, had been jettisoned and the original Indian name, *Kolkata,* restored. But had the city really changed? Of all the cities in the world, this was the city name that most strongly conjured up images and memories. I love cities; I am generally much more comfortable in cities than in the countryside. After all, I only really feel completely at home in New York. There are people who think New York is crowded or dirty or dangerous or overwhelming—and I don't know what they're talking about. But Calcutta had been too much for me when I was in my thirties. How would it welcome me in my seventies?

Perri, who with the Internet has the world at her fingertips, had this time booked us into the Fairlawn Hotel, an odd, historic landmark of the Raj. The hotel's dowager proprietor, Mrs. Violet Smith, an octogenarian, as perfectly turned out as a mannequin in Madame Tussaud's, sat near the front desk. In the impeccable accent of a bygone London she never knew, she sorted out the newcomers. Welcoming us, she was both loquacious and gracious, and she knew her city cold. She would tell me what was what.

I ticked off a list of old haunts I hoped to revisit.

The Maidān, that lovely park in the heart of the city with the Victoria Memorial, and its pony rides and other delights for children? Of course, it was readily available during daylight hours.

The Free Jewish Girls School—which actually charged fees and took boys—and had obligingly enrolled Perri and David during our first month in India? It still existed, a fine school, but all the students now were non-Jewish. In fact, there was but one single Jew left in the entire city! This last Jew in Kolkata was Mr. Nahoum, who owned the bakery in the market. We must look in on him, Mrs. Smith urged. He was in charge of the two great synagogues: empty now, but beautiful.

Mrs. Creet's guesthouse, the Bengal Chambers, on Park Street, where we had lived in 1963, in cool, dark, cavernous rooms? Alas, Mrs. Creet was dead. She had been a particular friend of Mrs. Smith's, for they were both children of Armenian immigrants. Though, Mrs. Smith reminded us immediately, she had, of course, married a British soldier. Mrs. Creet had gone out of business years before and sold the Bengal Chambers to Indians. "They ran it down," Mrs. Smith said mournfully, as she released us to go exploring.

Perri: Mrs. Smith seemed mildly interested, though not at all surprised, to hear that my mother had lived for a while in Calcutta. She talked at some length about her husband, mentioning several times that he had been a returned British soldier. He had passed away, and the children were all in England, except for her one daughter who helped run the hotel. She gestured at the various Indian hotel employees who were bustling back and forth. "They take care of me," she said. "If I were in England, I would be in a home, I know. But here, they take care of me." Back forty years ago, there had apparently been a whole set of Armenian Calcutta landladies, boardinghouse chatelaines, and it wasn't hard to picture them sitting together, calling to the servants for more tea. Mrs. Smith had been one, and another had been Mrs. Creet, proprietress of the Bengal Chambers boardinghouse. Now only Mrs. Smith was left.

And yes, the Jewish girls' school was still a going concern, and we would have to go and meet Mr. Nahoum, from the last Jewish family in Calcutta. He ran the family pastry shop in the Old Market—and I imagined him supplying the pastries to the busily gossiping set of Armenian boardinghouse landladies. Had Mrs. Creet, back in the 1960s, ever told the story of the American family of four, the anthropologist and his wife the writer, and their two little children, who were living in a room at the Bengal Chambers while they got ready to go live for a year somewhere in the countryside? Had she told my mother's famous story of how she had agreed to charge half-board for the children, for my brother David and me, and then been horrified at the quantities of food we consumed? Finally, apologetically, she told my parents that they would have to pay full board—she could not afford to feed us at reduced rates. And my parents, mystified themselves at our ravenous hunger, and at the way we were continuing to lose weight while stuffing ourselves at every meal, finally had us tested and discovered that we had both, in our first month in India, acquired interesting intestinal parasites. My poor parents—their own mental map of India must have been heavily annotated with rabid dogs and intestinal worms and malarial mosquitoes. We were eating vast quantities of Mrs. Creet's food, but most of it was not getting to us. Instead, she—and we—were feeding a passenger list of exotic microscopic worms. Now that I am a pediatric infectious diseases expert, I wish, of course, that my mother had kept more careful notes about those parasites—I'd love to know what I had. She mostly remembers that I had something and that they got rid of it—and ever since, unfortunately, everything I eat goes only to me.

Sheila: We found Mr. Nahoum at the cash register in the pastry shop in the Old Market. He sent us off by taxi with one of his employees to see the synagogues. We were caught in massive traffic, and then I felt how much the city was like it was long ago: a frenetic metropolis of crowds and incessant car horns, beggars, peddlers, and anarchic traffic complicated by the variety of vehicles. Besides the cars and trucks, there were bicycle rickshaws, motorcycle rickshaws, animal-drawn carts, human-drawn carts, small herds of goats and sheep and cows . . .

Suddenly, an elephant pulled up beside us at one red light. "What's he doing here?" I wondered aloud.

"Probably returning from a wedding," Mr. Nahoum's man guessed. "Some Bengali bridegrooms still like to arrive on the back of an elephant."

"I won't mention it in New York," I promised Perri. "What congestion it would cause in the Lincoln Tunnel!"

At last, the taxi stopped. We were at the synagogues.

Immense, beautiful, and ghostly in their sealed emptiness, both buildings, maintained by trusts set up by former congregants, saddened me. Their communities were gone. But when I said this to Perri, she had a completely different take on it. "They all emigrated,

Mama. They got away to make better lives. Not so many synagogues have such endings."

We headed for the school. It was a gentle, sunny day and the walk was a pleasure. Park Street is a major thoroughfare with many fine shops. We stopped to watch a peddler demonstrating a kind of magic vegetable grater, peeler, French-fry maker, coleslaw shredder. His spiel drew him a large crowd, and his skill with the gadget was amazing. I was about to buy when Perri pointed out that what he was using was a kind of spinning razor and that I can barely see. I reluctantly had to forgo the bargain. What a great present that would have made!

Perri: Actually, what I pointed out, I think, was that this was not a device that could be carried onto a plane nowadays. It's true that as I watched the sidewalk peddler demonstrate it, slicing potatoes into flowerlike curls and beets into paper-thin discs, I could only imagine what havoc my mother might wreak with it in her own kitchen—but I was too polite to say that.

The streets of Kolkata were not easy. The crowds were intense. To find your way along the major shopping thoroughfare of Chowringhee, you threaded your way through close-packed mobs, everyone shopping in all directions, at the storefronts, the stalls along the curb, the random razor-swinging sidewalk people in between. But there was a strong sense of order and commerce—when I wanted to buy a notebook, I was directed from store to store, from stall to stall, everyone in complete agreement, until I did indeed come to the notebook section of the market, where I could take my choice from four or five notebook stores, side by side. There were no notebooks available anywhere else; here were all the notebooks, ready for my purchase.

And there were the pavement-dwellers, the families living out on the sidewalk, and there were the beggars who surrounded cars and taxis at every stoplight, many of them children, dodging among the cars, banging on the windows, pleading over and over for money. I thought about my parents, leading their two small children through these streets, through the railroad station, which my mother still remembers with horror from 1963. There were so many people living and sleeping in the station, she recalls, that it was impossible to step along the platforms. I wondered whether they had worried that this year in India was a terrible mistake—or whether they had felt oddly comforted by the peculiar institution at which they dropped us off each day—and for which we were now searching: the Free Jewish Girls School of Calcutta.

Sheila: We came to a massive iron gate, part of a high fence that bounded the schoolyard. Of course, I remembered it—remembered holding a three-year-old and five-year-old tightly by their hands and bringing them to this very gate. There was the sign, arching proudly over the gateway: JEWISH GIRLS SCHOOL OF CALCUTTA. But now the gate was locked. A sari-clad mother who had come to pick up her daughter was waiting. We told her why we'd come, and she called to the guard within, telling him that there was a former student out here asking to come in. The guard seemed dubious—and highly security conscious. He demanded a card or a passport to take inside, so the authorities could review it, but neither of us was carrying any useful ID. We had left our passports at the hotel, and because of the crowded, crazy streets, we had also left everything else important in the hotel safe. I looked through my wallet—a few dollars, a few rupees, no cards at all—except the little cardboard card that had come with the wallet, on which I had filled in my name and address. In despair, I gave him that, and after a little wait, during which it was presumably reviewed by the authorities, he came back and let us in.

The big open school courtyard was full of uniformed girls in red skirts and white shirts, dark cardigan sweaters worn against what seemed to me a very hot day, school ties around their necks secured with little metal badges. Most of them had the two long, dark braids that Perri coveted when she was a child. There were no boys at all. Back in 1963, boys had been allowed in the very early grades. The younger girls were running and playing in the courtyard. The older girls, more grown up and graceful and self-aware, walked in small groups and talked—and eyed us as we were escorted into the office. We met the elderly headmistress and her assistant, who were intrigued by our connection: Perri went to their school for a month forty years ago. "You are one of our girls," they said gamely, welcoming her.

The assistant took us around and showed us classrooms and books, adequate but shabby. She presented Perri with a JEWISH GIRLS SCHOOL OF CALCUTTA badge and several of their notebooks as souvenirs. I was awash in memories. The first day Perri came home from that school, she reported, "There are three children named Moses in my class. There's Moses Abraham and Moses Isaac and Moses Moses. And Moses Moses is a girl!"

I asked if the school still serves lunch. No more. I remembered buying individual aluminum cups for each child to take to school—and probably to drink the water that carried the intestinal parasites that they acquired. The school lunches had not been a hit with my kids: mashed potatoes, rice, and *dhal,* and water to drink. But the school had interested the children, and the staff had been kind.

As we left, a group of older students, high school girls, stopped us and questioned us politely. They were excited—and much amused—that Perri was an alumna. We took pictures of Perri and her schoolmates, to much giggling. Then I carefully snapped several pictures of Perri at the gate under the big arching sign: JEWISH GIRLS SCHOOL OF CALCUTTA. An alma mater is an alma mater.

"We're on Park Street, so let's see if we can find number twelve and see what's become of the Bengal Chambers," Perri suggested. She was remarkably indulgent. She knew that for me, the best part of any trip often is nostalgia. Modern Kolkata was bustling on around us in its crazy way, but I wanted the Calcutta of 1963, as much of it as I could get. Mrs. Smith, back at the hotel, would have understood, I felt sure, that in my own way, I was having fun.

Finding number twelve was easy; the entire block of stores and entrances were all Twelve Park Street, Queen's Mansions, one vast building encircling an inner courtyard. There was no one entrance. There was no sign for any guesthouse. Alphabetical designations were marked on some entrances, but no Bengal Chambers that we could see. Perri spotted a bespoke tailor shop: Barkat Ali & Bros, Tailors and Outfitters, established 1924. "Well, that's been there for a while," she said. In we went. Several personable gentlemen in Western dress headed for us. Perri explained our weird errand: two American women, looking for a guesthouse we'd stayed at more than forty years ago.

Bengal Chambers? Mrs. Creet? Of course! The shop owners nodded, not the least bit disconcerted. First, we had to sit down and have some tea—and a runner was sent out onto Park Street to procure it. Theirs was a family store, they explained, that had been there for more than fifty years. The two eldest brothers sat and talked with us over the tea and biscuits, and the other younger men handled customers. We watched a whole family march in behind their adult son, and soon he was pinned in cloth up to his ears, and all his relatives were commenting excitedly on the fit. Perhaps it was his first business suit or his wedding suit.

Our hosts confirmed that Mrs. Creet had left the business many years ago and had since died. But the Bengal Chambers, now Indian owned, was still very much in business and was an excellent place to stay. They gave us explicit directions; the entrance we needed was not on Park Street at all but hidden within the courtyard.

We found it and took a rickety elevator cage up. An Indian gentleman greeted us, and when we explained about long ago, he volunteered to show us the rooms. The place was quiet and spotless, the rooms huge. When he told us the rate, it was comparatively modest. We took his card and promised that if we were in Kolkata again, this was where we'd stay. And we meant it.

We headed back to the Fairlawn, stopping at the one-hour photography shop around the corner to leave our film. We'd been eating wonderful curries and other local foods, so this night we resolved to try the hotel kitchen. The menu was mulligatawny soup, sliced grilled beef, greens. The dessert was a trifle. Indeed it was. Even less than that. The message was one I had learned long ago in India and should have remembered well: Never, under any circumstances, look to the British for food.

We hurried to the one-hour photography shop, where our pictures were ready. There were all my bits of 1963 Calcutta—there was Mrs. Smith, holding court at the Fairlawn, and there were the synagogues and the girls in their school uniforms and the outside and inside of the Bengal Chambers. Perri had even taken a photo of the faded ancient list of rules near the elevator, which prohibited servants from riding. There was the proud family of tailors in their bespoke tailor shop. Only two photos had failed: I had disgraced myself with the shots of Perri at the school gate. I'd captured my daughter's vibrant enthusiasm and tourist dishabille as she stood before the gate, but in both photos, I had carefully chopped off the sign overhead so it read only WISH GIRLS SCHOOL OF CALCUTTA. Perhaps I was thinking of the deserted synagogues—perhaps I was just wistful about my own vanished past.

CHAPTER TWENTY-SIX

Waiting for Godot's Golf Cart

Perri: I would like to say that this was all my mother's idea. I find India a fascinating country, and I am eager to get a look at its complex present and to appreciate its multilayered past, to admire its art and artifacts, to broaden my acquaintance with its food—but I don't do gurus. There is not, and there has never been, any tiny little element of spiritual quest in my traveling—I skip over all the pages in the *Lonely Planet* guidebook that take you to ashrams or Vedic healing sites. I draw my spiritual sustenance from sightseeing and from eating, I suppose. I have read about spiritual seekers searching for timeless wisdom in India or Nepal or Tibet—and all I feel is a profound wish *not* to be stuck next to them on a long train journey.

But when I was trying to persuade my mother to come to India with me—when I was trying to convince her that she was not too old and too blind and too decrepit and too immobilized by routine and inertia and depression to make one more trip to India—well, the first thing that seemed to draw her was the idea of going to see Sai Baba. The echoes of past trips or pieces of her past life pull her more power-fully than the idea of things she's never seen, and Sai Baba had preoc-cupied my father for several years. And during those years, my mother had gone along to ceremonies and meetings, had met the followers of the holy man, had heard my father, who always discoursed on his enthusiasms, speculate and analyze and describe.

My mother was curious to see Sai Baba. My father's interest in him had never been religious; he had been interested, anthropologically, in the phenomenon of this holy man from India whose followers included both West Indians and East Indians in Trinidad—and also wealthy North Americans and Europeans. My mother was interested in him because my father had been. It was another trip, I suspected, that we were making because he would have liked to make it.

I wasn't sure how hard Sai Baba would be to locate on the vast map of India, but I had underestimated his importance. There he was, in the index of my guidebook. The place to go was Puttaparthi, a small town a few hours to the east of Bangalore, where he had built a giant ashram. And when we landed at the airport in Bangalore, there were numerous taxi drivers waiting, looking for Sai Baba pilgrims on their way to Puttaparthi. We were immediately offered rides by two different gentlemen at two different government travel-agency desks, and when I stepped away from the desk to consider, a third gentleman approached me and assured me that the government agencies were overcharging me; he had a whole fleet of modern taxis and could get us to Puttaparthi for significantly less.

I was happy to find that it was easy to get to Puttaparthi, but I have to admit that as we sat in the backseat of the taxi, I was thinking cynical thoughts about gurus and the business they generate. There was something unappetizing, it seemed to me, about this whole pilgrimage business. I guess I expect gurus to be on the make; I expect holy sites to be surrounded by opportunists, if not by outright crooks.

Sheila: Here we were, at last, waiting to see the Divinity Incarnate. Simply put, we were waiting to see God.

"I can't help feeling I'm in Beckett's play," I told Perri.

"Nah, you're too well dressed, Mom," she said, laughing. She always knows what to say.

Sai Baba's enterprise is a big one, but we had chosen not to stay in the ashram's huge ten-thousand-bed dormitories. Instead, we'd spent the night in a modest hotel. Waking early and breakfasting deliciously on vegetarian samosas and green-coconut water, we hastened to join the crowd of Indians, tourists, fashionable Europeans, and backpackers hiking briskly in the brilliant morning light to the major activity of the day: *darshan,* when Baba appears. His presence confers a blessing on his audience.

The town seemed a clean, pleasant, prosperous place. Sai Baba's visage stared back from every store window, from posters, T-shirts, coffee mugs, pillowcases, stationery. Obviously, he was the major industry, the underpinning of local tourism, supporting the souvenir shops and stands, the many restaurants, and Internet cafés. A small local airport had even been built to handle the pilgrims who came by private plane or charter flight. This was a bustling town with no beggars visible anywhere, which is remarkable for India.

Puttaparthi was a small, poor village eighty years ago when Sai Baba was born, and it was here, under a tree, that it was revealed to him in adolescence that he was the incarnation of an earlier holy man, that he was, indeed, divine. So it was here that he established his ashram, Prasanthi Nilayam, the Abode of Supreme Peace. He built schools and a great hospital as well, and the town boomed.

We entered Prasanthi Nilayam through a wide gate with abundant warnings posted that there were to be no photographs. We were in a vast, campuslike compound, low buildings and fenced lawns, with neatly dressed devotees policing the grounds. Perri noted that every woman, no matter whether her dress was Western or Indian, wore a scarf draped across her shoulders, and she asked a devotee if that was required. Turned out it was, so we headed back out the gate to the nearest shop.

"You are going to *darshan?*" asked the shopkeeper, who must have flourished on the scarf trade. He leaned over close, and said to Perri, "Pair one of your shoes and one of your mother's shoes together, and then put their mates together, elsewhere. That way they won't be stolen."

In the Abode of Supreme Peace? I didn't say it.

Thanking him, we paid for our two cheap holy scarves (or *shmattes*, as they might be called in my own faith), and then rejoined the huge throng heading for the *mandir*, the worship hall where Baba was to give *darshan*.

At the entrance shoe pile, Perri kicked off her flip-flops as I looked around for a bench. Nothing but an old tree to lean against. I squatted to unlace my shoes.

You know how *Waiting for Godot* starts with Estragon the tramp sitting on the ground, trying to pull off his troublesome boots? Well, that was my situation exactly, at this shoe pile. Only worse. Estragon had only Vladimir there to witness his struggles, while I was in the midst of a mob. And with knotted laces. Oh, to be able to traverse India in flip-flops! But never, even during the best days of my youth, could I walk happily in anything but lace-ups. I was born doomed to English-teacher/librarian shoes. Perri waited, a monument of filial patience, till I was unknotted at last.

Perri: Actually, although my mother thinks I was a monument of filial patience, I remember quite clearly that I was standing there and worrying. Could the man at the scarf store possibly be right? What if someone stole my mother's shoes? Was it possible that her black lace-up orthopedic walking shoes, in which she had tramped energetically through the streets of Delhi and Kolkata, would look expensive, imported, desirable, here amid these heaps of sandals and flip-flops? *What if someone stole my mother's shoes?* What were the chances of finding anything that would work as well for her, here in rural Andhra Pradesh? I began to think apocalyptically—the trip would be over, everything would be spoiled, unless I protected her shoes. They seemed to me for a minute to be the repositories of my mother's strength and power. Without those particular shoes, she would not be able to keep up the pace that she had been managing, almost without effort. Everything depended on protecting those shoes—her independence, her sure-footedness, her ability to enjoy the trip.

So I took the scarf-man's advice, and I paired one black lace-up shoe with one pink flip-flop, and deposited the mismatched set carefully at the base of the tree. Then I paired up the two remaining shoes and carried them some distance away, to leave them against a wall. I marked both places carefully in my mind. All around us were devotees, most of them European, young and old, each woman draped in a scarf, leaving their shoes to join a line entering the place of worship. I felt suspicious of them—who knew which one might be an evil shoe-snatcher?—and more generally suspicious of the whole enterprise. But I took my mother's arm and, barefoot and *shmatte*-wrapped, we joined the line.

Sheila: We headed for the curtained separate entrance for women, where we lined up so stern female devotees with metal detectors could search us thoroughly.

Then at last we were inside, sitting cross-legged on the marble floor, surrounded by prosperous European matrons, many of whom had brought cushioned floor-chairs. There we two sat amid the thousands of silent women in the *mandir*, a brightly colored, festive open-air pavilion with an ornate gold-leafed ceiling and gorgeous chandeliers. Alas, we had not been early enough to be among the first-comers, so we were crowded in quite far back from the high stage. And more women were crowding in behind us. Soon every space was filled.

On the far side of the *mandir*, across the great divide of floor, sat a horde of silent men, awaiting Baba's presence as well. In India, such quiet in such a crowd was awesome. But here in Baba-land, if a miscreant so much as whispered to a neighbor, a devotee-usher quickly shushed her or hand-signaled a threat of expulsion. Were the ladies around me meditating? Who knows? They had faraway looks in their eyes. Baba communicates with his devotees through dreams and portents. My own thoughts wandered, most often returning to Mort. Here, more than anywhere else in India, I thought sadly: *If only you were with us.*

It was from Mort I had first heard about Sathya Sai Baba and his multitude of followers, millions all over the world. Mort had spent years researching and writing about Baba, who, believers say, heals the sick and sometimes brings back the dead, who materializes gold objects—watches and bracelets—from the air and presents them to devotees, who drips sacred *vibhuti*—gray perfumed sandalwood ash—from his fingertips into eager cupped hands. For years I had listened to Mort talk about this strange-looking Hindu guru with his wild Afro, clad in flowing saffron robes, who sings hymns of adoration and teaches brotherhood and love of God.

His own teachings are vague and comfortable: Be the best you can be. All religions are good. Stay in your church and worship as you will. All your prayers will come to me anyway, for I am God.

His message is subtle, indirect. Often he speaks to his followers in their sleep, and in symbols that they interpret idiosyncratically.

Baba also has his detractors, the doubters and the bitterly disaffected former devotees who accuse him of fraud and heinous crimes, most often pederasty.

Mort, ever the scholar, withheld judgment. I wasn't sure exactly what his real opinion had been in the end, but I was eager to see Sai Baba for myself.

So we waited to see him. And we waited. For the next two hours, nothing happened. We just sat. At one point, Perri boldly whispered to a neighbor, "What will happen?"

"Baba will come," the lady said, with confidence.

Perri: So there we were. We were sitting on a marble floor, comfortably shaded by the roof, in a silent crowd of female devotees. The woman I asked was in her twenties, from Germany, and willing to chat a little bit in whispers, though we were periodically shushed by a fierce monitor. She said that she was from Frankfurt and had had many friends who were devotees of Sai Baba, but she had never believed in him herself. "And then one day, I had a good meditation, and Baba came to me," she said, and laughed in delight at the memory. "And then I understood, and now I am here almost three months!"

The monitor shook her finger at us, and we quieted—but then her attention was drawn by someone who was standing up over on the side, and off she went, moving low to the ground like a crab, to restore order. My neighbor asked whether I was a devotee myself, and I said no, just a visitor. "Maybe you will have a good meditation," she said. "Maybe Baba will come to you and tell you also!" And again she laughed, as if that would be kind of funny, and I have to admit, I laughed as well. I mean, it *would* be kind of funny, at that.

Now, I also have to admit that there was something rather peaceful and compelling about sitting there quietly in this group of women, waiting. The shade was pleasant, the pavilion was pretty, and the atmosphere was calm. And maybe there was even something larger, stranger, harder to quantify—something in the air—the kind of element that is hard to identify or hard to acknowledge for someone like me—some kind of spiritual peace and goodness. After all, here were all these people, many of them from the other side of the world, who had trekked to this quiet, peaceful place and who sat here together, each exploring her own mind, waiting for nothing more than the appearance of someone they believed held great wisdom and great good. Everything we had seen of the ashram so far suggested sincerity and simplicity. I had no idea whether Baba was actually innocent or guilty of the various charges brought against him, and I had no real opinion of the man himself (except that, of course, I don't believe that he's God), but the devotees we had met were kind and serious about their own spiritual quests. Also, like the German woman beside me, they seemed full of laughter and good humor. And no, I didn't really get the joke, but I also respected the lightness and the gentleness of it all. This was a religious site that was built to hold everyone's own journey. You each pursued your own relationship with the divine, meditating, going to lectures, attending the ceremonies if you wanted—no one kept score, no one made rules (except about the importance of the sacred *shmatte*), no one tracked your progress.

There seemed something rather noble and beautiful about it all as we sat there on the cold, hard marble in the early-morning light. I don't know if I was Meditating (with a capital *M*), but I was certainly meditating on my parents, on my mother's determination now to follow down the threads of her life with my father, on the way that this idea of hers had brought us to this rather remarkable place that I would otherwise never have thought about. And here I was, waiting for the guru to appear. I had finally stopped worrying about my mother's shoes.

Sheila: Long after my gluteus muscles had given up the ghost, there was a sudden clanging of a gong, as if it were warning us of a fire, and then a superb sound system broadcast Baba's voice singing hymns he had written (to himself?). The devotees were alerted. They sat up, and many began to clap rhythmically to the music and sing along in Hindi. The music went on for some time, then the gong again, and then more hymns, and this time there was activity on the platform up front. A red vehicle—well, not to mince words, a bright red golf cart—appeared on stage, and there was Baba seated in it. The devotees were galvanized. There were gasps and sotto voce acknowledgments: "Baba! Baba!" Four male acolytes dressed in white accompanied the unlikely chariot as it very slowly traversed the stage and then traveled out toward the audience, made a circuit, and ponderously turned to make the trip back. Baba waved gently to the crowd. "He looks feeble," Perri whispered to me.

I, who see so poorly, could barely make out the distinctive, diminutive, dark-skinned man with the wild Afro. All around me, women's heads moved slowly as if magnetized, inching along with the vehicle. Many held up their hands, cupped, to receive his blessing. And I could tell that many of the women around me seemed to feel some kinetic or visceral or spiritual effect, some energy. I did not. I felt nothing.

Suddenly, I thought of my youngest child, Judy, who was at that time in Nashville, Tennessee, trying hard to sell her original country music, so I asked Baba, silently, to help her. I figured it couldn't hurt.

The red cart and Baba rolled backstage and out of sight. A scant number of people rose to leave. Mostly, everyone else sat still. Perri asked her neighbor what would happen next. She shook her head. Again, she seemed on the verge of mirth. "You never know what Baba will do! He is giving private audiences now, but he might come back!" She smiled fondly, speaking of her god. "Sometimes he speaks—and sometimes he sits right in that chair!" She pointed to a chair up on the dais. "One day this week, Thursday, I think, Baba came, and then he went to give audiences, and he was there very late, and we waited and waited, and finally, after three hours, many, many people leave. And then, Baba came, and he sat right in that chair!" she pointed again, and her laughter bubbled over as she contemplated the fools who had gone away too early and missed the treat. We would not be of their number; we went on sitting.

So we waited. An hour and a half later, the gong and the hymns began again, and we were treated to a second *darshan,* identical to the first, the devotees drawing sustenance from the presence of their avatar. The red golf cart rolled slowly away, out of the marble pavilion. We rose and thanked our informant, who had come from Hamburg with her friend, who celebrated her birthday every year in Puttaparthi.

"Well, shall we go?" I suggested to Perri.

"Let's go," she agreed.

That's exactly the way Samuel Beckett ends his play—except his characters don't go. But we did. We retrieved our shoes and went off to have the ashram's glorious fifty-cent vegetarian lunch. Then we went to an Internet café, where I e-mailed Judy that I'd asked Baba to intercede for her.

The next day she sent a jubilant message. Perhaps he had. She'd gotten contracts for five songs!

CHAPTER TWENTY-SEVEN

You Let Mama Do What?

Perri: Now it can be told: My mother traveled all through India without changing her underwear. She bought a new suitcase for the trip, at my urging, a small wheeled suitcase, and she packed it very lightly: a nightgown, a few clean shirts. She was immensely pleased by the small, compact (and, need I say, cheap) suitcase; she felt she was truly traveling light. Of course, at the last minute, she almost doubled her luggage. Since there was snow on the ground in Boston in January, she wore a heavy parka on the drive to the airport, planning to leave it in the car, and then, in the excitement of saying good-bye, she forgot completely about leaving her coat behind. As Larry and the kids pulled away in the car, my mother cried out, "My coat! I still have my coat!"

And then, of course, she tried to insist that it was perfectly okay to be taking a heavy winter coat with you on a trip to India. "I'm always cold," she insisted. "You know how I'm always borrowing a sweater in your house. I'll just take the coat along—it doesn't weigh that much. No, don't call Larry, don't make them come back—that's so much trouble!" But I did call him. And he did come back, and he took Mama's winter coat, and she was able to get on the airplane with her tiny little rolling suitcase. And every so often in southern India, as we clung to little patches of shade or as we toughed it out under the broiling sun, I would say to Mama, "Good thing we didn't bring your winter coat, huh?" And she would say, "Well, it *did* get chilly at night in New Delhi. . . ."

Anyway, it's not that my mother didn't bring a few extra pairs of underpants to India. Of course she did—there was plenty of room in even that modest little suitcase for a couple of pairs of Mama's modest cotton briefs. The interesting thing was, she couldn't bear to use any of her extras. They were so nice and clean and neatly folded—why ever would she want to take them out and get them all dirty and wrinkled? Each evening she would consider the question as she unpacked her nightgown and gazed fondly at the few small, neatly folded garments beneath it in the suitcase, and then generally she would decide that whatever she was wearing would do fine for another day.

Sheila: "Ma, how old are you?" a stranger asked me in Delhi. Of course he was a stranger. Who did I know in Delhi? His was an unusual conversational gambit because Indians are so private. I'd just landed on the top step of the Jamma Masjid, the largest mosque in all India. I was dusting pebbles from my bruised, scorched soles when this young man—nicely dressed, personable, smiling—detached himself from his group of friends and confronted me. He wasn't selling anything, and he certainly wasn't begging. I didn't get it.

His companions hovered close by, listening. I've never minded telling my age. Not so many people are interested. Except, apparently, in India.

"I'm seventy-seven," I said. Whereupon he put forth his hand enthusiastically to shake mine, and his three friends lined up to follow suit.

I felt as if I'd just been awarded my elementary school diploma. "What's going on?" I asked Perri softly. "Why am I being congratulated?"

Like any hard-of-hearing person, when I speak softly, it's never soft enough. The young man heard and hastened to explain. "You understand how it is, Ma; we do not see many women like you"—he pointed to my white hair—"standing up. We do not see them climbing. They are mostly lying down." He stiffened and held his arms rigidly at his sides, feigning rigor mortis.

I was being congratulated for being a survivor.

So the next time it happened, I understood. And the next. Always young men, always polite and frequently using the honorific *Ma,* just as the guard at the Indian consulate in New York had done. It was sweet, an expression of Indian men's fondness for their mothers.

But that didn't prepare me for the gallantry of Hampi.

Hampi is a village in Karnātaka where, in a strange, boulder-strewn landscape, villagers live amid the glorious ruins of the Vijayanagar kings, the sixteenth-century capital city of a destroyed empire. I had expressed the desire to travel south and visit Sai Baba, and then Perri had researched that part of India, and we'd ventured on to Hampi, which neither of us had heard of before. This turned out to be a brilliant move. Think ancient Rome and Greece. Think temples—one still used for worship—think colossal elephant stables, and gateways, palaces and statues, a royal zenana, and a bazaar.

However, to get to the major sites, it is necessary to cross the Tungabhadra River, and the only means is by coracle. I'd never heard the word before. A coracle turns out to be a shallow, circular reed basket with waterproof material stretched over it, a kind of giant, water-repellent, wicker saucer that holds about twenty people (fewer if a motorcyclist brings his bike aboard or a passenger carries sacks of rice). To get into and out of the coracle, one sloshes ankle deep among muddy rocks, somehow holding shoes aloft. During the voyage, passengers squat in a couple of inches of water while a boatman stands and paddles. Several coracles operate as ferries on the Tungabhadra River; that's mass transportation in Hampi.

"Okay, Mom?" Perri asked, soon after we'd arrived and inspected the place. She looked a bit anxious. She's usually on the chill side of cool.

A paean to Perri as the tough-love travel mate for the handicapped! Mostly, she leaves you alone. She doesn't hover or restrict or needlessly warn. I was aware that she was constantly alert, but she allowed me to be a grown-up, to determine what I thought I could do.

How I hate being restricted and advised and cautioned. "Hold on to the banister. Button your sweater. Better not eat that." Well meant, infantilizing, and insulting. There is something about being allowed my own judgment that is vital to my life. Perri, who can be bossy and often thinks she knows better, nonetheless respects independence. God knows she claimed it early for herself and has kept careful watch over it.

In India, when it was dark and we walked on broken pavement, she took my hand and guided me. She warned me about concealed steps and led me around potholes. She watched the traffic lights, which I sometimes couldn't see. She reminded me about not drinking the water or even washing my toothbrush in it. But just once. Occasionally, she checked to see if I had my medicines in hand. But she really trusted my common sense. I ate what I wanted to, slept as I pleased, went where impulse led me, and shared in the major travel decisions. I even paid for what I pleased.

There were only two issues on which we differed early and radically: how often travelers should change their underclothing (a much more genteel word than *underwear*, Perri) and the necessity of nightly showers. I changed my underclothing whenever it was necessary and convenient. When it was not too much trouble—a phrase that means when I wanted to. Not automatically, not daily. My suitcase had plenty of clean underclothing when we left and plenty of clean underclothing when we returned. My shower policy is pragmatic. At home, I shower every morning. When traveling, the diurnal splash for me— as someone whose childhood was amply sanitized by weekly baths— is just too much trouble. Perri, child of the middle class who grew up with hot water on tap, scrubs her body and washes her hair every night, no matter what. We managed an uneasy truce, and otherwise, she never questioned my judgment. I have to say I never caught her sniffing me, either.

So on the banks of the Tungabhadra River in Hampi, when I saw the coracles filled with merry passengers, it seemed a lark to sail that way. Besides, there was no other means of getting over to those ruins. To me, it appeared perfectly doable, adventurous, and much more fun than a rocking chair. The coracle meant wet, mucky feet and pants, that was all.

I did just fine going and coming on the first day, wading, shoes in hand, climbing in, squatting, then climbing out. But on the return trip the second evening, the coracle had to "dock" in much deeper water, through which the passengers then needed to wade to shore. I was not happy; I can't swim and I am scared of water. It wasn't deep water, only about knee high, I told myself, and I tried to figure out how I could climb out carrying my shoes and socks with only one hand free to maneuver and steady myself.

The boatman must have spotted me as a possible weak link on our earlier trips. I never exactly hopped out of his coracle quickly with grace. Rather, I lumbered out like a klutz.

Now, he—a small, wiry man half my size—climbed into the water to supervise the unloading, and then immediately motioned to me to follow. "I carry you, Ma," he said, grinning, and turned around and offered his back, crouching slightly so I could hop on and ride piggyback.

I weigh 135 pounds. He was smaller than I and didn't look like he weighed that much. "No," I protested, "I can do it by myself."

"Climb on his back," the other passengers murmured. "Go ahead. He wants to help you."

I shook my head.

Twenty people squatting in a muddy coracle waited for me to move. "I can do it," I said again, but I didn't move.

"Mom," Perri urged softly behind me, "you have to get off . . ."

Piggyback! I hadn't been carried that way for seventy-five years. Oh, how I didn't want to. I felt humiliated. But I wasn't sure I could manage getting into and then out of the water. And I was holding everyone up.

Perri put out her hand for my shoes, and I surrendered them. Several male passengers edged closer, hoisted me up, and helped me onto my rescuer's back. Then, sure-footed and with arms extended like a tightrope walker, he stepped lightly over the slippery rocks, with the encouragement of his appreciative audience. Minutes later, he deposited me safely on the grassy bank, to general applause from the coracle steerage crowd.

His eyes sparkled with pleasure. "I carry my ma all the time," he said to me with great pride. Just then, Perri arrived on the riverbank, holding our shoes. "I carry your ma," he told her joyfully. "I carry my ma, and today I carry your ma." Proudly he strode back into the water, heading toward his vessel.

"Thank you," I called after him lamely. I hated the piggyback, but, oh, how I owed him.

Without turning, he raised his arm to wave graciously.

Perri: Actually, my mother kept up quite an impressive pace on our trip through India. I tend to be greedy, especially about sightseeing— well, especially about food and sightseeing. And there is so much to see in India! We had made it to Hampi and back, on two overnight train rides. We had made it to Mysore and visited its sacred hill and its rajah's palace—and by a piece of excellent luck, which my mother, of course, insisted on attributing to my excellent planning, we had been there on the right evening to see the palace illuminated at night, out-lined in golden lights. And now we were heading back to Bangalore, and from there, we would fly back to Delhi—but of course, I had tried to cram too many other things in along the way.

We set out early in the morning from Mysore in a car we had hired, a big old white Indian Ambassador. It was spacious and theoretically air-conditioned (useful because of that broiling south Indian sun that makes heavy winter coats so unnecessary), and the driver drove it at a careful fifty kilometers an hour. It was a long day of driving, and a hot day of sightseeing. We went to see the giant Jain statue at Sravan-abelagola, and when we got there, we discovered that to see the statue, it was necessary to climb 637 steps up the mountain, under, you guessed it, the noonday sun. There was a small group of gentlemen waiting at the bottom of the steps for elderly or less energetic visitors; they were bearers with sedan chairs on poles, eager to carry pilgrims up to the shrine. "No way," said my mother. "That's much too much trouble. I don't want them to carry me—they'll drop me. I'm not get-ting in one of those things. Don't be silly, I can climb steps." And as we climbed, slowly, up all 637, I had two voices playing in my mind.

One was Noel Coward's voice singing, "Mad dogs and Englishmen go out in the midday sun." The other was my brother's voice, saying accusingly, "You let Mama do *what*?" Anyway, it was that kind of day. Six hundred and thirty-seven steps up in the sun—and then the statue of the Jain saint. On to the temples of Belur and Halebid, admiring their amazing intricate carvings—in the hot sun. Hours and hours in the back of that bouncing, slow-moving Ambassador, creeping toward our final destination, the city of Bangalore. A full and interesting and effortful and exhausting and downright sweaty day.

Sheila: The "Ma situation" escalated on Vindhiagyri Hill, the Jain holy site, which has a massive statue of hero Bahubali at its peak. Arriving there, as Perri says, we unexpectedly faced the prospect of climbing 637 steps carved out of rock—barefooted. And whatever doubts she may have privately suffered, it was here that Perri metamorphosed into World's-Best-Travel-Companion-for-an-Aged-Relative. Yes, here she showed her mettle. The day was hot; we'd hired a car and we'd been touring temples since early morning. We were particularly eager to see this legendary statue, which looks out over the entire countryside.

It was noon when we arrived. We hadn't quite understood that the only way up the mountain was a staircase. At the foot of these massive steps were *dholis* (straw sedan chairs) and bearers, to carry up the lazy or the infirm—or elderly mothers. The mountain was incredibly steep—it looked almost vertical—and the very idea of those unreliable-looking bearers carrying me up in a straw basket was laughable. I knew they would drop me. I weighed more than they did. Looking down would make me so dizzy, I'd be sick. I'd die of vertigo. I saw that Hitchcock movie. I'm a daughter of the working class. I never ride in palanquins, not even shabby ones.

No, I decided. I would climb, slowly. I would do it all on my own. "You're sure?" Perri asked.

I gave her "the look." Every mother and child knows what that means.

We had an unbelievably protracted, hot climb, made more difficult by the increasing heat of the steps as the sun baked them. My soles were soon melba toast, my toes croutons. Along the way, as we rested, several times, anxious young men who were drinking water and mopping their brows, as they also rested, inquired about my age. Perhaps they were thinking, *Wh-a-at? If that old lady can do it, I can do it, too.* Groups of schoolchildren on outings greeted us and seized the chance to practice their English. "Hello. What is your name?" they would start, and we would respond, but they were shy, so the conversations didn't get much farther.

At last, we made it to the summit, which was magnificent. There was the massive statue of the saint, gazing out into the distance. All around, for miles, was the flat, verdant surrounding landscape. There we rested, until we had the strength to start the descent, a relatively easy task. Aside from frequently passing me bottled water, Perri didn't hover. She trusted me to signal trouble—and I had none. We finished the descent in good, but tired, shape.

After admiring two more easily accessible temples, we settled luxuriously in the car and rode on to Bangalore, and in my languid state I reveled in thoughts about how much like their father my children are. When they were at college, not one of them took an anthropology course, though anthropology was Mort's passion. Perri was a biology major; David, an ancient-history major; and Judy, a political science major. (Of course, I couldn't sell many English courses either. The children went their separate ways.) But, in fact, all three of them grew up to travel eagerly and easily almost anywhere. All they need is a pretext to go. They try new foods with great pleasure. They are friendly and curious, truly interested in other people and their lives. And they read voraciously. The world fascinates them, as it fascinated Mort. They are very much his children.

So far, Perri is the only one I've traveled with extensively. I've learned the following about her:

- That she's a sucker for ethnic tchotchkes
- That she never eats breakfast, so her roommate has to forage on her own

- That she showers and washes her hair every night, no matter the temperature of available water
- That she is prompt and reliable, and can dress and be in a taxi in minutes
- That she is a quiet, thoughtful roommate, but she reads late into the night, so it is necessary to devise an antilight mechanism (Fortunately, I've figured one out. I close my eyes, and that works just fine.)
- That she has boundless energy and enthusiasm, can walk miles, and has superhuman sightseeing/museum endurance
- That she's a sucker for ethnic tchotchkes
- That she's a quick packer because she just crams everything into her suitcase any which way, an infuriating skill because she always seems to know where things are
- That she's a sucker for ethnic tchotchkes
- That she's a whiz at travel-booking on the Internet, especially good at ferreting out rare events such as Full-Moon Viewing of the Taj Mahal, which almost no one ever gets to see
- That if she ever invites me to join her on a trip again, I'll go (In fact, I've got my suitcase neatly packed, with minimal clean underwear all ready.)

Perri: So that long day of climbing the 637 steps and wandering barefoot around temples in the hot south Indian sun and riding for hundreds of dusty kilometers in the slow-moving old Ambassador car finally came to an end. We had made it back to Bangalore, the thriving city at the center of the Indian Internet boom. I had booked us into what was described as a "business hotel" in Bangalore. And it turned out to be quite a nice business hotel indeed, a luxe palace of high-speed Internet access and marble-floored conference rooms. We put down our bags and went out and found a very good dinner high up on a terrace overlooking the lights of the city, surrounded by upscale young Bangaloreans. It seemed far away from the great stone statue of the saint on his mountaintop, or the intricate ancient temples. And the food was great. And then we walked back to the hotel and took long, hot showers and put on our nightgowns. At least I did. My mother, on the other hand, looked at her compact little rolling suitcase and announced, "I packed everything up so beautifully this morning, I'm not even going to open my suitcase!"

"What do you mean?" I asked. "What will you wear to sleep in? What will you wear tomorrow?" I had already bundled my own dusty travel clothes into the hotel's plastic laundry bag, glad to be out of them, glad to be clean.

"I'll sleep naked," my mother said, cheerfully. "And the clothes I wore today will air out overnight, and I'll wear them again tomorrow. Anything so I don't have to go to the trouble of opening the suitcase, just when I have it so beautifully packed."

So my mother did not open her perfectly packed suitcase, and she slept naked in the bed in the Bangalore business hotel, and then the next morning she put on her aired-out, taken-off clothing, and we flew to Delhi, then took a car to Āgra and checked into a true luxury palace, a last-night-in-India extravagance, the Taj View Hotel. I hadn't told my mother that we were paying an extra twenty bucks or so for a Taj Mahal–view room—which was just as well, because in the hazy early evening, she couldn't see the Taj at all from our window, and I could barely make it out. Still, it was a very splendid hotel, full of employees attempting to deliver the kind of excellent, not to say obsequious, service that so upsets my mother. It was a hotel that was all about going to trouble. I felt it was the kind of hotel that warranted opening up one's suitcase—a nightgown, maybe, or a change of underwear for tomorrow. My mother, I could tell, didn't want to open her suitcase. It was so beautifully, so perfectly packed. But we were back in northern India, and the evening was getting chilly and she needed her warm overshirt. Not her North American winter coat, just her warm overshirt. And so eventually she gave in and unzipped her suitcase and took out the overshirt—and then there was no need to avoid the nightgown, or even the change of clothing for the morning. And so let it be known: On the last day of her trip to India, to see the Taj Mahal, my mother changed her underwear.

PART EIGHT

In Search
of a Storybook
Ending

CHAPTER TWENTY-EIGHT

The Taj by Moonlight

❧

Perri: From the moment that I began to imagine a trip to India with my mother, I knew how this book should end. It would end with Mama and me standing together in front of the Taj Mahal. I sat in front of my computer in Cambridge, Massachusetts, and imagined the closing scene of the book: mother and daughter before the Taj Mahal. I wasn't sure exactly what it would represent—or how it would resonate—but it seemed like such a perfect conclusion. I suppose I had in mind some poignant mix of the powerfully exotic—*the Taj Mahal!*—and the triumphant—*I've done it! I've brought my seventy-seven-year-old mother all the way across the world!* There would be the tinge of passing time, with dead empires and dead great loves represented by the marble dome and minarets, and there would be an element of personal farewell in my mother's return to a monument that had moved and inspired her during other passages of her life. I would bring her to the Taj Mahal to say good-bye—to India, perhaps, and to her memories of travel with my father. I wasn't exactly sure how and why, but it seemed to me that if I could orchestrate this Taj Mahal moment properly, I would bring the trip—and the book—and perhaps something more than that—to a dramatic and appropriate climax.

Then I found out about the full-moon thing. I had called an acquaintance to ask advice about planning a trip to India, and though we never actually connected, he left a long and enthusiastic voice mail for me about the full moon. The courts had recently insisted that the Taj Mahal be reopened for tourist visits at night, he said excitedly. Whatever else you do, be sure you take advantage—try to see the Taj by moonlight! No one has been allowed to do it for decades—what an opportunity! I e-mailed the official government of India tourism office, and sure enough, he was right. By court order, the Taj Mahal would be open for moonlight viewing, but only for the few days right around the full moon. And the last few days of our trip to India would coincide with the full moon—the first full-moon Taj viewing in more than twenty years. Tickets would be highly limited, said the government tourist office, and no, they couldn't tell me how to get them. Perhaps my tour company would be able to get them for me. But of course, I was my own tour company!

I became slightly obsessed with the project. I had originally planned that we would go to the Taj on our third day in India as a side trip from Delhi. That made geographic sense—but it hadn't really made dramatic sense; I wanted a grand finale. So, what with this full-moon schedule, suppose instead I left it till the end—till we came back from southern India—so that we could be there for the full moon? Suppose I booked us into a fancy hotel. Surely they would be able to get us moonlight viewing tickets! And there we would be, among the first tourists in decades, standing before the most beautiful white marble building in the world, watching it glow in the light of the full moon. A transcendent travel moment, a celestial convergence of politics and lunar cycles and Mama and me.

"Plan it any way you like," Mama said. "But don't worry too much about this moonlight thing—you know I don't see very well."

She would be amazed, I thought, when we stood there in the moonlight. She would think I could do miracles, locating the tickets, timing the trip. It would be magic.

And so we reshuffled the trip. I helped in this enterprise by getting my foot run over by a bicycle rickshaw on our very first full day in Delhi, as I led the way through the complex traffic near the Jamma Masjid in Old Delhi, the enormous mosque at the center of the old city. The streets were full of carts and taxis and little three-wheeled auto rickshaws and bicycle rickshaws—the old human-pulled rickshaws persist in Kolkata, but not in Delhi. I was blazing the trail, leading my mother through the complex mix of humans and vehicles, toward the mosque. But we were both slightly jet-lagged after the long trip and the time change, and the street was crowded, and at some point, a bicycle rickshaw rode over the very edge of my right shoe. It didn't hurt much at the time, but as we climbed the steps up to the mosque, my right little toe began to ache. And then it began to really hurt, and we ended up spending the afternoon back in our hotel room, with me elevating and icing my foot, and worrying that the toe was broken. It was better the next day, but by no means well enough for the long day trip to the Taj Mahal—so I definitely moved the Taj to the end of our trip.

Sheila: Okay, so Perri and I needed a fitting final destination. As novelists, we're both peculiarly aware of the importance of beginnings and endings. So a dramatic Indian setting was essential, an exotic landscape tinged with beauty and romance, with pathos and irony. We had made too long and arduous a pilgrimage for it to peter out with a whimper. In *Octopussy*, Hollywood settled cheap, plunging James Bond into a pool in a lake palace in Udaipur. Not for us. We wanted something epic.

Too much to expect in real life for an elderly-mother–indulgent-daughter–economy-class saga? Oh, no! Think what Homer could do with our adventures: a toe smashed by a rickshaw, a heroic mountain ascent, perilous voyages by coracle followed by a daring rescue at sea, a god with bad hair riding around his vast pavilion in a red motorcar while amplifiers blasted hymns he had written to himself.

Perri, particularly, had so wanted the end of the trip to be special for me because it was unlikely that I'd be wandering that way again soon. No question she'd be back; there was so much more of India to see. But for me to have done this now was a marvelous feat (of the heart as well as the feet). I was fully conscious of this because, occasionally, I glance at an actuarial table. Sometimes I can even read the numbers. So in our planning, we'd studied the guidebooks and considered various itineraries. We narrowed our search by asking ourselves the critical question: What's the most beautiful structure in India and, arguably, in the whole world? The answer had to be the Taj Mahal, the perfectly symmetrical, white marble mausoleum that was built by Shah Jahan to honor his second wife, Mumtaz, who died on a battlefield after giving birth to their fourteenth child. (He always took her along to battles. *Quelle sentiment!*) It was reported that on the night of her death his hair turned white out of grief. No doubt his two other wives and his huge harem of concubines attempted to comfort him.

It took twenty-two years to build the Taj, during which he found consolation in an incestuous affair with his daughter, Jahanara, who greatly resembled her mother. "The gardener has the privilege of gathering the fruit from the tree he has himself planted," said Shah Jahan, justifying himself.

Twenty thousand craftsmen labored on his Taj, then many of them had their thumbs amputated to ensure that they would never repeat this artistic triumph . . . or so the legend goes. My problem was, I knew too much. The first time I saw the Taj, I was young and romantic. I saw it with my husband, whom I dearly loved. I was so captivated by its beauty and its myth, I spent the next two years researching and then writing a novel about Mumtaz. So I know all the gossip. Arjumand Banu was my heroine's maiden name, and she was fourteen when she met the king. Too many tales of intrigue, incest, and murder were Shah Jahan's legacy. In fact, in my feminist eyes, he became something of a cur—with great riches and impeccable architectural taste.

I called my novel *The Marble Princess*. Publishers said nice things about it, but no one bought it. Sadly, I buried *The Marble Princess* in my bookcase of unsold manuscripts, not as beautiful but easily as extensive as the Taj. Maybe that's what really soured me on Shah Jahan.

But so what if the love story was not what it seemed? The Taj was no less beautiful. Tagore had eloquently described it as "a teardrop on the cheek of time." I remembered it fondly: the formal gardens, the gorgeous onion domes, the reflecting pool, the tapering minarets. Perfection!

Perri: For two weeks, as we traveled through India, I was in phone contact and then in e-mail contact with a manager at the hotel in Āgra. I called from Calcutta: Could they arrange tickets for the night viewing of the Taj on the night of the full moon, when we would be staying at the hotel? The manager told me he would look into it. I called again from Mysore, to see whether he had been able to arrange tickets, and he told me he would need our names, our residences, our ages, our passport information—and even then, he didn't know if it could be done. Security was tight, he told me, and he might not be allowed to book our tickets without actually showing the passports—but he would try.

I e-mailed him all possible information. In Bangalore, I checked my e-mail, and he had responded: the information was sufficient, the tickets were ours! We would be allowed in at nine-thirty P.M. for exactly thirty minutes! From then on, I became completely focused on our appointment with meteorologic destiny, our full-moon moment. We took an early-morning flight to Delhi; we hired a car and driver to take us to Āgra. We checked into the hotel by four P.M., in plenty of time. At the desk, we were handed an envelope containing two enormous tickets, printed with our names, our ages, our passport numbers. We were instructed, on the tickets, to present ourselves at the gates of the Taj Mahal at least an hour in advance to complete security procedures. So we told the driver to come and pick us up at eight P.M. The driver, experienced at escorting foreign tourists through their Taj Mahal experiences, was dubious: "It's closed at night," he told us. We produced the magic tickets, and he examined them, along with two doormen and a small group of hotel staff: The Taj will be open tonight for moonlight viewing! The two American ladies have tickets! They must present themselves at eight-thirty for security purposes! I imagined that everyone—the driver, the hotel staff—was looking at us with awe, the two foreigners who had figured out the system, who were holding the special tickets.

We went up to our room, and I talked my mother into opening her perfectly packed suitcase and taking out her warm overshirt. We looked out the window but were unable to see the Taj in the fading afternoon light. To tell the truth, I was slightly relieved; I didn't want to start out with a dim, faraway behind-glass view. We had come so far and made so many arrangements, and here we were, on the night of the full moon. We would see the Taj together from close up, in the moonlight.

Sheila: Perri, who in everyday life is realistic and clear-eyed, turned out to be an inveterate romantic. She was absolutely taken with the idea of stopping in Āgra—a long drive, a costly detour—and once she inadvertently discovered that on the night of the full moon, for the first time in twenty years, the Taj would be opened to a limited and select few (willing to pay fifteen dollars apiece for a half hour of spectacular viewing), she was hooked. We had to go. In fact, I quite agreed. It would be sweet to revisit the place where Mort and I had been so happy, and to look on such beauty again. It wasn't easy to acquire the tickets, but Perri persisted, sending frequent e-mails from our various hotels along the way and alerting concierges and bureaucrats by telephone.

She'd booked us a room with a view of the Taj in a classy Āgra hotel. We hired a car and driver in Delhi and set off. On the outskirts of Āgra, our driver stopped to pick up Krishna, an engaging young man who explained in loud (bless him) and excellent English, that he was the guide who came with the car. We had unknowingly already paid for him in a package deal. He turned out to be the best bargain of the entire trip.

"I was born here," Krishna said. "I know Āgra well and I am proud of it." He pointed out local landmarks as we drove to our hotel. The hotel and room were lovely, though the view of the Taj was, I thought, minimal. You had to position yourself at a radical angle in the right light to get the tiniest glimpse. I endeared myself to Perri by telling her the room reminded me of an old joke: An aged woman in New York summons the police, complaining that a man in an apartment across the street is indecently exposed. The policeman looks and says he doesn't see a thing. "Oh yeah?" says the indignant complainant, "Well, you just try standing on this ladder in the closet, and you tip your head all the way back, and you'll see plenty!"

That was our Taj view.

At eight P.M., our driver and Krishna returned to take us to an army staging area. They were allowed to come no further but would be waiting for us afterward. The full, round moon was already shining—but the sky was very cloudy. Our group was assembling; no one mentioned the clouds. We had paid fifteen dollars each; surely it would clear.

Perri presented our documents for the soldiers' scrutiny, and, after some waiting, we passed through metal detectors and were patted down thoroughly. Considerately, as always in India, the women were patted down in privacy, behind a curtain, by uniformed female soldiers. Our handbags all had to be checked, and our cameras were carefully investigated. Perri had to snap a picture to prove our camera was taking pictures, not carrying explosives. Cell phones and all other electronic devices had to be left at this checkpoint. More milling about and waiting ensued.

An aged army bus then took us—a motley collection of about thirty foreigners and two expatriate Indians, a couple from Toronto—quite a long way and then unloaded us in complete darkness. To my disbelief, we were then escorted into a small building where all the security procedures were repeated—the walk-through metal detector, the pat-down, the examination of our cameras. The soldiers, all carrying automatic weapons, seemed to me to take this very seriously. We tourists had whispered to one another about the fear of terrorism—about threats from militant Sikhs, who might attack what was, after all, a Muslim monument, and a tourist icon of the Indian government.

Finally, we were through our second full security check, and we congregated again outside. The moon notwithstanding, the night was very dark; at that moment, the clouds covered it completely. We followed a commanding voice—surely a drill sergeant—as we were quick-

stepped over broken ground, a particularly choice exercise for the vi-
sually impaired. It seemed to me that I stumbled along for a long way.
These security measures to ensure the safety of the Taj beat anything I
ever encountered in an American airport.

Once in a while, I glanced up at the sky. The clouds were skirmish-
ing merrily. We had several moments when the moon was clear,
round, and perfect and bright in the night sky—and then the clouds
moved again and we were in the dark. At last, the Promised Landmark
loomed in the distance! We were led along the walk to the viewing
platform, on which we were to remain. It was the most distant of the
several platforms from which you look at the Taj—a long way from
the actual building. We positioned ourselves, waiting silently. The
moon was still behind the clouds, but the sky was full of movement,
and surely, in a moment they would shift. The vast structure ahead
outlined in the dark was a lovely shadow, and it was exciting to think
of what was to come in the next few minutes when it would be fully
illuminated by the moon. As I rested, I began to think a little more
kindly of Shah Jahan. His artistic vision was flawless, at least, though
he had a lot else to answer for.

The clouds never shifted, not during our thirty-minute slot. The
sky never cleared; the moon never appeared. The clouds teased us by
dancing rapidly over the face of the moon. However, if I stared fixedly,
I got an occasional momentary glimpse of the shining white beauty
before me. About a blink's worth. That was it—a blink here and there.
Otherwise, it was the shadowy dim silhouette under a dark sky. The
result was profound disappointment.

Then it was over. Our half hour was up, and the sergeant's voice
summoned us. Our rather dispirited crew followed the voice in the
darkness back to the bus. At least we weren't quickstepping now.
There wasn't much conversation on the way back. The fiasco was nobody's fault; it just happened to be a cloudy night.

Perri: Well, there wasn't any way around it. I stood there, in the darkness, squinting at the shadow of the Taj Mahal. I couldn't pretend to
myself—or to my mother—that we were seeing anything extraordi-

nary. Yes, there was something faintly thrilling about standing there next to the most famous building on Earth, guarded by the Indian army, on a special secret night visit—but it was a long way from my full-moon fantasies. For our entire half hour, I was ready to celebrate. Only one moment of true moonlight, and I would have pronounced it all worthwhile. I leaned over the wooden barrier and tried to talk myself into it. Wasn't that a gleam, a little reflection off white marble? Well, no, it wasn't.

As our minutes ticked away, I began to wonder whether I could plead our right to a second go-round—our tickets were for the nine-thirty slot, but we had been so prompt at the entrance, so quick through security once and security twice, that we had been sent in with the nine o'clock group. Surely I could claim our nine-thirty places—perhaps the moon would come out. In fact, I suddenly thought, what if we leave, and then right at nine-thirty, when we should have been coming in, the clouds clear up and the moon appears? What if I had had it all set up perfectly, and then I had ruined it by letting them take us in too early?

I knew that the moonlight view had never been my mother's project—that she had been dubious from the beginning and would have been perfectly happy with tomorrow's regular daytime visit to the Taj Mahal—but I still felt that I had let her down. I had wanted to arrange a once-in-a-lifetime moment, a special mark for this particular trip to India. My mother had seen the Taj Mahal when she was young and in love—she had been inspired to research and write a novel about it—and I had wanted to come back with her and give her something she had never seen by arranging this special view. I was trying to sound cheerful and cynical, as we leaned on the barrier and hoped for the clouds to clear, and I knew my mother was worrying about me, not about herself. I knew she was trying hard to let me know that it was fine, that she didn't care a bit—but in spite of myself, I cared. I wanted the moon to come out for us—or at least I wanted the moon to disappear altogether for the rest of the night, so that no one, in the nine-thirty group or after, would have a chance of seeing the Taj.

Our time was up. The soldiers corralled us, all of us dejected and disappointed and longing, I suspect, to grab just another few minutes in hope of the moon, and they marched us back to our bus. There was clearly no hope of showing my ticket and arguing my case. They wanted us out of there before the next group arrived. They were not at all interested in whether we were disappointed, in how far we'd come or how long we'd waited, or in the fantasies and wishes with which we might have invested this moment. Marching back to the second security point, riding back on the little bus, passing back through the first security station, I made good-natured, adult conversation with my mother, but I was bitterly, childishly crushed. All that planning. All that effort. And a bunch of other disappointments and worries, large and small, came crowding in: My mother's eyesight was so bad—how much would she have seen even if we'd had the moon? What if her eyes got even worse? How would she manage? And my toe—it still hurt a little, two weeks after the rickshaw accident—I was sure it was broken. And would we get back okay to Delhi the next evening and make our plane, and would we make our connection in Milan, and would my mother be okay with the jet lag when I left her alone in her apartment in New York, and had it been too much to bring her all the way to India?

Sheila: Our driver and Krishna were waiting for us. Quickly, we bid the other hapless moon-gazers laconic good nights and started for the car. Krishna, noting our silent disappointment, moved next to me as we walked, and said softly, "You know, Ma, I am named Krishna for the god who is a prankster. If you like, I can take you to see the Taj in the moonlight. But that would be a prank because it is not legal. Would you like to go?"

"You bet," I said. "Perr—?" I repeated his offer.

Perri was all for it.

Krishna explained in whispers. "I have a friend in the army who sometimes guards the Taj from the back, from the bank of the Jumuna River just behind it. He is not on duty tonight, but I can sneak you up close from that side, and, if we are very quiet, probably no one will stop us. We are not supposed to be there. Should we try?"

"Can we really go?" I couldn't believe it. The main entrance had troops watching it and the tightest security measures I'd ever encountered.

"And you know," Krishna continued, in his tour guide identity, "the building is perfectly symmetrical—each side is the same. To see it from the back is the same, exactly, as to see it from the front."

"Let's go," Perri said.

Our driver sped rapidly through the ancient walled streets of the old city of Āgra, where there still live the descendants of the craftsmen who built and decorated the Taj.

"The riverbank might be muddy," Krishna warned. "Take off your shoes and leave them in the car." We did as we were told. We parked right on the bank. Barefooted and silent, we got out and stepped closer. January is the dry season in India, and the river was very low, the bank very broad. The narrow stream ran adjacent to the Taj, and as we approached the river, we were actually much closer than we'd been on the viewing platform.

We waited there on the muddy riverbank while the frivolous clouds rolled around above us. Then, there were several absolutely clear, cloudless minutes when the clouds moved away, and the perfect, round, full moon was shining above us, and the great pearl dome emerged from its cloak of night and gleamed. It was a truly transcendent sight, and I could see it perfectly. I squeezed Perri's hand in joy and victory. This was the way to remember India! We stood together on the wrong side of the Taj Mahal, where we weren't supposed to be, holding hands in the moonlight.

Perri Klass is a pediatrician at a neighborhood health center in Boston. She is associate professor of pediatrics at Boston University School of Medicine and serves as medical director and president of Reach Out and Read, a national early literacy program that makes books and the promotion of reading aloud part of standard pediatric checkups. Dr. Klass is the author of nine books, including a book for parents about quirky children, memoirs about medical training, novels, short-story collections, and a book about knitting. She lives in Cambridge, Massachusetts, with Larry Wolff, a professor of history, and their three children, and she spends a great deal of time thinking about traveling, eating, and knitting.

Sheila Solomon Klass is professor emerita of English at Manhattan Community College, CUNY, where she has been teaching creative writing for forty years. She is the author of sixteen adult, young adult, and juvenile novels, as well as one humorous memoir about the birth of her coauthor, Perri. Her two most recently published books are *In a Cold Open Field,* an adult novel marking the tragedy of the Korean War, and *Little Women Next Door,* a juvenile novel about Louisa May Alcott's bizarre and comic adventure at Fruitlands, where her parents attempted to create a utopian community. Professor Klass's three adult children are all professional writers. Born and raised in New York City, she endured exile in the New Jersey suburbs for two decades; she now lives in Manhattan, where she currently spends much time riding the New York subways, triumphantly, on a half-fare senior citizen MetroCard.

ABOUT THE TYPE

This book was set in Garamond, a typeface originally designed by the Parisian typecutter Claude Garamond (1480–1561). This version of Garamond was modeled on a 1592 specimen sheet from the Egenolff-Berner foundry, which was produced from types assumed to have been brought to Frankfurt by the punchcutter Jacques Sabon.

Claude Garamond's distinguished romans and italics first appeared in *Opera Ciceronis* in 1543–44. The Garamond types are clear, open, and elegant.